# THE ROLLING STONES

D1245848

# THE ORIGIN OF THE SPECIES

**The Rolling Stones**
**The Origin Of The Species**
**How, Why and Where It All Began**
by Alan Clayson

A CHROME DREAMS PUBLICATION
First Edition 2007

Published by Chrome Dreams
PO BOX 230, New Malden, Surrey,
KT3 6YY, UK
books@chromedreams.co.uk
WWW.CHROMEDREAMS.CO.UK

ISBN 9781842403891

Edited by   Cathy Johnstone
Cover Design   Sylwia Grzeszczuk
Layout Design   Marek Niedziewicz

Photographs courtesy of Starfile, Rex, Alan Clayson Archive,
Tony Lewis.

A catalogue record for this book is available from the British Library.

Printed and bound in Great Britain by William Clowes Ltd, Beccles, Suffolk

# THE ROLLING STONES

## THE ORIGIN OF THE SPECIES
### HOW, WHY AND WHERE IT ALL BEGAN

Alan Clayson

To Jim McCarty

*'I know this won't last.*
*I give the Stones another two years.*
*I'm saving for the future'*

Mick Jagger, 1964

## About The Author

Born in Dover, England in 1951, Alan Clayson lives near Henley-on-Thames with his wife Inese. They have two sons, Jack and Harry.

A portrayal of Alan Clayson by the *Western Morning News* as the 'A.J.P. Taylor of the pop world' is supported by *Q*'s 'his knowledge of the period is unparalleled and he's always unerringly accurate.' He has penned many books on music - including the best-sellers *Backbeat*, subject of a major film, *The Yardbirds* and *The Beatles Box* - and has written for journals as diverse as *The Guardian, Record Collector, Ink, Mojo, Mediaeval World, Folk Roots, Guitar, Hello!, Drummer, The Sunday Times, The Independent, Ugly Things* and, as a teenager, the notorious *Schoolkids Oz*. He has also been engaged to perform and lecture on both sides of the Atlantic - as well as broadcast on national TV and radio .

From 1975 to 1985, he led the legendary Clayson and the Argonauts - who reformed in 2005, ostensibly to launch *Sunset On A Legend*, a long-awaited double-CD retrospective - and was thrust to 'a premier position on rock's Lunatic Fringe' (*Melody Maker*). As shown by the existence of a US fan club - dating from a 1992 *soiree* in Chicago - Alan Clayson's following grows still as does demand for his talents as a record producer, and the number of versions of his compositions by such diverse acts as Dave Berry (in whose backing group he played keyboards in the mid-1980s), New Age outfit, Stairway and Joy Tobing, winner of the Indonesian version of *Pop Idol*. He has worked too with The Portsmouth Sinfonia, Wreckless Eric, Twinkle, The Yardbirds, The Pretty Things and the late Screaming Lord Sutch among many others. While his stage act defies succinct description, he has been labelled a 'chansonnier' in recent years for performances and record releases that may stand collectively as Alan Clayson's artistic apotheosis were it not for a promise of surprises yet to come.

Further information is obtainable from *www.alanclayson.com*

## Other Books
by Alan Clayson

Call Up The Groups *The Golden Age Of British Beat, 1962-67*
(Blandford, 1985)
Back In The High Life *A Biography Of Steve Winwood*
(Sidgwick and Jackson, 1988)
Only The Lonely *The Life And Artistic Legacy Of Roy bison* (Sidgwick
and Jackson, 1989)
The Quiet One *A Life Of George Harrison* (Sidgwick and Jackson, 1990)
Ringo Starr *Straight Man Or Joker?* (Sanctuary, 1991)
Death Discs *An Account Of Fatality In The Popular Song*
(Sanctuary, 1992)
Backbeat *Stuart Sutcliffe: The Lost Beatle* (with Pauline Sutcliffe)
(Pan Macmillan, 1994)
Aspects Of Elvis (ed. with Spencer Leigh) (Sidgwick and Jackson, 1994)
Beat Merchants (Blandford, 1995)
Jacques Brel (Castle Communications, 1996)
Hamburg *The Cradle Of British Rock* (Sanctuary, 1997)
Serge Gainsbourg *View From The Exterior* (Sanctuary, 1998)
The Troggs File *The Official Story Of Rock's Wild Things*
(with Jacqueline Ryan) (Helter Skelter, 2000)
Edgard Varese (Sanctuary, 2002)
The Yardbirds (Backbeat, 2002)
John Lennon (Sanctuary, 2003)
The Walrus Was Ringo *101 Beatles Myths Debunked*
(with Spencer Leigh) (Chrome Dreams, 2003)
Paul McCartney (Sanctuary, 2003)
Brian Jones (Sanctuary, 2003)
Charlie Watts (Sanctuary, 2004)
Woman: *The Incredible Life Of Yoko Ono*
(with Barb Jungr and Robb Johnson) (Chrome Dreams, 2004)
Keith Richards (Sanctuary, 2004)
Mick Jagger (Sanctuary, 2005)
Keith Moon *Instant Party* (Chrome Dreams, 2005)
The Rolling Stones Album File (Cassell, 2006)
Led Zeppelin *The Origin Of The Species* (Chrome Dreams, 2006)

Prologue
## Mightier Than The Scissors

*'We don't grow our hair like this for a gimmick, but I don't see why we should cut it off to conform' - Brian Jones*

The Rolling Stones came to the attention of an appalled nation as anti-Beatles after the weather vane of adult toleration, if not approval, had lurched in the direction of the Poor Honest Northern Lads who'd Made It to ITV's *Sunday Night At The London Palladium*, the very pinnacle of conventional British showbusiness, with its endless centuries of stand-up comics, crooners, The Tiller Girls dance troupe and the famed 'Beat The Clock' interlude. Eventually, the Stones would appear on the programme too, but they'd do so with the worst possible grace, leaving a bad taste, and were never to be asked back.

What should be stressed here is the conscious sense of scandal aroused by a mere pop combo. The extent to which they courted trouble, knowingly or not, may be measured in one detail: hair. Today's pony-tailed navvy would find it astonishing that, early in 1964, 'Well, he had long hair, hadn't he?' had been the plea of a man at Aldershot Magistrates Court, accused of assaulting a complete stranger, and that eleven boys were suspended from a Coventry secondary school for having 'Mick Jagger' haircuts - i.e. just about touching the collar and with ears still visible - and a general open-necked scruffiness that they imagined was shared with the Stones. A few months earlier, there'd been a slew of viewers' complaints about the group's appearance - neat by comparison - after they'd first flashed into living rooms on ITV's *Lucky Stars Summer Spin*.

The Rolling Stones weren't, however, created solely to upset. Visually, they seemed to be taking the next reasonable and logical step after the moptopped Beatles - as the more hirsute Pretty Things would after the Stones. Musically too, they were not so much innovative as the exploiters of already existing possibilities. Nonetheless, the flavour of deliberate rebellion cannot easily be dismissed - nor can Average Joe's historical fear of what he finds difficult to comprehend.

The accelerating if unwilling absorption of head-scratchingly artistic outrage can be traced as far back as the so-called 'Gay 'Nineties'. Since then, the associated bohemianism and *l'art pour l'art* asceticism propagated by the likes of Gautier, Flaubert and the persecuted Oscar Wilde had combined with the rapid increase in the minority embracing it as far as they were able. Call it an 'underground' if you like, but this expression, however, was becoming a misnomer as, by the 1960s, it was being pushed into your face and ears via television, radio and the cinema. On emerging from the security of London's more specialist clubs - and with many *afficianados* refuting vainly any suggestions that they were becoming a pop group - The Rolling Stones weren't about to mask the fundamental nonconformity that lurked beneath their brief concessions to how a TV producer in those naive times expected pop entertainers to look.

There was none of that self-aware amusement that Tony Hancock had displayed in the 1960 movie *The Rebel* when, for instance, he explains to a crowd of squatting Parisian beatniks, all dressed in the same black garb, that one of the reasons he had to leave London was because he couldn't stand the sartorial uniformity in the accountancy office where he'd worked. As he leaves them, one beatnik comments to another, 'It must have been very soul-destroying for him. Imagine: everyone looking the same.'

'Art' - if that's what you called it - wasn't somehow a proper trade to the ordinary working man, whether ledger clerk or navvy, laughing at Hancock's antics in *The Rebel*. If you shone at painting or music at school, it was often treated as a regrettable eccentricity - and, if you wanted to be a pop musician, trying to con money out of government aid to do so, or applying to take a degree course in pop, well, that belonged to an unthinkable future.

California State University's inauguration of a degree course in 'rock studies' in 1971 was to be a sign that academia was ceasing to sweep pop under the carpet, and it was soon to begin its infiltration of school curricula. It was remarkable that, unlike film, jazz and other disciplines pertaining to that Coca-Cola century, it had taken until then for higher education to take seriously music that has been recorded for the masses since before the death of Queen Victoria.

That's as maybe, but in the mid-1960s, fathers would switch off *Top Of The Pops* automatically if the Stones or anyone like them were on, and, as late as 1970, when I was nineteen, my own mother swore she'd die of shame if ever I walked on stage with a pop group. Her tone wasn't humorous, far from it.

Not long after that, an inner devil spoke to her when, to take the edge off her relentless and unforgiving moaning about my hair - which wasn't even as long as Jagger's had been in 1964 - I trusted her to trim an inappreciable few millimetres. Probably the fault's all mine for not getting over it, but that hateful morning and its prelude and aftermath will be with me to the grave. Even in my mid-fifties, I experience slight but definite trauma, and my hand wanders involuntarily to the nape of my neck, usually at twenty to eleven - the approximate time she seized the entire overhanging hank at the back of my thick blond hair in her fist, and hacked it off almost to the crown. My tone wasn't humorous either, far from it.

Such an incident - which she said 'did you some good' - epitomised indirectly how the reaction of an older public to the coming of The Rolling Stones and the long-haired creators of depraved cacophony that flowered - or not - in their wake, had become enduringly pathological as it engendered a belief that extreme strategy was a citizen's right, even some sort of moral duty as a defence against ...what? Communism? Anarchy? The end of western civilisation? Reading at the dining table? The Beatles being more popular than Jesus? Going to the cinema on the Sabbath? Having fun? For those disenfranchised by the Swinging Sixties, did an element of suppressed envy translate into the bitterest priggishness?

In Britain, nowhere was this emotion, whatever it was, more fiercely overt than in the provinces. While the pastime of shocking the 'establishment' took on at times a playful aspect in London and the bigger cities with accepted traditions of counter-culture, it was carried on with an uncompromising seriousness in towns like Cheltenham or Dartford where middle-class grammar school boys like Brian Jones and Mick Jagger had gazed glumly through lace curtains and wondered if this was all there was.

Before the Sixties began Swinging elsewhere too, local newspapers reported on whist drives, the Opera Society's production of *HMS Pinafore* and Jack 'PC Dixon' Warner opening a new High Street department store. There was fuss about the gypsies camped on the disused aerodrome and the Borstal runaway hiding somewhere in the everglades, and gossip sufficed for harder news that came via *Melody Maker,* the *New Musical Express* and *Record Mirror* for youths who, on a flaming August afternoon, would be shuttered up inside the coffee bar, making a cup of frothy liquid last for hours, while once upon a greensward buried beneath that very building, archers rehearsed for Agincourt. Though Bill Wyman became a National Serviceman, for Brian, Mick, Keith Richards, Charlie Watts and most of the other Stones who were to fall by the wayside before the group Hit The Big Time, there seemed to be nothing as horribly exciting on the horizon as the prospect of slaughtering foreigners, no apparent avenue of deliverance from mortgage-paying and humdrum jobs with a gold watch on retirement to tick away the seconds before the silence of eternity.

Yet, for all the suffocating mundanity they contained, these decades are at least as intriguing as any of the more exalted and chronicled eras that followed the period from the Stones' scattered wartime childhoods to 1964 when a world beyond Britain opened up and swallowed them like an anemone.

In my explorations, I was, as always, at the mercy of my source material - which provided me with only an infinitesimal amount of the detail needed by those who devote themselves to collating facts about the group. They want the impossible: DVDs, for example, of domestic scenes within the Chelsea flat where most of the Stones dwelt in the months prior to the national breakthrough with a 1963 chart entry, or sampling with their own sensory organs keyboard player Ian Stewart's feelings about being reduced from onstage Stone to glorified road manager.

No doubt they'll pounce on mistakes and omissions while scrutinizing this work. All I can say is that it's as accurate as it can be after what amounts cumulatively to over thirty years of intermittent study of what interested me about the Stones - and what didn't. Since becoming a published author in 1985, I have also desensitised myself to a considerable degree about asking questions that stop just short of open insolence.

*Rolling Stones - The Origin Of The Species* has resulted too from the frequently complex synthesis of over-stuffed files labelled 'Dartford', 'Cliftons', 'Decca', '1963 Tour' and so forth; exercise books full of doctor's prescription-like scrawl drawn from press archives ranging from journals purchasable anywhere in the country to the likes of the *Gloucestershire Echo* and *Kentish Times*; local studies departments of relevant libraries; numerous Internet web-sites, and tomes with contents ranging from the broadest outline to the most meticulous trivia

- including 2003's *According To The Rolling Stones* inside story, and *Stone Alone*, an autobiography of Bill Wyman, the group's most diligent archivist.

My index of probabilities became wider than first imagined, principally through the exploration of some previously unchartered territories in the light of both refinement and alteration of previously-held perspectives and new information gleaned from conversations - some taking place long before this project was commissioned - with such as Rick Huxley, Jagger's cousin by marriage, and bass guitarist with The Dave Clark Five, who I first met in 1981 when he was behind the counter of a musical equipment shop in South London; John Keen, musician friend of the teenage Brian Jones; Mike Cooper, who was approached to join the Stones in 1962; Brian Poole, Ricky West and Dave Munden of The Tremeloes, who Decca wished the Stones to regard as role models; Don Craine and Keith Evans from The Downliners Sect; Yardbirds Jim McCarty, Chris Dreja and Paul Samwell-Smith; Phil May of The Pretty Things, and, in particular, Dick Taylor of The Pretty Things too, but also a founder member of the Stones, and, in 2005, central figure in an edition of a BBC 1 series, *My Best Friend Is...*, in which he discussed former Dartford Grammar classmate Mick Jagger against a backdrop of old haunts.

With deceptive casualness, I entered Dick's life in 1984 when I was researching my first book, *Call Up The Groups!* However, fifteen years later, during what the Russians call 'the old wives' winter', my then-accompanist couldn't manage an engagement at Dimbola Lodge on the Isle of Wight - so I dared to ring Dick, who lives to the south of the island. He volunteered to help out, and I sent him a tape and music charts, and hoped for the best.

Of course, Dick was brilliant, the most accomplished guitarist with whom I've ever trodden the boards. I could scarcely believe it was happening as I'd first known him as a figure on a TV screen when I was about thirteen years old, but there he was, backing me at one of the most peculiar venues I've ever played. In Freshwater Bay - on a stormy night with the sea crashing outside and no street lights - Dimbola Lodge was less an auditorium than a tea house with antique porcelain on the shelves, a Steinway grand piano in the playing area and Pre-Raphaelite paintings on the walls. Tennyson used to give readings there and I wondered what he'd have made of this, the first of many recitals - a surprising number of them, in circumstances just as unusual -by our double act.

In this literary context, I am grateful to Dick for his reminiscences, clear insight and intelligent argument - as I am for those of Pat Andrews, Dave Berry, Alan Dow, Richard Hattrell, Trevor Hobley (president of the Brian Jones Fan Club), Twinkle Rogers and Art Wood, who died in November, 2006, aged sixty-nine. Three years earlier, Bob Taylor, a former member of The Downliners Sect, had summoned Art and I to a studio in Brompton to assist with his 'concept album' of the Anglo-Saxon Chronicle. Attending too were Dick Heckstall-Smith and two of The Downliners Sect. The five of us were required to congregate round an omni-directional microphone and to re-enact the Battle of Hastings by bawling scripted lines actually in Anglo-Saxon. It all got very fren-zied and degenerated into chaos, but Bob - who videoed our efforts - seemed pleased with the outcome and, in licensed premises afterwards, Art spoke for all of us when, dragging bemusedly on a cigarette, he cal-culated that it had been one of the strangest sessions in which he'd ever participated during a long, if sporadic, career as a recording artist.

I'd first encountered Art two years earlier at the opening night of the Eel Pie R&B Club, founded at the turn of the millennium 'to pre-serve and continue the heritage of Richmond Rhythm & Blues in the area where it all began in the 1960s'. Convened in a pub functions room in Twickenham, it was a celebratory occasion that, if not musically ambi-tious, had a friendly, down-home atmosphere. Yet no-one could pre-tend that this is what it must have been like when the Stones, The Pretty Things, The Yardbirds, The Downliners Sect and The Artwoods were at large in the Crawdaddy, the Marquee, Eel Pie Island dance hall and, earlier, at the 'Moist Hoist' in Ealing, where Art, Mick Jagger, Charlie Watts, Dick Heckstall-Smith and others who loomed large in the legend performed with Blues Incorporated, formed by Alexis Korner and Cyril Davies as the kingdom's first major all-blues ensemble.

In February, 2004, I spent a long afternoon with Art in his local, the Tide End in Teddington. Our conversation was centred on this present project, but it embraced too the taping of what neither of us knew was to be his final interview.

Please put your hands together for Art - and next, for Rob John-stone, Sylwia Grzeszczuk, Marek Niedziewicz, Cathy Johnstone, Angela Turner and the rest of the team at Chrome Dreams.

Whether they were aware of providing assistance or not, let's have a round of applause too for these musicians: Mick Avory, Roger

Barnes, Alan Barwise, Arthur Brown, Clem Cattini, Pete Cox, Paul Critchfield, Tony Dangerfield, Billie Davis, the late Lonnie Donegan, 'Wreckless' Eric Goulden, John Harries, Brian Hinton, Alan Holmes, Garry Jones, Graham Larkbey, Andy Lavery, the late Carlo Little, Tom McGuinness, Andy Pegg, the late Gene Pitney, Brian Poole, Mark St. John, Jim Simpson, Mike and Anja Stax, John Steel, the late Lord David Sutch, John Townsend and Paul Tucker.

As well as to those who'd prefer not to be mentioned, thanks are also in order in varying degrees to Jane Allen, Jack Belton, Stuart and Kathryn Booth, Robin Brooks, Tony Cousins, Phyllis Cox, Robert Cross (of Bemish Business Machines), Kevin Delaney, Jayne Down, Stefan Mlynek, Ian Drummond, Tim Fagan, Katy Foster-Moore, Paul Hearne, Michael Heatley, Verity Herrington, the late Susan Hill, Dave Humphries, Allan Jones, Mick and Sarah Jones, Elisabeth McCrae, Russell Newmark, Mike Ober, Sally Pillinger, Mike Robinson, Hilary Stafford-Clark, Mark and Stuart Stokes, Anne Taylor, Michael Towers, Warren Walters, Gina Way and Ted Woodings as well as Inese, Jack and Harry Clayson.

*Alan Clayson, April, 2007*

Chapter One
**East Side Stories**

*'We grew up in a wasteland' - Keith Richards* [1]

When talking to fans and media in Britain, Mick Jagger took to brutalising an accent born of a privileged upbringing to facilitate a 'common touch', usually via a florid sub-Cockney drawl. However, The Rolling Stones' only true workin' class 'ero was the remarkable Bill Wyman, formerly William George Perks, born in Lewisham Hospital on 24th October, 1936.

On this dry, windy evening, a cookery programme billed in the *Radio Times* as 'Cook's Night Off' was seen on the country's only television channel, which had begun transmission only weeks earlier as the first public service of its kind in the world, and novel enough to be regarded by censorious great-aunts as meddling with dark forces. Reception was confined to the small number of Home Counties families that could afford servants.

Most of south-east London, however, were within earshot of a wireless set, and, on the day of baby Bill's arrival, the kingdom's sole nationally-networked radio station was broadcasting an expected across-the-board mixture of light classical music, farming news, 'The Public Social Service', shipping forecasts, a keyboard recital by Reginald Goss-Custard (!) and music hall with Gladys Knight [2], Marriott Edgar, The Fol-De-Rols and The BBC Variety Orchestra. There was also a programme in Welsh, sport from the White City, and a play, *Ski Heil: A Tyrolean Interlude*, while the hour before the Epilogue - a short sermon - National Anthem and close-down was filled with Billy Cotton and his Band, whose burst of 'Waltz Intermezzo' from Masagni's 'Cavalliera Rusticana' was as wild as it got.

Yet nothing could follow Edward VIII's 10 p.m. abdication broadcast that December, and the BBC shut down for the rest of the night. The year was notable too for the 'Nazi' Olympics in Berlin; the whole of London rushing out to gawk at the first helicopters - and the long-running knitting contest in the *Daily Mail*, then a broadsheet. It also contained Kay Francis, 'the best-dressed woman in Hollywood', endorsing Bondor, 'the stockings of the stars', and a serial on 'characterology... with a kick in it', based on word-association and a questionnaire, and co-written by Prince Leopold Loewenstein, who 'has made an intensive study of psychology in its relation to character'. He was an offshoot of Austrian royalty, and was to father the Stones' future financial advisor, Prince Rupert.

There was also an advertisement about residential properties in '15 Lovely Districts' in London with 'electricity, gas and hot and cold water installed'. These did not include the suburb where the Perks family lived. Originally, they were from Stratford-upon-Avon, but when Thomas Perks, Bill's bricklaying great-great grandfather, moved south, the names of his descendants became imprinted on census rolls pertaining to the Deptford-Lewisham-Penge axis, where the capital bleeds into Kent.

His mother, Molly, was reared in 36, Blenheim Road, Penge, the parental address round which the lives of her and her siblings continued to revolve, even after they married. Before television became an indispensable domestic fixture, riotous and crowded Christmas parties there culminated with sing-songs round the piano, and perhaps a grandchild being led forth, glistening with embarrassment, to the centre of the front room to pipe out a song in an uncertain treble. Yet nothing suggested that any of them - including Molly's husband, William Perks, a builder like Thomas before him - would not dwell to death in the same district, once fashionable but on an irreversible slide into seediness since unwelcome nationwide coverage of a parochial murder - a woman was starved to death - in 1877.

This was reflected in the depressed forbearance of the majority of a populace for whom running water was still a council election promise; gas rather than electricity lit kitchens where margarine was spread instead of butter; backyards were dominated by outside lavatories and finger-crushing mangles, and kitchen sinks were where a mother would both bathe infants and wash up dishes from a Sunday lunch on a newspaper tablecloth. Households survived on perpetual mental arithmetic, eking out a low income and being forever on the look-out for means of supplementing it.

'My mother used to take in blankets to wash,' recalled the boy fated to be Bill Wyman, 'She also used to get these huge bags of elastic bands delivered to the house, and we had to sort them out into sizes and put them in packets. Piecework is really vicious because there's so much work involved and such little reward. She also started to take in onions and peel them for pickling. Of course, the whole house then smelt of onions. Our hands went bright yellow. I remember darning hundreds of socks too. We were all taught to knit and embroider and make rugs out of rags.' [3]

'We' meant Bill and the two younger brothers with whom he shared a bed, and his two sisters who slept together in the second of three upstairs rooms. Two siblings, however, were yet to be born when Bill, short-trousered and gaberdine-raincoated, began his formal education at Melvyn Road Primary School and an unimaginative regime epitomised by multiplication tables chanted *en masse* to the rap of a bamboo cane, and cross-legged music lessons around the upright piano in the main hall, which also served as gymnasium, dining room and the prayer-hymn-prayer sandwiches with which Church of England schools usually began the day.

This was interrupted by World War II and correlated evacuation to the Midlands, an uprooting that Bill found so onerous - partly because the local children mocked unmercifully the rather reserved boy's gor-blimey accent - that he was soon returned to Penge to risk the London blitz - during which his new school, Oakfield Road Juniors, was bombed while the school was in a summer recess.

The hostile shadows of the Luftwaffe were also falling over Kent's thriving Medway Towns - actually a conurbation fanning out from the estuary docklands and naval garrisons of Chatham and Gillingham - beyond the creeping smog and mile upon mile of Albert Squares in the part of London where Bill had been alive for seven years prior to the coming of the two fellows to whom he was to be advisedly subordinate, and through whom he was to enjoy a dotage rich in material benefits.

They were sons of Dartford, more immediately west of London, and as far from the White Cliffs of Dover's mythical bluebirds as it was feasible to be without leaving the county referred to as the 'Garden of England'. Yet neither Mick Jagger nor Keith Richards grew to man's estate in a fairy-tale arcadia of meadows and woodland. 'If you were a "war baby", it was a bit gloomy and grey, and everything was bomb-struck,' remembered Keith, 'It was nothing to turn a corner and see nothing on the horizon apart from one or two miracle houses.' [1]

With the German airforce's unofficial help and hindrance, an urban renewal programme would turn the area into an impinging riparian hinterland of stucco-fronted housing estates, windswept acres of playing fields, tangles of shopping precincts and industrial zones of engineering, electronics and chemical works with giant chimneys levelled at the sky like anti-aircraft guns - all connected by arteries of an ever-increasing volume of motorised traffic.

In the red-brick maternity wing of Dartford's Livingstone Hospital, the two arch-Rolling Stones were each prised into the world - Mick on 26th July, 1943, and Keith on 18th December - and so were two members of The Pretty Things and Jagger's cousin by marriage, Rick Huxley, who was to play bass with The Dave Clark Five, another pop group that was to rack up hefty achievements in the Swinging Sixties.

Rick knew Michael Philip Jagger as 'Mike' for most of the first two decades of his life - as would Mike's parents Eva and Joe, a physical education lecturer and author of *Basketball: Coaching And Playing*, a definitive tome about a North American sport that had just been introduced to Britain. His salary was ample enough to allow Eva to resign from a local hairdressing salon to become a most orderly housewife and home-all-day mother to Mike and Chris, his younger brother, in Wilmington, Dartford's leafiest and most upmarket outpost.

A few streets away in Morland Avenue, Keith Richards would be developing many of the common characteristics of the only child. Though self-contained and adept at entertaining himself, all he had to do was shed tears to gain undivided attention and be reassured by mother Doris how adorable and special he was. This perspective was not shared by Bert, his father, who was as stolid as his gradually more estranged wife was free-spirited. He was away from home most of the time for reasons to do with both eventual personal choice and a long daily commute prefacing longer hours on the assembly line of a light-bulb factory on the north-western edge of London. When not rendered too indolent by exhaustion to consider it, he thought that the zeal with which Doris championed Keith's chosen activities was excessive. She seemed to let him do whatever he liked on his terms, in his way, and whenever he felt like it.

Keith, however, wasn't as prepared as he might have been for confronting the competitive world of Westhill Infants School where he was delivered, grizzling in his mother's arms, on the first morning - unlike Mike Jagger, who betrayed no emotions whatsoever when first cast adrift in the playground at Maypole Infants in the adjacent educational catchment area.

On that same warm September week in 1947, Bill Perks entered the first form at Beckenham and Penge Grammar School For Boys, having been one of only three in an Oakfield Road Juniors class of fifty-two to 'pass' the examination known later as the Eleven-Plus, and thus not be consigned to a mixed-sex secondary modern - where the remaining forty-nine pupils acquired an intellectual inferiority complex. 'I was nervous about it because I was quite a shy and introverted kid,' recollected Bill, ' but I was absolutely thrilled because I loved learning.' [3]

For ambitious parents, grammar school was as much a social as an academic coup, but Mr. Perks had studied the letter informing him of his son's achievement grimly. 'He always looked on the worst side of everything,' sighed Bill, 'and what concerned him was forking out some extra expenses on clothes, not that I was getting this opportunity.' [3]

While he handed over crumpled and hard-earned banknotes for the regulation uniform of black 'bombhead' shoes, grey flannels, blazer, white shirt, tie and cap, Mr. Perks' largesse did not extend to the faster bicycle Bill needed to get to an establishment that wasn't a mere few minutes dawdle away as Oakfield Road had been. Indeed, he insisted that Bill surrendered half his earnings for various newspaper, milk and bread rounds to pay for the new three-speed, drop-handlebarred model that replaced the second-hand sit-up-and-beg that he'd outgrown.

During the following winter - the coldest in living memory - the icy roads were too slippery for bikes, and, in any case, fuel shortages closed the grammar and nearly every other surrounding school for up to a fortnight at a stretch. Around one million sheep perished in frozen meadows, snow halted entire rail networks, and the prohibition of street lighting was a flashback to the wartime blackouts, just as the shortages of even dried eggs and powdered milk were to the world of queues during the tightest period of the rationing that was to persist into the next decade to the benefit of the *spivs* - black-marketeers - at large in all the bigger cities.

Inside homes like Bill's, any number of saved-up ration cards still couldn't procure heating. 'We'd lie in bed with our breath coming out all smoky,' he shuddered, 'and in the morning, the *inside* of the window would have ice on it, which was quite pretty, but stepping out of bed to do my milk round, the lino was like ice. Even your socks were stiff with cold, and you had to knock some life into them before you could put them on.' [3]

When school resumed, there were occasions when, with hands supporting weary head at an ink-welled desk, his extra-mural employment took its toll. It wasn't quite Richard Attenborough as the poor boy winning a scholarship to an upper crust school in *The Guinea Pig*, a film drama on general circulation in 1948, but fellow pupils had no qualms about pointing out that Perks smelt of the onions that pervaded the air at home where he reverted to 'my normal *sarf* London semi-cockney' after speaking in more round-vowelled fashion when among youths such as the classmate who 'had a marvellous house. I'd never seen the likes before. It was in its own grounds, probably an acre of land, a huge lawn with a bird fountain and a little greenhouse at the bottom. I thought it was a palace, and I felt out of my depth completely. Of course, you're then supposed to invite your friend back to your house. Well, I couldn't. It would have been embarrassing.' [3]

There were, however, sufficient periods of prosperity for piano lessons to be arranged for Bill with a Miss Oppenheimer. Talented enough himself to pound out accompaniment at Blenheim Road musical evenings, Mr. Perks was delighted by his eldest's progress, apart from when he 'jazzed up' the classical pieces he was supposed to be practicing for the two Royal College of Music grades he passed. 'I thought it was fun,' grinned Bill, 'Then I became fanatical about football and cricket, so the lessons stopped. I was always in the park, and wasn't serious about my studies.' [4]

Sport was a principal means of escape from the overall post-war dreariness and social immobility. Yet, according to the mitherings of most parents and teachers, attempting to make a living as a musician wasn't a sensible option. The bloke murdering 'Ida Sweet As Apple Cider' or Ray McKinley's 'Down The Road Apiece' on the pub piano was no worse than Reginald Goss-Custard or any of that other rubbish on the wireless, but it was who you knew in the business, wasn't it? Two of Mike Jagger's maternal uncles had been on the periphery of the music hall, but neither made it to Drury Lane. Neither of them sang a prime-time radio duet of an old evergreen with Gladys Knight.

Theoretically, Mike, Bill and Keith were well-placed to pursue a showbusiness goal as the British entertainment industry was focussed, then as now, on central London. Yet on the city's frontiers you could daydream as much as you liked about topping the bill at the Palladium but the reality was the dull job waiting for you when you were through with being educated. It was never too late to give up messing about with football or music and try for a raise or even promotion instead of just waiting for Friday to come around, and lay the foundations for slipping into a comfortable and respected old age.

The translation of Bill, Mike and Keith to pop stardom, therefore, was mostly a gradual development of unconscious forces that weren't apparent in families in which no-one was groomed from earliest youth for showbusiness, and where a boy's choice of any of the liberal arts as a profession was a sure sign of effeminacy, what with the words 'artistic' and 'musical' being as much of a euphemism for 'homosexual' as 'gay' is now.

More than once, Joe Jagger had observed Mike spending too long combing, stroking and sculpting his hair in that 'quiff' style that was coming into fashion. Mr. Jagger was quiet and modest to the point of invisibility, and, as the 1950s left the runway, he had shared the common adult bemusement at the narcissistic exhibitionism of certain North American performers, particularly that of Johnnie Ray, 'the Prince of Wails', with his hearing-aid discernable from the gallery when he burst into tears during some agonised *lied* or indulged in an excess of pelvis-thrusting and microphone stand hand-ballets during a lewdness entitled 'Such A Night', his interpretation of the largely indecipherable lyrics implying that the conclusion of an evening out with a woman - if it *was* a woman - had gone further than a wistful embrace beneath the stars.

If Mike had to like pop singers, then let it be Tennessee Ernie Ford, Vaughn 'Ghost Riders In The Sky' Monroe, Frankie Laine or another with a heavily masculine image rather than 'musical' Johnnie Ray. Yet, as well as preening himself in the hall mirror, Mike was also inclined to cavort about to music on the Light Programme, the most popular of the BBC's three newish nationally-broadcast stations. Maybe he got that by osmosis from Eva's side of the family as much as reading about Johnnie Ray. 'The radio was usually humming with

Victor Sylvester or Edmundo Ros,' agreed Mike, 'Our mother sang and danced around, and our nan used to belt out a tune at parties.' [5]

Keith Richards' interest in music came from his mother and her blood relations too. Doris's father, Theodore Augustus Dupree, was a multi-instrumentalist versatile enough to have blown saxophone when dapper in immaculately stiff evening dress on a palais bandstand in the 1930s, and to have bowed weepy fiddle in a check-shirted post-war country-and-western band after a god had descended on London in 1947 when Roy Rogers rode *a* Trigger from his hotel to Leicester Square Odeon cinema for the UK premiere of *The Cowboy And The Senorita*.

To many youngsters, including Keith - and Mike Jagger - Rogers, Gene Autry, Hopalong Cassidy and other film-acting singing cowboys with guitars were significant early influences, even if they leaned towards the light 'sweetcorn' also adopted by Slim Whitman and Jim Reeves rather than the 'hard' approach of Hank Williams and his Drifting Cowboys with their unusual absorption with near-clockwork rhythms that, with the interlocking plain-and-simple riffs and singing composer Williams's own guitar chopping, left its mark on the output of Johnny Cash, a C&W artist who was to be as much admired by Richards - and Jagger and Brian Jones - as Williams had been by their younger selves for the 'big fun' of 'Jambalaya' and wounded 'Your Cheatin' Heart', and for the incorporation of what they were to perceive as blues into 'Howlin' At The Moon' and 1951's million-selling 'Moanin' The Blues', just as Ray McKinley and his Orchestra had done with 'Down The Road Apiece' and - so they were to discover too - bluesmen did with C&W.

As his fame spread beyond the USA's Deep South, Hank's records were covered for the pop market by Tony Bennett and Rosemary Clooney and evidence suggests that, but for his drug-induced death in 1953 at the age of twenty-nine, Williams might have shared the mainstream popularity of this syrupy elite - and that of the rock 'n' roll upstarts that superseded them.

'You should never underestimate the importance of country in rock 'n' roll,' Keith would pontificate later. [6] - and you could see his point if you accept that, in its blending of cowboy pessimism and Victorian broadness of gesture, what else is C&W if not white trash blues? Richards recognised too that the technique of US singing pianist Hoagy Carmichael - then in his late fifties - was 'very country, very laconic and dry. I like the ambiguity he gets. I want words to pull triggers.' [7]

Hank Williams' brand of C&W, Johnnie Ray's most uptempo outrages and infrequent spins of Hoagy Carmichael were among few 'songs with rhythm' - as Bill Wyman was to describe them [8] - heard on the Light Programme beyond, say, *Ken Sekora's Jazz Club* and, also on late in the evening, *Radio Rhythm Club*. 'There'd be one "folk song" per programme,' remembered Lonnie Donegan, an ex-serviceman, soon to be one of the country's leading pop icons, 'Sometimes it was a blues'. Sometimes too, it was sung with a resident vocalist's plummy gentility when surfacing on *Services Calling*, an Entertainments National Service Association (ENSA) series in which such a version of 'Down The Road Apiece' was introduced by interlocutor Sally Douglas as 'a good old good one'.

Blues cropped up occasionally too on the British Forces Network (BFN) whose opening transmission from Hamburg in 1946 had coincided with that of the Light Programme. Ploughing a similar light entertainment furrow, BFN staff included such future denizens of BBC Broadcasting House as Cliff Michelmore, Brian Matthew and Alexis Korner, then awaiting his destiny as 'the father of British blues', who moonlighted as presenter with Nordwestdeutsche Rundfunk - closed down in 1955 - and was recalled by Michelmore for his expeditions 'in search of jazz along the Reeperbahn.' [9]

Korner's BFN playlist was as extreme as it could be without being called to task by his superiors. Back in Britain, the staider BBC's broadcast diet of pre-rock 'n' roll pop was freighted with unchained melodies, Mambo Italianos, doggies in the window and Billy Cotton still blasting up 'Waltz Intermezzo' after all these years, as well as muzak arrangements of Handel, Offenbach and Rossini and light opera arias from such as Mario Lanza and Josef Locke: all aimed principally at the over-thirties and the old and square in general.

This policy was to persist on a law of diminishing returns into the 1960s. The music hall died as lingering a death too, even after television became a more convenient avenue for shutting out, however fleetingly, the nastier truths of the dingy lives most of its consumers led, grown-ups and youngsters alike.

It was called 'music hall' because each artiste made use of the pit orchestra if only for a rumble of timpani as a rabbit was produced from a top hat. Usually, the bill would contain an entirely musical act, a singer more often than not. These days, however, you'd be less likely to be serenaded with 'Ida Sweet As Apple Cider', 'The Spaniard That Blighted My Life' or a similar ancient chestnut than an entry in the *New Musical Express*'s 'Top Tens' of best-selling sheet music and 78 rpm discs.

Of the two lists, the sheet music one was then the most important as, for British artists anyway, record releases were mere adjuncts to earnings in variety - you were not yet 'only as good as your latest record' - and there were often several versions of the same composition, direct from the USA - 'Hey There', say, or, from the same film musical, *Pyjama Game*, 'Hernando's Hideaway' - jockeying for position. Nine-year-old Keith Richards, while pledging no allegiance to any specific star, preferred Nat 'King' Cole's less mannered version of 'Because You're Mine' to that of Mario Lanza, and specific items, such as Hoagy Carmichael's 'Hong Kong Blues' and Billy Eckstine's 'No One But You', twisted his heartstrings occasionally.

As for Bill Perks, he'd sold his stamp collection to buy a record-player and two singles, Les Paul and Mary Ford's 'The World Is Waiting For The Sunrise' - 'The first time I ever heard electric guitar on a record' [10] - and quasi-religious Frankie Laine's 'I Believe', which knocked Lita Roza's 'How Much Is That Doggie In The Window' from Number One in 1953, and spent a record-breaking eighteen weeks there throughout that summer when Queen Elizabeth II was crowned, Mount Everest was conquered and England regained the Ashes after nearly two decades.

Yet, if anything, funnymen such as Max Bygraves, Dave King and Bob Monkhouse were more likely objects of adoration than most pop vocalists then - although both Bygraves and King enjoyed chart climbs as a sideline - as were the Brylcreemed, 'sensible' likes of Eamonn Andrews, David Attenborough, sports commentator Peter West, Richard 'Robin Hood' Greene, crooner Dickie Valentine, newsreader Huw Wheldon and others omnipresent on British television when Mike Jagger and Keith Richards had graduated from their respective infants schools to Wentworth Juniors in 1950, where it was discovered that Keith, surprisingly, required little coaxing to participate, even sing solo, in class assemblies.

Of the teachers who warmed to the new pupil was a Mr. Clair. In charge of the choir, he included Keith in an ensemble destined to appear in the finals of an inter-school competition at no less than the Royal Albert Hall. That a future Rolling Stone was also amongst the massed choristers - so the (probably erroneous) story goes - at the Queen's televised coronation in Westminster Abbey on 2nd June, 1953, was not appreciated at the time either - though Keith himself was to acknowledge that 'Jake Clair taught me a lot,' albeit with the reservation, 'After my soprano went at thirteen, singing was over for me. I only got into singing again after finding out that I could write songs.' [7]

By the final year at Wentworth, Keith and Mike's paths had diverged, owing to the former's family uprooting from Morland Avenue to Spielman Road in Temple Hill, a council estate built by the book for those who had no choice. As early evening street lamps were lit on this desolate cluster of streets, a lone pedestrian might cross over to avoid an aimlessly swaggering phallanx of youths - assessed at a glance as secondary modern sorts who wouldn't work - out for more than boyish mischief, and styled by both the media and themselves as 'Teddy Boys'.

In 1954 on a London heath, a meek if vulgar reproof - 'You flash cunt' - by the victim would precipitate the first Teddy Boy murder. After that, there'd be questions in Parliament, hand-wringing vicars in pulpits and films such as *Violent Playground* and *Cosh Boy* that suggested that flogging was the only way to tame these 'Teds' – sartorial hybrids of Mississippi card-sharps and Edwardian rakes who wrecked Church youth clubs, snarling with laughter as a with-it curate in a cardigan pleaded ineffectually. Though they made themselves conspicuous too in details like brilliantined, vaguely girly cockades offset with scimitar-like sideburns, and brass rings decorating their fingers like knuckledusters, if you so much as glanced at them, the next piece of action could be *you*.

Unaware as yet of rock 'n' roll's increasingly less distant thunder, their attitudinal role models were mostly up-and-coming US *film noir* thespians such as James Dean - the Rebel-Without-A-Cause - and Marlon Brando, leather-clad leader of a motorbike gang, mumbling his way through 1954's much-banned *The Wild One*: a 'fast boy' from the wrong side of town, oozing sullen introspection. Sucked into the vortex, Keith Richards, who was to name his elder son Marlon, began aping the aping of older sham-tough lads, sauntering down to corner shops with hunched shoulders, hands rammed in pockets and chewing gum in a half-sneer.

If on the cusp of adolescence too, Mike Jagger wasn't to absorb the mannerisms of the new youth cult as deeply. Mainly, it was because, like Bill Perks before him, he'd joined an academic elite. Seated at arms-folded attention on his first day at Dartford Grammar School, West Hill, he seemed to have adopted the party-line that there were more constructive things to do than knot bootlace ties round your collar and squeeze into the circulation-impeding drainpipe jeans that went with the rest of the Teddy Boy costume of crepe shoes, velvet-collared drape jacket and frilly shirt like whipped cream. This was, he was led to believe, in readiness for slitting cinema seats or, less secretively, barging *en bloc* into a dance hall without paying.

Nonetheless, Teddiness rippled across Dartford Grammar to such an extent that it provoked a fad for luminous socks, albeit suppressed immediately at the decree of the headmaster, 'Lofty' Hudson. A smaller rebellion would be epitomised by the growing of sideburns as soon as he was able by a Richard Clifford Taylor, up from Brampton Primary in Bexleyheath.

Destined to loom large in the Stones' early legend, Dick Taylor's walk with destiny began on 28th January, 1954 with an eleventh birthday present of a plastic ukelele. His mastery of both this and 'a tiny, ancient drum kit' inherited from his grandfather was surpassed by that on the steel-stringed acoustic guitar of indeterminate make that he acquired at the age of fourteen from a musical instrument stockist along Denmark Street, London's Tin Pan Alley.

Amused by the memory, he would reconjure a first impression of classmate Mike Jagger as 'a fresh-faced, sporty type - bright, lively without being the form's fool. I was the quiet one in what one teacher judged to be the brightest form, but the most vicious verbally.'

Just under middle height with a slender frame and auburn-to-mousy hair kept unwillingly to regulation short-back-and-sides, Jagger's most distinguishing feature was inherited from his mother: wide, loose and over-generous lips that, in repose, drooped to an expression construed as insolent by those teaching the top arts stream he and Taylor were in by the third year.

Genuine surliness contorted Mick's face through a dislike of the uniform (especially the cap) and physical exercise, 'but I know I have to do it'. [11] Yet, despite seeming to despise an inbred ability, he shone at cricket, rugby and badminton, was a luminary of the basketball team, and was to obtain a holiday job assisting with physical training instruction at a US air base just beyond Dartford. Moreover, four years earlier, Mike had made a mute television debut in the ITV children's magazine, *Seeing Sport*, with Joe, also its technical advisor, for an edition broadcast from Tunbridge Wells. They scaled a rock face and erected a tent, but the clip to be most commonly used in these before-they-were-famous TV compilations that rear up periodically nowadays, would be the presenter pointing out the practicality of Mike's hard-wearing plimsolls.

To classmates, he spoke no more about *Seeing Sport* than he would about being obliged to go to Church. Indeed, he proclaimed himself an atheist, and spoke confidentially about sex-before-marriage as if had inside information about it - and about certain of the pupils at the girls' school, also along West Hill. No-one wanted to believe him, but Dick Taylor noticed that his friend 'always seemed to have multiple girlfriends, and was very active in that department before the rest of us. He was forever in the coffee bar in Dartford, chatting up some girl.' His main targets were females more dauntingly 'fun-loving' - to use a tabloid cliché - than the usual 'nice' girl of the mid-1950s, 'saving herself' for her wedding night.

Not quite so precocious was Jagger's appreciation that the United States of America seemed the very wellspring of everything glamorous from Coca-Cola to Johnnie Ray. With the arrival of numbers like 'Such A Night' and then rock 'n' roll from the same source, mainstream pop's libidinous content was no longer as cloaked in stardust and roses. Like all but the most serious-minded children of the 1950s, he - and Dick and Keith - had been thrilled, superficially anyway, by 'Rock Around The Clock' by Bill Haley and the Comets. Yet on watching *Don't Knock The Rock*, a celluloid vehicle whereby Haley could mime to his hits, when it reached Dartford in 1956, Jagger had been entranced totally by the second-billed Little Richard's far more unhinged go-man-go sorcery. In a billowing drape suit and precarious pompadour, Richard's bombastic vocal delivery swooped from roar to shriek in 'Rip It Up', 'Long Tall Sally' and, climactically, 'Tutti Frutti' - sexual doggerel sanitised to joyous gibberish and, therefore, palatable to a white public - while punishing a grand piano with parts of his anatomy other than just his fingers.

Out of touch with Mike now, Keith, caught 'Long Tall Sally' - yet to be released in Britain - when tuning into static-ridden Radio Luxembourg that summer on one of these new-fangled pocket transistors. During the same few evening hours, Keith Richards also heard Elvis Presley's debut UK chart entry, 'Heartbreak Hotel'.

'It was an electrifying night for me,' he reminisced, 'I knew from the minute I heard Elvis that that's what I wanted to do.' [12] When the leaves turned brown, his resolve would be hardened further on encountering the heart-stopping second guitar break in Presley's 'Hound Dog', and, predating that chronologically but issued in Britain later, a solo by the same musician, Scotty Moore, in 'I'm Left You're Right She's Gone'. 'I could never work out how he played it,' marvelled Keith, 'And I still can't. It's such a wonderful thing, I almost don't want to know.' [6]

Once, the instrument had been associated mainly with Latinate heel-clattering, but now it was what Elvis - and, if you read the small print, Scotty Moore - played. In a time-honoured ritual of thwarted eroticism, Keith would get into possition in front of a wardrobe mirror, his left hand gripping the fretboard and his right slashing the strings of an imaginary guitar. He'd pretend to shape chords and pick solos with negligent ease, perhaps feigning a collapse and crawling to the edge of a stage to the delight of thousands of ecstatic females that only he could see: 'I got the moves off first, and I got the guitar later.' [12]

While he could spare less time than Keith for Presley's embroidered shout-singing, Mike Jagger wondered from whence it and Little Richard's more glorious row were traceable. If there was a specific road-to-Damascus moment for Mike, it was - according to another school chum, Peter Holland - when one of the catering staff at the US encampment where he helped with PE, spent an afternoon spinning the blues for Mick on a record player in the sergeants mess. Something enormous took place. Yet, though transfixed instantly, the young man had no idea at first how to set about obtaining discs that couldn't be had from any ordinary high street record shop in England.

'There was very little on wax - or shellac as it was then,' shrugged Lonnie Donegan, 'Nevertheless, in 1947, I fell in love with Josh White's 'House Of The Rising Sun' backed by 'Strange Fruit' on black label Brunswick. After that, I really got into jazz - and there were a lot of jazz records available with blues titles and the likes of Bessie Smith singing blues within the jazz bands.'

Mike Jagger hadn't much more than that to go on either until he learnt from Dick Taylor - already a blues connoisseur - of the existence of Dobell's, a shop in the same part of central London as Denmark Street. It specialised in a wide spectrum of imported merchandise from black America that included both country blues and the citified *rhythm*-and-blues - R&B - that had been among the chief points of stylistic reference for Little Richard, Elvis Presley, Jerry Lee Lewis, Chuck Berry, Gene Vincent and further wild men, whose records were arriving by the month in the *NME* record chart - now containing as much vinyl at 45 rpm as more breakable 78 product, and about to swell to a Top *Thirty*.

In his parallel dimension across town, Keith hadn't been especially keen on Jerry Lee, regarding him on first acquaintance perhaps as just an Elvis who substituted piano for guitar - though decades later, Richards, along with Dave Davies of The Kinks, Van Morrison and other now illustrious fans, paid pragmatic respects to Lewis by joining him on stage during a London concert. [13] As self-obsessed as a genius can be, the self-styled 'Killer' profited from an electrifying stage presence that displayed plurality of taste, unpredictability and a forgivable arrogance in compatible amounts. Serenity wasn't Jerry Lee's way offstage either, riven as his years were with high living, destitution, stimulant abuse, arrests, more marriages than Henry VIII, last-minute tour cancellations, his shooting of a bass guitarist and the accidental deaths of two sons and a wife. There were also the bouts of loud piety that recurred from a poor upbringing within the clang of the Assembly Of God Church bell in Ferriday, Louisiana.

Independently, Richards, Jagger and Taylor saw Lewis pounding out 'High School Confidential' from the back of a flat-bed truck in the film of the same name, and, earlier, Little Richard doing much the same with the title song of 1957's *The Girl Can't Help It* in the same Dartford cinema - though it would be the next Richard single that convinced Richards that rock 'n' roll was going to last far longer than hula-hoops, the cha-cha-cha and previous short-lived fads: '"Lucille" is the one that first turned me on, that made me think rock 'n' roll's here. England was black and white, and, suddenly, everything went technicolor.' [6]

Of all the Grand Old Men of classic rock, the first and foremost for Keith was - and always would be - Chuck Berry, despite no major penetrations in the British charts for years. As his name will surface as regularly as rocks in the stream in this account, it may be useful to outline Berry's background in some detail. He was born Charles Edward Berry in 1926 - or 1931, depending on which press releases you read - and raised in St. Louis, Missouri. With the onset of puberty, he became a singing guitarist and began composing. His output was flavoured with the most disparate ingredients in the musical melting pot of the Americas: zydeco, calypso, vaudeville, Latin, country-and-western, showbiz evergreens, and every shade of jazz, particularly when it was transported to the borders of pop via, say, the humour of Louis Armstrong, the rural stumblings of the Mississippi delta, and Chicago and New Orleans rhythm-and-blues.

Berry turned professional at the age of twenty-six in a group named after its pianist, Johnnie Johnson. When rechristened The Chuck Berry Combo, the outfit worked local venues with occasional side-trips further afield to the Cosmopolitan Club in Chicago, where blues grandee Muddy Waters was so sincerely loud in his praise that Berry was signed to the Windy City's legendary Chess label in 1955.

After 'Maybelline' - which owed as much to C&W as it did blues - peaked at Number Five in the *Hot 100*, 'Roll Over Beethoven' climbed almost as high. Next, 1957's 'School Days (Ring! Ring! Goes The Bell)' came close to topping the list. With melodies and R&B chord patterns serving as support structures for often erudite lyrics celebrating the pleasures available to US teenagers, another fat commercial year generated further smashes in 'Rock And Roll Music', 'Sweet Little Sixteen' and Chuck's 'Johnny B Goode' signature tune.

He had been first experienced by the world beyond the States when he appeared in *Jazz On A Summer's Day*, a US movie documentary about a turn-of-the-decade outdoor festival. Derisively 'duck-walking' with his crotch-level red guitar, Chuck offended jazz purists but captured the imaginations of those European teenagers who were able to watch a flick that was the stuff of film clubs and arts centres rather than general circulation.

Thus, Bill Perks first experienced Chuck Berry at the Beckenham Regal when he gave 'em 'You Can't Catch Me' in 1957's *Rock Rock Rock*, a conveyor-belt of lip-synched pop diversity connected by a vacuous story-line. Afterwards, Bill vanished into the spring night as lost in wonder as Keith Richards had been when he saw the same sequence when it came to a Dartford flea-pit the following week.

Bill had now entered the world of work. Four years earlier, when he was two months away from sitting his General Certificate Of Education - GCE - 'O' level examinations that June, his father had decided to withdraw his son from the grammar school. He'd already spoken to a bookmaker in the West End, who had a vacancy for a junior clerk, and was willing to take on Bill straight away. The sub-text of this sudden upheaval was that work had been slack in the building trade, although the weather had been mostly dry, if rather cold, since January. Underemployed for too long, Mr. Perks had been driven to break into the family's savings. Finding Bill a full-time job made sense, even in the teeth of a letter from the headmaster imploring a change of heart.

The boy was more directly aggrieved, feeling that his father 'did it out of spite. There was that resentment about me going to a posh school, trying to talk posh and wearing a uniform that he had to pay for. He was a very cold person.' [3]

As it had been when Bill was amassing cash to pay for his bicycle, most of his wages were tithed by his parents. This, however, was discontinued after the dreaded official-looking envelope that hung like a sword of Damocles over every young Englishman fluttered onto the doormat one dark morning in 1955. The war office, anxious about the deadlock the Geneva Summit had reached over the reunification of Germany and an associated abandonment of east-west defences, had sent for Bill Perks.

As he hadn't been brought to his assigned camp on a stretcher, the induction medical was a mere formality. Next, his hair was planed halfway up the side of his skull with electric clippers, and he was kitted out with a uniform that had the texture of a horse blanket. During basic training - in which square-bashing, rifle drill and boot-polishing invaded his dreams - he was bawled at from dawn to dusk prior to a posting as a Royal Air Force statistics clerk - 'all charts, graphs, means and averages' [4] - to Hereford and then to the transport section in the British zone of still-occupied West Germany, one hundred miles from the Russian border: 'we had to keep trucks fuelled up to supply three fighter squadrons and in readiness to evacuate four thousand people in four hours.' [4]

As his ordained two-year patriotic chore was turning out to be as agreeable as it could be, particularly after its vile beginning, Bill volunteered for an additional year. 'National Service teaches you camaraderie and to care about other people,' he enthused, 'It taught me to fend for myself and deal with things that I'd never had the necessity to do before. I flew for the first time and heard rock 'n' roll for the first time. It was in Germany that I first began to get into music.' [14]

How could Bill have known how fateful it was to purchase for a few *deutschmarks* from a shop in Oldenburg, Lower Saxony, an acoustic guitar with taut strings so high off the fretboard that *barre* chords proved painful to the yet-uncalloused fingers on his small hands. Another portentious consequence of this period was his membership of one of the base's football teams. The team's leading light was a truck driver whose name, Lee Whyman, was, reflected Bill, a damn sight more glamorous than the one with which he himself had been stuck.

Bill Perks, eh? When times were hard, you'd imagine a road sweeper being called that. At a better moment, 'Bill Perks' might be a mid-field footballer whose team was about to be relegated to the fourth division. In the normal course of events, however, our Bill Perks was, following a return to civvy street in January, 1958, a storekeeper for an engineering firm in Streatham, a relatively well-paid job accepted gladly when the old one at the bookmaker's wasn't waiting for him, and the short-lived one after that - in an office within the East London docks - was too poorly waged.

The only 'proper job' Keith Richards was to do was when he functioned as a relief postman one Christmas just long enough for the early mornings to not cease to be a novelty. At thirteen, he had been enrolled at Dartford Technical School, an educational option that was more likely to lead to a trade apprenticeship than any kind of further education. Keith was an uninvolved student, unblinking in the monotony of lessons. Into the bargain, though he'd lasted a few weeks as a Boy Scout, he had long nurtured an animosity towards any form of hearty clubbism inherent in this and similar after-school activities, and a distrust of adult authority figures.

This impacted on his sojourn at the Technical School where there was too-frequent turmoil over his speech, his manners, his slouch and the 'crude' drainpipe jeans he wore every day to go with the perpetual winkle-pickers, denim jacket and purple shirt. He hadn't yet started shaving, so sideburns hadn't appeared yet, but, because he could rarely pass a mirror without making a quick adjustment with a comb, his hair now cascaded naturally into a ducktail and gravity-defying quiff akin to those on the scalp of one of those Teddy Boys, who still prowled the neon streets in packs, looking for things to destroy, people to beat up.

Comparing notes in the staff room, teachers agreed that that Richards lout had an 'attitude' as bad as the pimples that erupted constantly on his face. Not standing when he could lean, he was a known truant with the *leitmotif* of petty shop-lifting and seeking refuge in amusement arcades and snooker halls, or having his nose glued against motor-bike showroom windows. More long-term was the smoking that - as it was with Bill Perks too - he'd never have the will to stop.

In class, Richards tended to lounge in the back row, dumbly insolent and indifferent to a given pedagogue's chalky expositions. Relieved when he was absent, both wrinkled senior master and trainee on teaching practice found it less stressful to bite back on the sarcastic *bon mots* and, as far as they could, ignore him altogether.

Yet they may have been surprised at the slothful and disorderly youth's industrious application to extra-curricular pursuits that had little bearing on what he was meant to be studying. Almost as if he was embroiled in formal research, Keith voyaged evening after evening, often into the small hours, cataloguing and gloating over his growing collection of vinyl treasures, some of them ten- or twelve-inch 33 rpm long-players - LPs - making myriad private observations and finding much to notice, study and compare in sleeve notes, composer credits and listings of personnel.

This led him to the canons of associated artists. Elvis Presley's first regional hit, for example, had been a xerox of 'That's Alright Mama' by Arthur 'Big Boy' Crudup, also a resident of the blues capital of Memphis in the early 1950s. Keith also dug deeper into the cultural bedrock of Chuck Berry and, to a smaller degree, other US icons: 'Jerry Lee Lewis and Chuck Berry were a lightning bolt to kids of my generation, and they led you to other things. Chuck was on Chess Records, and so was Muddy Waters, so you go through the roster of Chess, Sun, Red Bird... Then I looked at the names of the musicians on Chuck Berry records, and the ones for Bo Diddley, Muddy Waters... same cats. So you want to be one.' [15] Having invested an amount of cash the equivalent of two weeks earnings as a Saturday boy in a parochial supermarket for every LP, Keith Richards intended to get his money's worth. Listening hard to them over and over again, he'd focus on maybe only the guitar or bass, then just the piano.

Yet Keith's beginnings as a record collector had been humble. Purportedly, the first disc he ever owned was 'Poor Little Fool', not the 1958 million-seller by US boy-next-door Ricky Nelson, but as duplicated by a hireling of Embassy, a domestic budget label that contracted artists whose very lack of individuality was ideal for cranking out workmanlike copies of other people's hits. Even when an Embassy session player copied Scotty Moore note for note, it was somehow too bland and inhibited with no 'feel' for rock 'n' roll. When this light dawned, Keith decided that it was a false economy to save nearly two shillings for, say, an ersatz 'School Days (Ring! Ring! Goes The Bell)' that bore as much relation to the Chuck Berry template as low-fat margarine did to dairy butter - and a full-price version for EMI, a company of greater merit, by Don Lang and his 'Frantic' Five, led by a singing trombonist from Halifax wasn't much better. So it was that Richards started buying Berry discs without first listening to them in one of the isolation booths that record stores had in those days and it was a magazine picture of Chuck on the wall that greeted him when he first yawned and stretched in the grey of morning.

Emulation of heroes is a vital part of growing up, and the essence of Keith's fretboard style was formed with Berry lurking in the background after Doris conjured up from her wages as a part-time shop assistant, the down-payment for a hollow-body six-string - possibly a Rosetti - on hire-purchase. Accepting it as his due rather than being beside himself with gratitude, Keith practiced daily, labouring late into the evening, to the detriment of even that modicum of homework necessary to avert trouble the next day. His fingertips hardened, and, from a favoured place at the top of the stairs, there emerged half-hidden clues of the guitarist he was to become.

Mike Jagger had also acquired a guitar, but was nowhere near as advanced as Keith, let alone Dick Taylor who had an expertise and theoretical insight that seemed stunning to one who used a pyjama cord as a strap so that it could hang on his shoulders when, in front of a bedroom mirror and with one of his small pile of records on the turntable, he posed - as Keith had once done - curling his lip, shaking his hips and mouthing the lyrics, yeah-ing and uh-huh-ing to imaginary thousands of girls.

Dick had taken the trouble to learn properly, even as he revised for his 'O' levels. His exam successes would be more than sufficient to enable him to start at an art college in nearby Sidcup, more London than Kent, in September, 1961 while Mike, who'd passed more of them, stayed on at Dartford Grammar in the Sixth Form.

Conversely, Keith Richards at the same stage had gained no official academic qualifications whatsoever, and had been slacking among pupils a year his junior prior to his foreseeable expulsion from Dartford Technical School at sixteen, then the minimum school-leaving age. He was advised that the Youth Employment Centre might not find him beyond redemption. Alternatively, though National Service was no longer compulsory, he could do worse than join the Regular Army. At the opposite end of the spectrum, however, was the art college in Sidcup. Someone told him that, for certain courses there, entry standards were lax to the point of being non-existent beyond evidence of a slight artistic turn - though a Phil May, who began at Sidcup in September, 1960, qualified this with 'The only way you could get into that art college without GCE 'O' levels was by doing graphic design. I got in when I was fifteen after they'd seen my Bexleyheath secondary modern school portfolio. It was obvious from the beginning that Keith was on the course so as not to have to go to work. He had no real interest in it.'

With the aid of a kinder written testimonial from the Technical School than he might have deserved, Keith Richards was able to keep that most noxious of human phenomena, a decision about the future, on hold for a while longer.

Neither had Mike Jagger much notion about what to do next, except that he hoped that it would be more exciting than, I dunno... Teacher training? Chartered accountancy? Junior management or any of the other financially secure but otherwise uninviting options that were typical for a grammar school leaver with the so-so grades Mike anticipated for his GCE 'A' levels? If he was fed-up now, what was he going to be like then?

He'd felt the vague lure of metaphorical greasepaint already. Before the Huxleys had moved to Kentish Town in north London in 1958, Mike and cousin Rick had sometimes tried in vain to 'sit in' with combos that played at the Railway Hotel, a Dartford pub with a music license. Mike also drank in accounts of the progress of a couple of rock 'n' roll groups formed by some chaps at school. One of them, The Southerners, had so proved themselves in regional heats for *Search For Stars*, organised by Carroll Levis, spiritual forefather of fellow Canadian Hughie Green of *Opportunity Knocks* notoriety, that they had seized the ultimate prize of a spot on 'Mr. Starmaker', Levis' ITV series. While a subsequent EMI recording test had to be postponed until the next school holiday – by which time the company's initial keenness had faded - the real benefit from this episode was The South-erners' date sheet stretching further into the future.

It might have provided a shadowy link to 'higher' artistic expres-sion, but the strongest motive for even the most ill-favoured lad to join such a group was sex. On the boards, there was licence to make eye-contact with the 'birds' who ringed the edge, ogling you with unmaid-enly eagerness. During an intermission, see, or even between numbers, a tryst after the last major sixth had reverberated could be sealed with a boyish grin, a flood of libido and an 'OK then. I'll meet you after the last encore.'

Buying into what was mostly a myth then about this *droit de seigneur* that prevailed for those on the bandstand, Mike, fired with envy, hovered when, in readiness for a dance organised jointly with the Sixth Form at the girls school, The Southerners were setting up puny amplifiers to power their guitars. The drum kit fended for itself, but some kind of public-address system had appeared by magic to magnify voices yet to spit out the Home Counties plums. From the dusty half-light beyond footlights still being tested, Mike Jagger stepped to the lip of the stage to ask meekly if he could sing with them that evening.

Politely rebuffed, he bore no grudge, and next approached Danny Rogers and his Realms, another outfit formed within a school that, slightly less shrouded in the draconian affectations and futile rigmarole prevalent in other establishments, wasn't completely malevolent towards pop music (as a hobby, of course).

The Realms' drummer Alan Dow - who was also, with Mike, a member of the basketball team - would remember 'Jagger coming up to me as I was walking down the stairs during an interval in a sixth form concert. He asked, "Can I do a few numbers with you?" I said, "No, Mike. I think we are all right." He was known for listening to all these weird records that no-one else wanted to listen to.'

It wasn't quite no-one. Mike plus fellow sixth formers Alan Etherington and Robert Beckwith were chief among a small coterie who dropped names like 'Muddy Waters', 'Howlin' Wolf', 'Jimmy Reed', 'Sonny Terry and Brownie McGhee' and others from the pages that few they knew read in *Melody Maker*, a more erudite pop music weekly than the *NME* or *Record Mirror* in that it covered blues and jazz too. Hardly any piece of information was too insignificant to be less than totally absorbing. It also became their habit to fall out of bed at five on selected mornings to catch a half-hour blues show on the American Forces Network.

They weren't that far removed from diehard supporters of a football club. Changing hands for weeks among them had been someone's copy of Paul Oliver's *Blues Fell This Morning*, hot off the press and to be recognised later as a standard work. [16] The Dartford blues disciples turned to it as monks to the Bible, working their way through as much of its bibliography as could be ordered from the public library, and fanning out to erudite tomes concerning, say, plantation field hollers and the African roots of blues. In the Sixth Form Common Room each could dwell very eloquently and with great authority on this interest, but couldn't grasp why the likes of Alan Dow were not as captivated.

In common with Keith Richards, the tactile sensation of handling the packagings of perhaps the *Rhythm And Blues With Chuck Berry* EP (extended play) or 1958's *Little Richard Vol. 2* LP had precipitated a spiral from pleasure to obsession to being addicted as surely as someone else could be to heroin. Vinyl? I can handle it. Records of the influences that influenced the influencers, and scrapbooks that kept track of them lent more resonance to Mike Jagger's lecture on 'blues-and jazz-influenced pop singers' to Dartford Grammar's history society. While he drew puffy smiles from those masters and their toadies present, there was no doubting Jagger's enthusiasm as he alluded to 'the strange and cruel origins of the blues' [17] and used as a case study an artist whose very name prompted amusement.

None of this Bo Diddley character's early UK singles - commencing with 1959's maraca-driven 'Crackin' Up' - had made the charts, but the tracks on the *Rhythm And Blues With Bo Diddley* EP - 'Bo Diddley', 'I'm A Man', 'Bring It To Jerome' and 'Pretty Thing' - which leaked into Britain three years before, had become as well known as many that had.

Such discs and others from untold North American independent labels were either taped from sources like the US Forces Network or else wended their way across the Atlantic by means as mysterious as a particular brand of footwear had to St. Kilda, the most remote Hebridean island, barely a year after its appearance in Victorian London. Often desirable for their very obscurity, many were spun time and time again on the turntables of the Dartford Grammar crowd as well as at Sidcup College of Art's Music Society gatherings - initially, no more than record playing sessions - after lectures on Fridays.

One evening, somebody brought in 1958's 'I Put A Spell On You' by Screamin' Jay Hawkins, who, so those present understood, was a macabre black Elvis from Ohio. With the best of intentions, Hawkins had bustled into the studio with a light romantic ditty that might have stood a British cover by Dickie Valentine. The recording wasn't going very well, and some liquor was procured to loosen the tension. Several takes later, the song had mutated into the goggle-eyed ravings of a man so drunk he was recording flat on his back, and swooping from warbling mock-operatics, half-spoken recitative, low grumbles - 'wurrrrrr' - and insane falsetto shrieks.

By fair means or foul, Keith Richards had to have 'I Put A Spell On You', just as he'd had to have the Bo Diddley EP and, to be found nowhere in any run-of-the-mill record shop in Britain, Elmore James's 'Rollin' And Tumblin' - something of a blues 'standard' - after Dick Taylor had made him aware of their existence. Deeply half-educated already in the music of black America when he started at Sidcup, Keith learned too that, in the decades that preceded rock 'n' roll, a white radio listener in the United States might have tuned in by accident to muffled bursts of what segregationalist pamphlets denigrated as 'screaming idiotic words and savage music' on some negro-run station - and that it had been possible for releases by such as Arthur Crudup, John

Lee Hooker, Jimmy Reed, Muddy Waters and Howlin' Wolf to sell by the ton in Uncle Sam's 'race' or 'sepia' (or 'rhythm-and-blues' as it became) market without figuring at all in the parallel dimensions of the corresponding country-and-western chart and mainstream pop *Hot 100* in *Billboard*, the Bible and Yellow Pages of the US music trade.

That had been how Hooker's 'I'm In The Mood' and 'Boogie Chillun' had each been registered as million-sellers in 1948. These and later discs stamped with the same droning blues-boogie undercurrent were available only on import, as were the exorcisms of Robert Johnson, a bluesman tormented by an inferno of ectoplasmic monsters. Most of these were taped in 1937, a few months before his slow death by poison at the age of twenty-four. For all his youth, there are those - such as noted pop historian Charles Shaar Murray - who seem to reckon that poor Robert was the greatest musician ever to have walked the planet. Keith Richards wouldn't go that far, but he was to avow that 'if Robert Johnson had lived into the era of electric guitar, he'd have killed us all. When you listen to him, the cat's got Bach going on down low and Mozart going on up high. The cat was counterpointing.' [17]

Johnson was mentor to Elmore James, whose records had also proved instructional years previously to Muddy Waters, whose in-concert *At Newport* album was to obtain a UK release in 1960. Seen by Richards as the missing link between Johnson and Berry, Waters had been taking the stage with an electric six-string and, also amid much criticism from blues purists, lewd movements akin to those of Ray and then Presley. What more did he need to earn the admiration of one such as Keith - whose vision was shared with other students, some of whom joined him in attempts to reproduce the black music themselves? 'There were jam sessions in the cloakroom with Keith, Dick Taylor and me,' affirmed Phil May, 'We wanted something that was ours, Muddy Waters, John Lee Hooker, Bo Diddley and so on.'

In Britain, see, blues in all its sub-divisions remained, to all intents and purposes, the exclusive property of a knotted-brow fringe. It was a comparatively unknown quantity even in the USA, hovering as distant thunder at most in mainstream pop. Furthermore, blues wasn't particularly popular amongst the Union's cosmopolitan young blacks, being music their migrant parents still liked. 'As far as white people were concerned, especially suburban kids,' confirmed Mike Jagger, 'It was interesting because it was underclass music that they'd had no experience of or, in fact, that didn't exist by the time they had got to it anyway, almost. It was disappearing. That culture was on its way out.' [18]

With no direct contact, the function of Mike and his Sixth Form blues boys - and Dick and Keith over in Sidcup - was just to listen, appreciate and absorb the signals, such as they were, as they came - like they would in hitherto unimagined abundance in 1958 when Sonny Terry and Brownie McGhee and then Muddy Waters performed in central London. Mike, barely fifteen then, was not permitted to attend either concert.

Neither had he been allowed to experience in-person North American rock 'n' roll when it had first reached England after a faintly pathetic fashion in 1956 via the twirling sticks of swing drummer Lionel Hampton, whose raucous nod to the form during a concert at the Royal Festival Hall prompted Johnny Dankworth - 1949's Jazz Musician of the Year in *Melody Maker* - to voice his disgust through cupped hands from the audience. Next up, we got Pat Boone at the Kilburn State and the Tooting Granada during a European tour. He wasn't much like the imagined real thing either, being, for grown-ups, a clean, well-mannered alternative to that ghastly Presley. Revelling in his married state, Pat preached that your parents' word was law; get your hair cut, and don't talk dirty. These worthy ideals would be incorporated into *Twixt Twelve And Twenty*, the Boone manual for wholesome boys and girls. When he, like Elvis, moved into films, he'd further parade his dearth of major vices by refusing to kiss his leading ladies. Well, you never know what these things lead to...

Thus Pat came and went, and, after the breakdown of discussions about Elvis coming over to England too, Bill Haley and his Comets rolled up early in 1957, paunchy, dad-like and begging pardon at press conferences for their knockabout stage routines, but what with this 'rock' nonsense going so well, it'd have been bad business not to have played up to it, wouldn't it? Anyway, one of the band had served under Benny Goodman.

Yet, if only fractionally more suitable ambassadors of rock 'n' roll than Hampton and Boone, they were well-received after a superficial fashion by snowblinded audiences that included nine-year-old Michael Kevin Taylor from Hatfield, twenty miles beyond London's northern suburbs, brought to see Haley and his Comets at the Edmonton Regal by his Uncle Paul, young enough to have bought a guitar, and to be as enthralled as his nephew by the country's most spectacular visitation thus far by gen-u-ine US rock 'n' rollers. If of reticent nature, the boy, known to the family as Mick, was wild with excitement, and was to recount the event at the top of his voice when he and the voluptuously weary Paul got home that night.

In the cold light of morning too, this biggest treat of his childhood resonated still - to the degree that Mick Taylor asked Paul to teach him all he knew on the guitar because, although he had a serviceable singing voice, Mick could not see himself donning the mantle of domestic Bill Haley or Elvis Presley. However, it would occur to him one day that, not only was it hard for him to put the instrument down when he started practicing, but also that he'd become a better guitarist than Paul.

Neither Bill Haley's singing and guitar playing nor his presence in the country had had such a mesmerising effect on Mike Jagger. Indeed, he'd been unimpressed by what he'd read and heard of performances by any of the US so-called rockers who'd plugged gaps in their tour itinerary with British dates - until his father, so Dick Taylor remembered, 'agreed in a bemused kind of way' to let him go to a show on Friday 14th March, 1958 by Buddy Holly and the Crickets at the Coronet in Woolwich, ten miles away.

Jagger and Dick Taylor had been lending an intrigued rather than completely fascinated ear to Holly, a weedy, bespectacled white Texan, who, with members of his backing Crickets, composed simple but atmospheric songs tailored to his elastic adenoids. Part of the attraction was that his take on rock 'n' roll - 'half country, half blues,' reckoned Dick Taylor - could be simultaneously forceful and romantic, and could progress without getting too complex. While 'I'm Looking For Someone To Love' was based on standard blues chord changes, another B-side, 'Not Fade Away' hinged on Bo Diddley's trademark *shave-and-a-haircut-six-pence* rhythm. 'We both thought that "Not Fade Away" was the best thing Buddy ever did,' recalled Dick - and, in Taylor and Jagger's eyes too, neither did Holly and the Crickets make idiots of themselves when tackling black non-originals. More intense than gut-wrenching, if Holly broke sweat on, say, Little Richard's 'Slippin' And Slidin'', sonorous wordless harmonies from his colleagues kept him cool so that the song could surge to a climax all the more rewarding for the predetermined constraint that preceded it.

Yet a *New Musical Express* reviewer was to write 'How these boys manage to make such a big, big sound with such limited instrumentation baffles me.' [19] It pre-empted the two-guitars-bass-drums prototype of the British beat explosion that lay five years away when Mike Jagger, Dick Taylor, Alan Etherington and Robert Beckwith experienced their closest encounter with in-person US pop during what turned out to be Holly's only visit to our sceptre'd isle, perhaps the most pivotal of all the events that coalesced to produce the beat group boom - for among other lads who found Buddy and his musicians' stage act and compact sound instructive were Dave Clark, Brian Poole, Jeff Beck, Keith Relf and Eric Clapton - who all caught the show in and around London too.

At the Manchester stop were future Hollies Allan Clarke and Graham Nash, and a gawky youth named Garrity, lately parted from a girlfriend who'd disapproved of him singing in a new outfit called Freddie and the Dreamers in which he wore Holly-like spectacles - as would Brian Poole after he'd approached lads at his Barking secondary school about forming his own Crickets with himself as Buddy.

Crucially, after the Crickets and Holly played Liverpool's Philharmonic Hall, John Lennon and Paul McCartney's nascent efforts as a songwriting team became less of a sideline. Previously, they too had been fans of 'really good-looking performers like Elvis,' smiled McCartney, 'Any fellow with glasses always took them off to play, but after Buddy, anyone who really needed glasses could then come out of the closet.' [20] Not lost to Mike Jagger either was that Holly was no Presley, true enough, but girls still screamed at him.

Notes

1. Sleeve notes to Hoochie Coochie Men: A History Of British Blues And R&B, 1955-2001 (Indigo IBBX 2501, 2002)
2. Not the US soul singer
3. *Sunday Times*, 5th July, 1999
4. *The Independent*, 11th October, 2001
5. *Sunday Times, 1990 (precise date obscured)*
6. *Keith Richards In His Own Words* ed. M. St. Michael (Omnibus, 1994)
7. *Q*, November, 1992

8. *Stone Alone* by B. Wyman and R. Coleman (Viking, 1990)

9. *Hamburg: The Cradle Of British Rock* by A. Clayson (Sanctuary, 1997)

10. *Record Collector*, No. 261, May, 2001

11. *New Musical Express*, 2nd September, 1989

12. *The Guardian*, 5th September, 2003

13. Furthermore, when recovering from a near-fatal stomach operation in 1983, Lewis had to refuse a kind invitation - made largely at Keith's insistence - to play on the Stones' *Undercover* album.

14. *Mature Times*, December, 2004

15. *Blues Fell This Morning* by P. Oliver (Cassell, 1960)

16. Quoted in *The Land Where The Blues Began* by A. Lomax (Minerva, 1999)

17. *Blues Guitar*, ed J Obrecht (Miller Freeman, 1993)

18. *Best Of Guitar Player*, Rolling Stones special, December, 1993

19. *New Musical Express*, 7th March, 1958

20. *Buddy Holly; The Real Story* by E. Amburn (Virgin, 1996)

*Chapter Two*
## West Side Stories

*'Brian was from Cheltenham, where it used to be fashionable to go and take the baths once a year. Now it's a seedy sort of place, full of aspirations to be an aristocratic town. It rubs off on anyone who comes from there' - Keith Richards* [1]

Beyond the pale of London and its dormitory shires, British pop was so parochial that, as the decade turned, there seemed to be no halfway between obscurity and a qualified national celebrity - as exemplified by the quantum jump to be made early in 1961 by Shane Fenton and the Fentones; one week denizens of youth clubs that convened mostly in musty Victorian monstrosities in glum Mansfield, the next, residency group on *Saturday Club*, a new two hour pop show, hosted by Brian Matthew, on the Light Programme. Fortune smiled less brightly when, after weeks of dogged negotiation the previous year, Dave Berry and the Cruisers, Mickey and Johnny, The Twin Cities Rhythm Group and two coachloads of fans brought Sheffield pop to London with a bold if vocationally disappointing concert at the Shepherd's Bush Gaumont.

Consolation for the failure of this and other provincial endeavours to stoke up interest amongst record company talent scouts or important impresarios was often the guarantee of a full workload within easy reach for such acts in a growing array of local jive hives. Yet the smallness of the ponds in which such big fish could swim was such that you could be as renowned in a particular neighbourhood as Buddy Holly and his Crickets were on a world-wide scale, but be able to stroll unrecognised a few streets away.

In Andover way out in the wilds of Hampshire, for instance, The Astrals were the boss group of Enham-Alamein, the military district on the edge of the town, while The Griefs held Tidworth, and Pete Mystery and his Strangers ruled Clatford, another outlying village. However, reformed as The Strangers Rhythm Group, the latter combo tried in vain to crack the harder nut of central Andover - as Chris Britton and the Redwoods had already, cramming in two separate engagements - at Abbots Ann Memorial Hall and the Andover and District Young Farmers Club - in the space of one evening. Those boys certainly got around, but being enormous in somewhere like Andover had to be enormous enough unless you pulled some far-fetched Shane Fenton-esque stroke.

Andover, therefore, produced no hit parade contenders prior to British pop's 1963 watershed - and neither did Cheltenham many miles further west from London where, realistically, it was necessary to head in order to tilt for the Big Time. That's what Chris Britton did - after his Redwoods had mutated into The Troggs by 1965 - and so did Brian Jones, as eternally, if reluctantly, Cheltenham's as The Troggs will be Andover's.

Wales was close enough for Brian, as a round-eyed toddler, to have watched the RAF's diamond formations zooming towards the Luftwaffe's bombardment of the docks in both Newport and Bristol - facing each other across the Severn - where the horizon glowed with ton upon booming ton of death and destruction. Moreover, on 28th February, 1942 - a cold but dry day during a year of meteorological extremes - he'd entered the world as Lewis Brian Hopkin-Jones, embracing the two most common surnames in the principality.

The border settlement that vied with Cirencester and Gloucester as stone-built 'capital' of the Cotswolds was remote enough from London, even after World War II, for the distance to the metropolis to be measured in years as much as miles. Yet Cheltenham had thrived in its isolation and built-in resilience as an agricultural centre from the pre-Christian era, and as a Roman settlement, exemplified today by period pavements uncovered for public scrutiny then buried again to preserve against deterioration. After the discovery of the medicinal properties of its waters, Cheltenham became a spa in 1719 - and 'the most complete Regency Town in England', it reads in the borough council's guide booklet.

Nonetheless, to Britons elsewhere, Cheltenham and its environs were merely another far-westerly point on the train route between London and Wales, no different from anywhere sufficiently large to warrant a railway station by the mid-nineteenth century. Likewise, its inhabitants were presumed to be a mingling of huntin'-shootin'-fishin' squireachy and brutish yokels who said things like *ooo-arrr* and *pshaw*, and rendered 'I' as 'oi', 'were' as 'was', 'was' as 'were', 'we' as ''us' (and vice-versa') and 'ain't' as 'bain't'.

That might have been so once, but after the Great War, though some open country remained just so - such as that within the estate of the aristocratic Mitfords - vast areas of woodland and meadow were lacerated by further clattering railway lines, or buried beneath bricks and mortar to cater for an encroaching overspill of incomers from the south's bigger cities. Yet conservatism and long residency in Cheltenham remained prerequisites for entry into polite society, which contained broods connected either to old money or an officer class that, after a life of service to the Empire - particularly in India - had retired there. In the aftermath of a civic reception, brigadier, baronet and *nouveau riche* town councillor sipped a fine old port put down by the baronet's great-great-great-grandfather while the councillor's respective ancestor was a collier clerk checking coal baskets at a pit near Bristol. Money was the leveller that permitted them to converse as equals, and to have married each other's sisters.

On the periphery of this upper crust were those who dwelt in the roomy semi-detacheds along Hatherley Road in one of Cheltenham's more genteel districts. Brian Jones spent most of his childhood at Number 355 - 'Ravenswood' - whose interior reflected the prescriptive, honourable - and severe - manner of his upper middle-class parents' domestic life. With geometrically-patterned linoleum in the kitchen among few hints of domestic personality, it was, recalled Pat Andrews, perhaps Brian's first 'serious' girlfriend, 'modern, if quite Spartan furniture-wise'.

'One of his grandfathers was a schoolmaster in Wales,' added Pat, 'The family background was "Chapel", and enjoying yourself in any way played no part in their lives. You were born, you went to school, you made sure you got good marks, you found yourself a good profession, you got married, you had children - and that was it. There was no time in between for any fun.'

As well as instilling into their son - and daughter, Barbara - what ought to be admired about quiet dignity and achievement by effort, Lewis and Louisa Jones paraded them to and from divine worship at nine-hundred-year-old St. Mary's Parish Church. Once there, Mum, Dad and Barbara took their seats in their usual high-backed pew while Brian went round to the vestry where cassock, ruff and surplice were to cover the detested and sober suit that, when he began wearing spectacles and was old enough for long trousers, made him look like a miniature version of his father. As a matter of course, he had been obliged to join other boys who cantillated every Sunday and, when required, at weddings and in St. Cecilia's Day oratorios. As he rose through the ranks, he'd be privileged sometimes to bear the processional cross as priest and choristers filed in and out. He also doused the altar candles after the General Confession during Matins.

Despite - or because of - this, coupled with drummed-in knowledge of the Bible and associated religious works, Brian decided he'd had enough Church to last a lifetime, and was to lose his faith during compulsory years of glowering resentfully from the choir stalls into the tedium of psalms, prayers, responses, communions, apostles' creeds, readings, catechisms, the whine of the pipe-organ and the vicar sermonising at a flock that, like him, were not worthy to gather up the crumbs under the holy Lord's table.

If Brian knew few who lived much differently from himself, from a motor-car window, he'd noticed rough - and, he guessed, godless - boys and girls hopscotching and footballing in Cheltenham's greyer streets. More intriguing, however, were the GIs on passes who burst upon the fun-palaces of Cheltenham in garb in which only blacks, cartoon *spivs* and homosexuals would be seen dead - padded shoulders on double-breasted suits with half-belts at the back, 'spearpoint' shirt collars, two-tone shoes and hand-painted ties with baseball players or Red Indians on them. At one stage during the hostilities, it was reckoned that North Americans stationed in the town had outnumbered the English addressees.

The Yanks were still around in the pre-rock 'n' roll 1950s, though, as sartorial visions, they were being outshone by Teddy Boys from the new housing estates, resplendent in their seedy-flash finery and quiffed glaciers of brilliantine. Gormlessly hostile stares, which the GIs acknowledged with waves of fat wands of cigars, became open grievances, and one evening, some Teds, wielding bicycle chains and flick knives, attacked a cluster of the US aliens outside the bus station toilets, a melee that left one GI dead, and the whole town declared off-limits to all North American servicemen.

The US presence marked too the genesis of Cheltenham's participation in Britain's attempts to get to grips with jazz, understood by Lewis Jones to be a slang expression to describe the improvised extrapolations prevalent in negro dance halls. Moreover, to both Lewis, sometime organist at St. Mary's, and Louisa, a piano teacher, jazz fell far short of their dictates about what constituted 'decent' music.

56

There was also a moral sub-text to their disapproval. 'To Brian's parents, jazz was black music, played in speakeasies,' explained Pat Andrews, 'Anything to do with it was connected with drugs and sex. Brian had problems listening or playing any sort of music at 'Ravenswood'. It wasn't to be too loud. He'd rarely practice at home, apart from piano which his mother taught him, and clarinet. He played piano in a duet on a school open day, and his father was very proud of Brian's rendition of Weber's clarinet concerto.'

Via a repressive cultural atmosphere as well as the general ennui of 'Ravenswood' and church, Brian had been sheltered as far as possible from any sort of social or cultural non-conformity as the country paid for its victory, and the West Country continued to be pictured in metropolitan breakfast-rooms as a corner of the map where nothing much was guaranteed to happen, year in, year out; where the 1940s weren't to really end until about 1956, and bored teenagers with hormones raging wondered what to do until bedtime just as they had since Cain slew Abel. All the alleged excesses of a wider world belonged to speculation whilst sharing a communal filter-tip behind school bicycle sheds, and infrequent sightings of the odd male student emerging from the Art College carrying a huge painting of a nude, and accompanied by a girlfriend who was identifiable as its subject.

There was nothing teenage in the national newspapers, and only the music press, such as it was, and the electric media aligned Cheltenham adolescents with trendsetting London - and even that was imbued heavily with what adults thought you *should* like. BBC television's *Six-Five Special* series just about passed muster because it balanced the 'pop' (by such as Don Lang and his "Frantic" Five, the most regularly featured act) and traditional jazz - 'trad' - with string quartets, features on sports and purposeful hobbies, and such upstanding interlocutors as former boxing champion Freddie Mills. Effusing an even more wholesome, self-improving reek, *Teleclub* too was 'a magazine programme for the under twenty-ones', embracing as it did 'acts by young professional entertainers, sport, interest, a personal problem, and "your turn"' [2] with music directed by the avuncular Steve Race. The inclusion of Humphrey Lyttelton's Jazz Band on *Round About Ten*, shortly before the immovable Epilogue, was as racy as it got after Independent Television (ITV) began in 1956.

Inevitably, Brian Jones became an avid watcher, whenever he could of such few TV broadcasts when a passion for any type of pop music would bring condescending smiles to the lips of the most open-minded grown-up do-gooders who presided over botany, charity work, the Great Outdoors and further hearty pastimes intended to distract young minds from what Robert Baden-Powell described in *Scouting For Boys* as 'the secret vice of beastliness'. [3]

'Never before have so many young people made their own music,' chortled one such pillar of society on *Six-Five Special* [4], seizing upon a new craze called 'skiffle' as a means of guiding tomorrow's adults along the straight-and-narrow. Yet it had been born of the rent parties, speakeasies and rowdy Dust Bowl jug bands of the US Depression, and had sprung up in Britain during a rummaging for a riposte to Elvis Presley. The job had gone to Tommy Steele, a merchant seaman of the same age, and from the next London suburb to Bill Perks, but his 'Rock With The Cavemen' had been shut down in 1956's autumn Top Twenty by 'Dead Or Alive' from Lonnie Donegan, who milked this gratifying turn of events for all it was worth, and came to be enthroned as 'The King of Skiffle' throughout its 1957 prime and beyond.

Though Donegan was to offend purists by striving for wider acceptance with such as the Boy Scouts campfire ditty, 'Does Your Chewing Gum Lose Its Flavour (On The Bedpost Overnight)' and 1960's chart-topping 'My Old Man's A Dustman', his impact would be carried across aeons of British pop through his impregnating an impoverished and imitative scene with energetic and imported idioms, and an alluring nasal tenor far removed from the docile plumminess of earlier indigenous pop singers.

On *Six-Five Special*, however, Donegan toed a clean, amiable line and so did visiting black North American Big Bill Broonzy, whose vocal lines were fired by the impetus of a then-novel *twelve*-string guitar, after the programme's brief extended to the 'ethnic' blues that was a major content of skiffle, given that the likes of 'Midnight Special', 'Rock Island Line', 'This Little Light Of Mine', 'How Long Blues', sweetly sinister 'Careless Love' and further items from the repertoires of Broonzy and fellow bluesmen had become set-works of a genre that had spread across Britain like bubonic plague thanks to Lonnie's record success and, more obscurely, to when trad jazz cornetist Ken Colyer's seaman brother Bill spotted one such outfit working in

Chicago, Dan Burley's Skiffle Boys, featuring a black singing guitarist called Brownie McGhee.

Manchester's Bogeda Jazz Club had, as early as 1950, hosted the debut of a blues outfit led by seventeen-year-old youth clubman John Mayall. However, Ken Colyer is generally accepted as the musician who formed the UK's first *bona fide* skiffle combo, albeit within his Crane River Jazz Band, who traded otherwise in 'Bill Bailey', 'Tiger Rag', 'Ida Sweet As Apple Cider', 'Who's Sorry Now' and like favourites from the ragtime portfolios of Louis Armstrong, Kid Ory, Sophie Tucker *et al*. As a novelty intermission from the interweaving extemporisations of front-line horns too, The Washboard Wonders - a trio led by Donegan - were granted a spot during performances by a similar London-based ensemble, Chris Barber's New Orleans Jazz Band. It became the highlight of the show.

Accepted advice from Donegan in *Melody Maker* was reiterated in a school essay on skiffle by Mike Jagger in his contention that 'before any group is started up, there should be someone who can sing really well, and a couple of guitarists who can play good, strong chords'. [5] Nonetheless, like punk after it, anyone with the most marginal talent who'd mastered basic techniques could have a crack at skiffle - and the more ingenuous the sound, the better. In sniffy *A Guide To Popular Music*, written by staff at Decca, one of the country's four major record companies, this was defined as 'a makeshift kind of jazz, played on standard instruments mixed with the home-made'. [6] While orthodox percussion instruments and maybe three bedrock chords strummed on an embarrassment of acoustic guitars were certainly at the core of the ideally contagious backbeat, no-one howled with derision at a washboard tapped with thimbles, tea chest-and-broomstick bass, dustbin-lid cymbals, biscuit-tin snare drum and further vehicles of musical effect, fashioned from everyday implements. The highest aspiration was to forge an individual style by making even 'Rock Island Line', Donegan's chart breakthrough - which also harried a US Top Forty upon which UK releases seldom trespassed - *not* sound like any other outfit's version.

Such displays had been generally for the benefit of performers rather than onlookers, but the proprietor of the Odeon, Cheltenham's principal cinema, interspersed *Tarzan And The Lost Safari, Idle On Parade* and the latest Norman Wisdom comedy with occasional in-person performances by amateurs - with a preponderance of groups fronted by youths enjoying hardly polite spatters of applause as they make-believed they were Lonnie.

Would-be Donegans were everywhere, stretching the limits of their abilities at wedding receptions, youth clubs, church fetes, birthday parties and every talent contest advertised. Back in the Medway Towns, for instance, a Peter Smith, strumming a home-made guitar, made a public debut with The Hard Travellers at a hospital's staff party. The group leaned towards country-and-western, though it also embraced the expected classic rock and Light Programme 'hit parade' preferences as well as one or two of Peter's first offerings as a composer.

After assuming the *nom de theatre* ' Crispian St. Peters', Smith was to flower momentarily as a 1960s pop star - as would a skiffler from Croydon, Ralph May in the 1970s, having adopted the stage surname 'McTell' in genuflection to a Mississippi bluesman, before taking to the road like dustbowl balladeer Woody Guthrie, 'armed only with a guitar and a pocketful of dreams'. [7]

When skiffle started losing its flavour on the bedpost overnight, other of its practitioners who'd meant business would be running up hire-purchase debts for the amplified guitars and orthodox dance band drum kits that were to supercede the finger-lacerating acoustic six-strings and pots-and-pans percussion that were becoming old hat. Stylistically, many backslid gradually to rock 'n' roll - 'a more commercial form of skiffle,' shrugged the authors of unconsciously humorous *A Guide To Popular Music* [6] - and a US-dominated UK Top Thirty.

The more 'sophisticated' of former skiffle players became, nevertheless, ostensibly snooty about the hit parade. Such a person throwing a pseudo-*demi-monde* party - usually when his or her parents were away - ensured that the artless scattering of LPs around the record-player were the coolest modern jazz, what with 'The Story of Folk Song with a Jazz Beat' being the sub-title of clergyman Brian Bird's *Skiffle* [8], the style's chief work of reference. Guests might also be treated to glimpses of unconscious comedy during 'impromptu' in-person musical entertainment involving, maybe, scat-singing, bongo-tapping and a saxophone honking inanely.

At student union shindigs, other exhibitionists would don boaters or top hats, and a variety of hacked-about formal wear, drink heavily of cider, and launch into vigorous steps that blended skip-jiving with the Charleston in a curious galumphing motion to the plinking and puffing of a trad outfit. According to the sleeve notes to a 1958 EP entitled *Chris Barber In Concert Volume Three* trad jazz was 'gay and carefree music' [9] - on paper, the antithesis of blues. There was also something vaguely collegiate about an apparent 'appreciation' of trad, principally because it had been claimed initially as the near-exclusive property of undergraduates flirting with bohemia before becoming teachers.

It is intriguing to tally how many famous groups from both trad and every phase of 1960s pop had roots in further education, particularly art schools. While the origins of both The Rolling Stones and The Pretty Things is traceable to Sidcup Art College, The Temperance Seven, The Rockin' Berries, The Beatles, The Animals, The Kinks, The Creation, The New Vaudeville Band, The Bonzo Dog Doo-Dah Band, The Move and The Pink Floyd were hatched in like establishments all over the kingdom.

Guitar hero-in-waiting Jeff Beck was on a two-year course at Wimbledon, even as he twanged the wires for The Crescents, just like Hank B. Marvin of The Shadows, who began as backing unit to Cliff Richard, Tommy Steele's successor as the English Elvis, prior to notching up instrumental hits in their own right, and spawning countless imitators like, well, The Crescents. In the neighbouring town of Kingston, Pentangle's John Renbourn and future Yardbirds Keith Relf, Eric Clapton and Jimmy Page also honed their musical skills in an atmosphere of coloured dust, palette-knives, hammer-and-chisel and lumpy impasto.

Harrow School Of Art was the *alma mater* of Charlie Watts, whose membership of The Rolling Stones will always remain central to any consideration of him as a figure in time's fabric. While drumming overshadowed Charlie's adolescence as much as his art studies, there were other interests such as the Wild West, which he researched beneath its Roy Rogers-and-Trigger veneer, maintaining an abiding interest into adulthood, particularly in the Civil War. He was, too, a keen listener to radio comedy, where his tastes ran to the *Hancock's Half Hour* sit-com rather than the more off-beat and childish *Goon Show*. He was also given to drawing cartoons supplemented with fragments of verse and prose.

61

This was symptomatic of a flair for art - as was the fluttering of a General Certificate of Education 'O' level pass in the subject onto the Watts family's doormat in August, 1957, gaining him a place on a three-year course at Harrow, commencing the following month. Thus, as it was with Keith Richards, the world of work could be held at arm's length for a while longer, enabling the fancy that he'd like to make a living as a musician to enter Charlie's index of possibilities.

Charles Robert Watts had entered the world in Islington's University College Hospital on 2nd June, 1941, the overcast and unseasonably cool day that wartime clothes rationing was introduced. He and sister Linda had already caught and held *norf* London accents before they, mother Lilian and father Charles, a British Rail delivery driver, moved into one of Islington's small and look-alike 'prefab' bungalows constructed between 1945 and 1949 for an estimated 'life' of fifty to sixty years after erection in six pre-assembled sections of aluminium alloy, in one day, by a gang of six with the assistance of a crane.

Remembered by Charlie as 'tiny but very cosy', [10] his home as an infant was situated on the edge of pasture in rural London, not quite the contradiction in terms it might seem in the capital's present-day austere and functional aesthetic of tower blocks and right-angled grids of inner distribution roads. Indeed, as Charlie observed half a century later, the district where he'd grown up had 'gone back to fields again now - which is very unusual.' [10]

In 1948, however, the family moved to Kingsbury, as much Middlesex as London, where the patches of green were not farmland, but country parks, sports grounds and play areas within earshot of the North Circular Road and, more so, the *diddley-dum-clickety-clack* of the national and internal rail links across a lugubrious suburb that was becoming indistinguishable to outsiders from any other on the western fringes of the metropolis divided by a Thames a few miles from its polluted flow through the dockland wharves, refineries, metal works, clerking offices and warehouses.

When Charlie Watts was a boy, dray horses still dragged cargos onto clippers poised to catch the tide. Then they'd become smudges on the horizon of the North Sea or the English Channel. Further myriad consignments - from crane-buckling girders to pen-nibs to rubble from bombed East End terraces - were transported down river on domestic tugboats steered by men like Arthur Wood, whose family - and that of his wife - had been 'river people' for at least two centuries.

'My mother was born on a barge in Paddington Basin,' recounted the eldest of Arthur's three boys, 'Her parents used to work on the Grand Union Canal. Although my dad was a tugboat captain, we were the first generation to live in a house rather than afloat. I was named Arthur after my dad.

My mum, Mercy Leigh - everyone called her 'Liz' - packed records at the EMI factory in Hayes. All us boys - me, Ted and Ronnie - went to the same primary schools in West Drayton. When I was fourteen in 1951, I passed a scholarship to go to Ealing Art School. Ted and Ronnie were to go to art college too, and all of us ended up in bands. It seemed normal to us until people pointed out how strange it was that we all followed the same path.

We were quite an artistic bunch. Mum used to do embroidery, and us kids would be drawing all the time. In the 1920s, my dad had been in a twenty-four-piece harmonica band who played at race-tracks and pubs. At art college, I formed a group, and then I joined Ted's trad outfit, The Candy Bison Jazz Band. I played guitar and banjo, but I wasn't very good. We rehearsed in our parlour - which we used to call "The Jazz Room". Ronnie was only little then, ten years younger than me, and we'd send him out, but he'd keep coming back in to interfere and pick up any instruments lying about. Nowadays, he can play piano, sax, guitar, anything.'

The talented Wood boys' and, in spite of the upheaval of moving to Kingsbury, Charlie Watts's respective upbringings were as undramatic and free from major calamities as Brian Jones's wasn't after he finished at fee-paying Dean Close Primary School in 1953, having sailed through the Eleven-Plus. As a first-former in the top academic stream at Cheltenham Grammar School, he'd settled down almost eagerly to classwork, but, as it was with boring, boring Church, he soon tired of it. His disinterest could not, however, remain passive, and 'somewhere along the line, he decided he was going to be a full-time professional rebel,' sighed Keith Richards, 'and it didn't really suit him - so that when he wanted to be obnoxious, he had to really make an effort, and, having made the effort, he would be *really* obnoxious.' [11]

No, it wasn't easy, but by the end of his second year at the Grammar, Brian Jones was a known nuisance. The most overt offences included an appearance behind an inkwelled desk in football boots, more comfortable, he argued, than the regulation black 'bombhead' shoes; instigating a widespread but swiftly suppressed practice of drinking bottled beer instead of the third-pints of lukewarm milk then provided at morning break, courtesy of the Welfare State, and earning a week's suspension for ringleading a mutiny against the prefects.

His bravado was at odds with him turning his back on the havoc he created at school - and home - to roam the pastures and woods of the Cotswolds alone, perhaps chasing what he'd absorbed at Church about St. Francis and his 'hidden solitude where I can listen in loneliness and silence to the secret treasures of God's conversation.' Such a yearning became piquantly apparent when Jones, with terror in his grey-green eyes, was summoned to be confronted with one or other of his infamies in headmaster Dr. Arthur Bell's study.

Yet, when gazing appraisingly at shame-smitten Brian's bowed head, Dr. Bell recognised a pupil that was as troubled as he was troublesome. In an informed obituary in the school magazine in autumn 1969, Bell concluded that 'Brian Jones seemed to be essentially a sensitive and vulnerable boy, not at all cut out for the rough-and-tumble of the commercial world.'

The headmaster agreed too that 'he always seemed quite clever, and he did in fact do quite well - though nothing like as well as he might have done had he been attracted to an academic career.' Whatever the stomach-knotting repercussions of his calculated pranks, Brian answered barked questions in class correctly and succinctly, often without seeming to awake from a daydream, and didn't lose a knack for passing examinations, even those most important ones held during summer when, shirtsleeved in the heat, and with pen sliding in sweaty palm, his chronic asthma allied with hay fever.

Lewis and Louisa were never over-loud with praise, but they were pleased that, paralleling reports of his irritating and futile escapades, there was talk of university. Furthermore, for parents for whom the good opinion of their peers appeared to matter more than their children's happiness, it was eminently satisfactory for Brian to be seen in the grammar's black-and-white-striped blazer and cap rather than the uniform - if there was such a thing - of a secondary modern where all the Eleven-Plus 'failures' were sent - 'failures' like Charlie Watts, who attended Tyler's Croft Secondary Modern as a self-effacing, seeming non-entity who could 'give the impression of being bored, but I'm not really. I've just got an incredibly boring face.' [1]

To his surprise, however, Charlie forged ahead at school where he was recognised, for instance, as a talented soccer player who preferred cricket. Actually, his ambidextrous bowling was impressive enough to gain a try-out for the Middlesex county club. He also won trophies for sprinting, and proved to be sound academically too - with end-of-term prizes for Art and English. If he didn't do particularly well at music, well, it might have run in the family. 'I reckon the only instrument any of them could play at home was the gramophone,' laughed Charlie. [12] Yet music started to become central to his life from around the age of eleven.

When the tip of classic rock's iceberg was sighted, he, in common with Jagger, Richards and Taylor in Kent, found most of its white executants less astounding than their black counterparts, somehow making this judgement while confessing 'I never listened to rock 'n' roll - or I refused to - until I was about twenty-one. I never followed the charts. I always took myself seriously, and thought Buddy Holly was a great joke.' [10]

He had been, however, very taken with 1952's million-selling 'Flamingo' by saxophonist Earl Bostic, former sideman with Lionel Hampton - the drummer who so annoyed Johnny Dankworth - who had surfaced from the big bands of the 'swing era' that was fizzling out after the war. Within months of hearing 'Flamingo', Charlie's imagination had been captured by jazz as surely as Crazy Horse's had been by the boundless expanse of the Great Plains. 'I never had any trouble listening to it,' Watts explained, 'It was very easy for me.' [10]

Charlie came to love all its roots and branches - ragtime, traditional, mainstream, modern, avant-garde, 'cool', 'hot', New Orleans, Kansas City, New York, Chicago - whether the orchestral euphoria of Duke Ellington and Count Basie, the white swing of Benny Goodman and Woody Herman, vocal dare-devils such as Buddy Greco, Frank Sinatra, Billy Eckstine and Anita O'Day, and the differing textural complexities of Ornette Coleman and Roland Kirk. Charlie travelled too the vinyl road to the 'hard bop' of The Jazz Messengers and, inevitably, free form via the 'be-bop' - or just plain 'bop' - of John Coltrane, Charlie Mingus, Theolonius Monk, Dizzy Gillespie, Miles Davis and, above all, alto saxophonist Charlie 'Yardbird' Parker. Indeed, so far as

Charlie Watts ever had a boyhood hero, it was the endlessly inventive Parker. 'He sort of epitomised an era in my life. Even now, although I may only play him once a month, I still get that good feeling.' [13]

More life-changing than catching 'Flamingo' on the wireless was when a fourteen-year-old heard 'Walkin' Shoes', a 1956 instrumental of 'cool' persuasion by The Gerry Mulligan Quartet. Charlie homed in on the scuffed snare and tom-tom propulsion of Chico Hamilton, 'the first guy that I ever heard on record that made me want to play the drums'. [10] As a result, he began concentrating less on Ellington, Goodman, Parker, Davis, Monk *et al* themselves than a particular fellow wielding the sticks behind them on respective LPs. Chico Hamilton notwithstanding, Charlie's first drumming idol was Joe Morello - 'all taste and elegance' [14] - best known to Joe Average for accompanying Dave Brubeck, one of few modern jazz pianists to reach the pop charts without compromising his stylistic determination.

Everybody who sat at the head of the table in the Valhalla of North American jazz percussion could command the attention of a young man half a world away, but, in reveries that none could penetrate, Charlie Watts was not Buddy Rich or Gene Krupa commanding the stage alone under his own voodoo spell for minutes on end, but Kenny Clarke, ministering unobtrusively to a genius like Parker. Rather than being particularly thrilled by drum solos, Watts came to realise that, while it was perhaps a trumpeter or saxophonist who gave an number its outward shape and direction, it was often the drummer that made the truest difference - and that the best of them did not merely maintain a precise backbeat, but lifted a band off the runway, allowing it to glide easily on the strongest musical winds.

Watts decided to put action over daydreaming. Somehow or other, he'd acquired a banjo, and one day, he removed the strings and the connecting screw to the neck, and was left with an object with metal rim, vellum skin and resonator: an approximation of a small snare drum.

After constructing a stand from a Meccano set, he bought a pair of not sticks, but wire brushes - because those were what Chico Hamilton had used for the subtleties of 'Walking Shoes'. As Charlie's consequent rhythmic experiments in his bedroom didn't either disturb the rest of the household or interfere with school, Mr. Watts didn't object to his son's hobby and that Christmas, he gave Charlie a basic second-hand kit of bass drum, snare and cymbal.

The neighbours were extraordinarily tolerant - 'A boys-will-be-boys kind of thing,' smiled Charlie [12] - when, on first acquaintance, he attacked his present with gusto, showing no signs of ever stopping. Fortunately for them, Charlie realised quickly that 'one of the great things with drums is to be able to play quietly.' [10] As the New Year got underway too, his strivings brought forth hand-and-foot co-ordination, accurate time-keeping, a clean roll faster than *moderato*, and the first indications of a impactive personal style.

There were instructional manuals available, but he's never been able to get to grips with standard music script, and drum tutors were few and far between then, even in Greater London - so Charlie gathered what he could by trial and error when playing along to records - 'which I hated. It seemed so synthetic' [15] - and through watching other drummers either on television or at local palais.

Yet, though it was known that Lonnie Donegan had drummed with a jazz band when on National Service and that mere ownership of a kit attracted overtures for your services all over a given area, Charlie Watts's ventures into skiffle were to be irresolute. David Green, a next-door neighbour - and lifelong friend - had manufactured a tea-chest bass, but the two never progressed further than talking about starting a group. More so than the Dartford Grammar Sixth Form and the Sidcup College Music Society, they spent a larger part of the time spinning discs than contemplating any reproduction of the sounds themselves.

Bitten by the skiffle bug too, Brian Jones had taught himself to play acoustic guitar, and had actually assembled a combo, albeit one so short-lived that, as with David and Charlie's duo, it never reached the stage. Nevertheless, he had the same all-powerful hold over it as Lonnie Donegan had over the entire movement.

Attracted to the rural blues ingredient in skiffle's melting pot, Brian became so ardent a devotee that listening to and playing the stuff turned into a craving, almost a religion. He was to be especially 'gone' on the grippingly personal styles of rural bluesmen like Snooks Eaglin, Champion Jack Dupree, Robert Johnson and the equally resourceful Lightnin' Hopkins as well as Huddie 'Leadbelly' Ledbetter and one-man-band Jesse Fuller, who both drew from a bottomless repertoire covering not only blues - Leadbelly's 'devil's ditties' - but also country square dance and children's play rhymes.

Brian had also developed a cautious way with alto saxophone based on his knowledge of the clarinet, also in the woodwind family. So much so that, even with GCE 'O' levels looming, he was able and willing to 'sit in' non-committally with outfits who were semi-professional at best, with too few bookings to stay the chill of workaday reality. In a similar situation were Cheltenham's first homogenous rock 'n' roll ensembles, banning themselves from dances at the more prudish youth clubs as well as the stuffy dinner-and-dances upon which they might have depended for virtually all paid work had they traded in 'decent' music in the heartland of middle England in which Gloucester city burghers had forbidden an Evesham combo, The Sapphires, from ever defiling its Guildhall again because lead vocalist Rodney Dawes' trousers were deemed 'crude' round the thighs and crotch.

Cheltenham's boss rock 'n' roll group was The Ramrods, a quintet who differentiated between the instrumentalists - the now-customary two guitarists, bass player and drummer - and Philip Crowther, a four-eyed vocalist, notable for a light-coloured jacket in contrast to the others' darker ones, though all sported black bow-ties against white shirts. Outwardly, they appeared to model themselves on Cliff Richard and the Shadows. Yet, though Phil Crowther might have been a passable Cliff, the rest strove to sound less like The Shadows than Duane Eddy, New York-born pioneer of the 'twangy guitar' approach, who boomed his instrumentals solely on his echo-chambered guitar's lower strings. 'Rebel Rouser', 1958's 'Ramrod' and further of his and his backing Rebels' many hits also showcased a saxophone blasting a semi-improvised counterpoint.

There came, therefore, an invitation from The Ramrods for Brian Jones to join them, and two equally plausible but opposing accounts of his involvement. According to Pat Andrews, he attended a mere couple of rehearsals, but Barry Miles, entertainments secretary at the Art College, maintained that 'the local band I always hired for our dances was The Ramrods - which had Brian Jones on saxophone.' [16]

Bespectacled, taper-thin and of beatnik persuasion, Barry - who encouraged people to address him by his surname - disliked Brian, partly because Jones was prone to boasting about his romantic conquests, to the extent of being dismissed by some as a total fantasist.

However, in an era when boys were spotty and girls untouchable, there was not exactly evidence, but reluctant educated guesses that Jones, a most heterosexual young man, was actually getting away with more romantic conquests than most - which may have led green-eyed monsters to whisper to his detractors. It helped that he looked a bit like Adam Faith, the latest pretender to Cliff Richard's crown, with his firm jawline, gaunt Viking cheekbones and brushed-forward grease-less haircut.

Carrying himself with a ruttish swagger onto the boards, Brian Jones was well on the way to completing his first sexual pilgrimage by the time his 'O' level results arrived. He'd passed all nine of them, but, while satisfied by the raw statistic, Lewis was disgruntled by the boy's 'bad attitude' at both home and school. This was reflected most obviously by his appearance. Take when he started growing his hair Adam Faith length, i.e. maybe an inch or two beyond the short-back-and-sides limit that marked self-discipline and masculinity. His father added this to a list of complaints about what he had detected to be the school's lax discipline - that, as Brian grew more burly, he was less able to enforce himself - during too-frequent and fraught discussions with a heavily patient Dr. Bell.

Beneath the gathering storm that would rage over what was left of his schooldays, the bookworm in Brian absorbed a hidden curriculum via a restless and omnivorous debauch of reading during which his understanding of who was worthwhile and who was not became more acute. His brow might have furrowed over Soren Kirkegaard, the Danish mystic, and certain of his existentialist descendants, chiefly Jean-Paul Sartre, but he was less enraptured with the US connection, epitomised by Kerouac and Burroughs, foremost prose writers of the 'Beat Generation', and associated bards such as Corso, Ginsberg and Ferlinghetti.

This was to be a subliminal point of contact when Brian Jones entered the orbit of the similarly well-read Charlie Watts in 1962, even if the latter was disinclined to air his learning. Indeed, for much of his first terms at Harrow School of Art, Charlie had rarely spoken an unnecessary word during tutorials when completing an all-purpose foundation year before specialising in graphics and lettering. Yet he began to fix on details that most others in a given lesson might be too lackadaisical to consider or even notice. He seemed also to be more *au fait* with the historical traditions and conventions of art and its interrelated philosophies than they.

Seen as slightly eccentric, he distanced himself further by not conforming to the unofficial art student - and 'beatnik' - uniform of army-surplus duffel-coat draped with a long scarf, polo- or turtle-neck pullover down to the knees, sandals or desert boots, a CND badge, and corduroy trousers that looked as if they'd hung round the legs of a particularly disgusting builder's labourer for the past three years.

Charlie based an understated dress sense on that of US jazz drummers from the pages of *Downbeat*, the jazz periodical. Family approval of this choice was attested in Linda cutting her brother's hair as regularly as he wished, and her father offering advice about and paying for Charlie's elegant and narrow-lapelled suits with plain shirt and tie - 'and I wore them as smartly as I could. I didn't like jeans and sweaters in those days. I thought they looked untidy and didn't feel somehow as good as I did in my suits with the baggy trousers.' [12]

He was, however, at one with beatnik friends at college in his taste in music - though 'modern' was more Charlie Watts's bag than trad, as demonstrated by his dropping of buzz-words like 'Coltrane', 'Monk', 'Brubeck' and, of course, 'Parker' into conversations in the refectory. He did not, however, allow himself to be introduced to the late 1950s equivalent of glue sniffing that was prevalent in certain student circles - such as Keith Richards and Dick Taylor's over in Sidcup. Purportedly, the former was already able to conduct a masterclass in the science of isolating that part of a Vick or, preferably, Nostrilene inhaler - each purchasable from the chemist's - that contained strips of an excitant called benzadrine. These, you then ate.

An equally impressionable youth in Cheltenham had discovered for himself that this tacky way of getting 'high' was the nearest you could get to sharing something with - sometimes doomed - musical icons. Heroin had taken Charlie Parker to a mental institution in 1948; substance abuse had killed Hank Williams, and weren't amphetamines the subject of Bo Diddley's 'Pills'?

Brian Jones wasn't especially *au fait* then with Diddley's disc output, or that of Chuck Berry, who, in 1959, served the first of two jail terms that would put temporary halts to his career. This incarceration, however, only boosted his cult celebrity in Britain now that its weekly hit parades were heaving with insipidly handsome US boys-next-door, all doe-eyes, hairspray and bashful half-smiles, matched by their forenames (mainly Bobby) and records. If they faltered after a brace of chart strikes, queuing round the block would be any number of substitute Bobbies - or Jimmies or Frankies - raring to sing any piffle put in front of them, just like British opposite numbers such as Ronnie Carroll and Mark Wynter with the Moon-June ballads that your mum liked.

Another indication of stagnation was dance-craze discs. Little dates an early 1960s film more than the obligatory Twist sequence after this 'most vulgar dance ever invented' [17] burst as the latest rave world-wide after Chubby Checker, a vocalist from Philadephia, penetrated 1960's Top Twenty with an exhumation of 'The Twist', an entry in the US 'sepia' chart two years earlier.

Worse, the Twist wouldn't go away, probably because you were too spoilt for choice of newer offerings such as the Fly, the Jerk, the Locomotion, the Slop, the Mashed Potato, the ungainly Turkey Trot, the Mickey's Monkey, the Hitch-Hiker, the back-breaking Limbo, the Hully Gully, the Madison - and even a revival of the Charleston commensurate with a revival of traditional jazz in places where its originators might least expect to find it.

Notes

1. *The Rolling Stones In Their Own Words* ed. D. Dalton and M. Farren (Omnibus, 1985)
2. *Radio Times*, 14th July, 1956
3. *Scouting For Boys* by Lord Baden-Powell (C. Arthur Pearson, 1949)
4. *Six-Five Special*, 18th January, 1957
5. Quoted in an interview with Chris Jagger (*New Musical Express*, 25th June, 1965
6. *A Guide To Popular Music* by P. Gammond and P. Clayton (Phoenix House, 1960)
7. *Streets Of London: The Official Biography Of Ralph McTell* by C. Hockenhull (Northdown, 1997)
8. *Skiffle* by B. Bird (Robert Hale, 1958)
9. *Chris Barber In Concert Volume Three* (Pye NJL 17, 1958)
10. *Rhythm*, June, 2001
11. Translated from *Folk And Rock* (French journal), summer 1987
12. *The Rolling Stones: The First Twenty Years* by D. Dalton (Thames & Hudson, 1981)

13. *The Big Beat* by M. Weinberg (Billboard, 1991)

14. *Best Of Guitar Player* (Rolling Stones special), December, 1993

15. *Downbeat*, February, 1987

16. *Days In The Life: Voices From The English Underground 1961-1971* ed. J. Green (Heinemann, 1988)

17. *Melody Maker*, 8th January, 1962

*Chapter Three*
**Parallel Lives**

*'There was always this joke that you went to art school to learn to play blues guitar' - David Bowie* [1]

The rising sap of puberty found Dick Taylor as well as Mike Jagger looking for an opening among pop groups in and around the Medway valley. His mastery of his grandfather's miniscule drum kit had attracted offers for his services from several such outfits, though it was made clear that, rather than the crazy, far-out music that he played on guitar at college, reputations were made doling out assembly-line mainstream pop in regional ballrooms, imagined to be halfway houses between amateur bashes in the local youth club, commandeered lecture theatre or the back room of the Dog-and-Gluepot, and nationwide 'scream circuit' tours - with recording contracts thrown in as an afterthought.

*Circa* 1961, the prongs of a triumvirate that ruled pop in northwest Kent were Erkey Grant and his Tonettes, Terry Lee and the Checkers, pride of pington, and, becoming to the Medway Towns what The Ramrods were to Cheltenham, Bern Elliott and the Fenmen, whose bass guitarist was ex-Southerner Eric Wilmer. They were named after Eltham's Jolly Fenman pub where, fresh out of school in 1960, the personnel had been regulars. The Fenmen's *forte* was, however, not Duane Eddy-esque or Shadowy instrumentals but a breathtaking four-part vocal harmony behind heart-throb Bern.

In a lower league then in the area's pop hierarchy, Group X, The Quiet Five, The Trojans and so many other outfits - more and more of them with no singled-out lead vocalist these days - battled with hire-purchase debts, unreliable transport and rough nights at, say, the Bromel in Bromley Court Hotel, Bexley's Black Prince and the Gun Tavern on Church Street, Croydon. The roads they travelled didn't look as if they led anywhere important, but there was always a chance - extremely slim, mind - that one might. Why, just over the county line in Surrey, Bobby Angelo and the Tuxedos had somehow reached the Top Thirty - just - with 'Baby Sittin'' in summer 1961, and, while their 'Don't Stop' follow-up had flopped, they'd extended the commercial yardstick by which the most unassuming local group could judge itself.

Showing what was possible too, John Baldwin, a seventeen-year-old who thrummed bass guitar with other amateur musicians at a Church youth club in Sidcup, was to shake off parochial fetters the following year by auditioning successfully for a group being assembled to accompany drummer Tony Meehan and Jet Harris, who was to pluck a given instrumental number's melody on a bass guitar tuned an octave higher than John's. Jet and Tony were hot property then, having just quit what many regard as the 'classic' line-up of The Shadows.

On stage at many a back-of-beyond town hall shindig in the early 1960s, you'd witness a quartet happily presenting a set consisting entirely of deadpan Shadows imitations, complete with the uniform suits and the guitarists' intricately synchronized footwork. The grinning fellow with the Stratocaster might be sporting Hank B. Marvin-via-Buddy Holly black horn-rims, while the peroxide-blond bass player was a Jet Harris *doppleganger*, transfixing the girls with his Brooding Intensity.

Such displays had been logged by Bill Perks on the evenings when he shut a front door on the lodgings in Penge where he'd started married life in October, 1959 with Diane Cory, a rather innocent bank clerk he'd met at a dance. Theirs was to be a generally unhappy espousal, ending in divorce after eight years. Diane never said much about it, but Bill knew from her silences what she felt about him buying on credit a Burns electric guitar and, after a period of feeding it through a tape recorder, a gleaming new state-of-the-art Watkins Westminster amplifier. Cumulatively, these came to over six weeks' wages.

Now ledgering in a high street department store, Bill had made friends with a chap named Steve Carroll, blessed with film star handsomeness and, crucially, advanced fretboard skills. 'He was a magical jazzy guitarist,' confirmed Bill, 'who could hear a Chuck Berry riff once and just play it straight off'. [2] Another work colleague, Dennis Squires, sang a bit, and the three began rehearsals mostly in the living room of the poky Beckenham flat Bill and Diane had found in autumn 1960. As a group smouldered into being, more musicians came and went, among them electrician Stewart Wealleans, who, deciding that he was one guitarist too many, left to form his own outfit.

For an audible but private gauge of their efforts alongside that of others, the group who were considering calling themselves The Squires - because Keith, Dennis's brother, had now joined on drums - committed to tape 'Blue Moon' and, also the recent subject of an alarming hit arrangement by the USA's Marcels, 'Summertime' plus a rocked-up version of a Cuban evergreen, 'Taboo'.

By then, Bill, Steve, Keith and a disinclined Dennis, still undecided on a corporate name, had been auditioned and not found wanting by the bookings manager in Penge's otherwise empty Starlight Ballroom with its midday essence of disinfectant and echo of the previous night's alcohol and tobacco intake. He engaged them for the following January week, thus allowing breathing space for a structural adjustment, *viz* the replacement of Dennis with an Elvis Presley fanatic called Andy. During a curate's egg of a maiden performance, Andy was waved in as hip-swivelling 'featured singer' while vocals for the remainder of a set that veered fitfully from jump-blues to classic rock to the current Top Twenty were shared between Steve and Bill - who broke a string and then a plectrum.

That they'd gone the distance at the Starlight was sufficiently heartening for the combo to accept immediate further bookings at a wedding reception in Thornton Heath and, next, someone's birthday party near enough for the gear to be walked there - though soon afterwards, Keith Squires drifted away. As well as lacking a drummer now, the group had missed from the very start the fourth part of the now standard two-guitars-bass-drums. An electric bass guitar was beyond the group's pocket, so Bill was cajoled into winding bass strings onto his Burns when he, Steve and Cliff Starkey, a guitar-playing brother-in-law of Bill's sister Anne, entertained at a Blenheim Road knees-up.

They struggled on with a new lead singer, Dave Harvey, whose big onstage moment was when he launched into 'I Love You' or 'Poetry In Motion', successive Number Ones for Cliff Richard and the Bobbyish Johnny Tillotson. As the increased volume born of gradually more splendid equipment precluded rehearsals in front parlours, the group convened in a pub functions room every Thursday evening, hiring it in the first instance to try out drummers, settling on Tony Chapman, a civil servant from Bromley, whose kit was compact enough to be transported on his mother's basket-prowed bicycle.

Tony made his debut on 17th June, 1961 at a private function. At another, the next Saturday, the group played for the first time under a name upon which they'd all agreed: The Cliftons - an amalgam, sort of, of Starkey and Chapman's forenames. While Carroll went on a summer holiday for two weeks, the others cooled their heels, but dates resumed with a vengeance in mid-July, beginning with a friend's lavish wedding do at Anerley Town Hall, and a residency in a youth club deep in urban Essex. Every week this involved a terrible, loss-making four-hour journey in a van that might have been maybe one oil-change from the scrap yard. Matters mended, however, when The Cliftons convinced someone with a more roadworthy vehicle to drive and help lug gear which now included a thirty-watt build-it-yourself bass guitar amplifier which tended to overheat, and a coffin-like speaker with a concrete base that, supposedly, fattened the tone, but also cured its inclination to creep forward or even keel over on rickety stages. Thus was powered a second-hand instrument procured for Bill by Tony, and then customised, chiefly by the removal of all the frets.

Bill had taken the plunge on returning from a weekend with sister Anne and her husband in Aylesbury, Buckinghamshire. On the Saturday, they'd attended a bash by a local combo, The Barron-Knights, a polished and hard-working professional unit with dates as far a-field as Essex and Somerset. The Knights also appeared regularly at Dunstable's California Ballroom, a key venue on the southern England circuit. Not yet wearing the comedy straitjacket that was to define the chart runs that sustained a long career, the group stunned Bill with an infinitely greater depth of sound than The Cliftons - or, indeed, any other outfit he'd ever heard. It boiled down to the boom of leader Barron Anthony's bass. 'Something really hit between the ears that night,' gasped Bill Perks, 'I watched very closely, and I made up my mind that I'd get a worthwhile bass guitar and really work at it.' [3]

Slipping back into the trivial round of engagements in and around Penge, plus side-trips into Essex and Kent, Bill - and Tony - began looking out for vacancies in groups with higher ceilings of ambition, but no-one's tomorrows yet appeared more promising than those of The Cliftons who, give them credit, wouldn't play Bobby music now unless some idiot or his girlfriend requested something specific, preferring to be a rock 'n' roll throwback now that pop was at its most harmless and ephemeral.

Yet, in a desert of Bobbies and Twist variations, there were scattered oases. Joey Dee's 'Peppermint Twist' was actually quite enthralling, while Ray Charles's 'Hit The Road Jack' in 1961 traded call-and-response with his female vocal trio, The Raelettes, like a spiritual's exhorter-congregation interplay. Of like persuasion, The Marvelettes' 'Please Mr. Postman' and Barrett Strong's 'Money' were among the first fistful of entries for Tamla-Motown, a promising black label from Detroit, in what US compilers had now stopped styling the 'sepia' charts.

These were among the 'weird records' of which, so Alan Dow observed, Mike Jagger was inordinately fond, and often purchasable only when imported by outlets like Dobell's and Carey's Swing Shop in Streatham. Mike was also receiving mailed lists and order forms from untold US independent labels like Excello, Aladdin, Atlantic and Imperial, and had been writing directly to the chief proprietor of Chess. Even when British labels began issuing R&B singles such as James Brown's 'Think' - on Parlophone in 1961 - and - via Pye International's R&B series - material in all vinyl formats by Bo Diddley, Howlin' Wolf, Muddy Waters and other executants of the sacred sounds, epistles arrived from Jagger in Wilmington entreating the companies to issue more.

Quoting blues titles and lyrics as if they were proverbs, and in the thick of every common room controversy to do with the music of black America, Mike also entered into occasional debate on the letters page of *Record Mirror*, ready at any moment with a corrective tirade against other correspondents. Neither did he hesitate to attack the paper's very journalists. He was certainly more knowledgeable about the subject than most of them.

Being mad about the blues might have been a more socially acceptable pastime than, say, accumulating information about donkeys' false teeth or annotating the reference matrixes of electricity pylons, but, with a madcap Jagger-esque devotion beyond mere enthusiasm, a Newcastle-upon-Tyne art student named Eric Burdon ritually inked the word BLUES in his own blood across the cover of an exercise book in which lyrics of the same had been compiled.

Brian Jones risked cutting a finger inadvertently when following the same star. Striking a conspicuously resonant chord with him was Elmore James, who, with Muddy Waters and Howlin' Wolf, now dominated the Chicago blues scene. While James's records were obtainable outside North America if you were prepared to be patient, he would always be something of an acquired taste for most white blues fans via his trademark application of pre-war bluesman Robert

Johnson's rural bottleneck (or slide) technique to electric guitar. Furthermore, as Jones deduced, James did not either play in orthodox fashion or use standard tuning.

'He used to play me Robert Johnson and Elmore James records,' reminisced Pat Andrews, 'and explain how they got their sounds. He believed they used actual bottle necks to get the slide effect - so he broke a bottle neck off and tried it. He got the sound, but it was a bit dangerous. One day, we went round to a number of garages, and Brian found a bit of pipe cut to fit his finger.'

After fitting his guitar with heavy-gauge strings too, he learned what he could from discs and by trial-and-error about how to obtain resonant effects - from sustained shimmer to undulating *legato* - from an appliance that had hitherto been heard only in the contrasting sphere of Hawaiian music. Yet, though Elmore James lurked in the shadows as he practiced, Brian's slide technique soon became as distinctive a musical signature as the mark of Zorro with an exactness of phrasing and a ringing, if sometimes stentorian, clarity that was all the more rewarding for its studied restraint.

In the haphazard cell of blues archivist-performers in Kent, bottleneck hadn't entered the equation to such a committed degree, nowhere near. Neither had anyone reached even Bill Perks' low level of public visibility. However, listening sessions by the Dartford Sixth Formers and Dick Taylor had evolved at last into endeavours to replicate the unpopular sounds themselves, principally at the Taylor family's semi-detached because 'My parents were most tolerant of the racket - and the lady next door was deaf.'

Acoustic six-strings were picked by Taylor, Robert Beckwith and Alan Etherington - with Alan and Dick doubling respectively on maracas and Taylor's antiquated drum set. After Beckwith screwed an electronic pick-up over his instrument's hole without any damage, Taylor and Etherington did likewise, plugging into available domestic inputs such as Dick's older sister's record-player - which was further overloaded with a cheap microphone through which Mike sang and blew a mouth organ, neither of which imposed restriction on movement. 'My Mum was fascinated by him,' laughed Taylor, 'loved his singing and dancing around. He was leaping about like a lunatic. He was dancing and chucking himself about even then.'

During pauses when he lubricated his throat with *Bing*, a fizzy beverage peculiar to Kent, there was little discourse about the quality of Mike's vocals. From the beginning, it was close enough in pitch and timbre to some of the black icons he admired that the others treated it as a matter of course. Consciously trying to imitate, say, laconic Slim Harpo, bestial Howlin' Wolf or unruffled Chuck Berry, his still-breaking voice was corrupted for all time, resulting in a delivery devoid of vowel purity and nicety of intonation. Instead, you got slovenly diction, disjointed range and a natural vehemence dredged up from the constrictions of his neck rather than the flexibility of the diaphragm, a capability that would render it beyond remedy by European *bel canto* standards.

Mike's mother didn't like it much and said so on the two occasions when she let the boys fool around with their guitars in his bedroom, perhaps assuming that they'd tire of it as they had of the pastime that had preceded it - shooting tin cans with an air-rifle in the back garden. If Mrs Jagger put her head round the door, the music - which had a ragged dissimilarity to any pop she'd ever heard - would shudder to a halt.

Thereafter, sessions took place at the Taylors' or, less often, the Etheringtons'. To what purpose was never clear. Certainly, no-one attempted to procure a booking or consider the directive concerning 'visual effect' of Bob Cort, one of skiffle's lesser icons: 'Some sort of uniform is a great help, though casual clothes are perhaps the best, as long as you look exactly the same'. [4]

As skiffle latecomers, however, they agreed with Cort's pontification, 'That's where half the enjoyment lies - in experimenting with ideas.' [4] Though they'd educated themselves in their preferred aspect of what lay beneath and fluttered above the form's chewing gum-flavoured surface, the Dartford group made one irresistible concession to in-yer-face pop with an arrangement of 'La Bamba' by Ritchie Valens, remembered mainly as one who'd been killed in the same aeroplane crash as Buddy Holly in 1959. Otherwise, it was blues - of urban rather than rural persuasion - and *almost* nothing but.

Though they were less sure of themselves with Wolf and Waters, there was a lot from Jimmy Reed and Bo Diddley, but, statistically, Chuck Berry won hands down. Still serving his sentence, he couldn't get a hit to save his life then, so how could Mike, Dick *et al* have guessed then that all the misses he'd suffered since 'Sweet Little Sixteen' had tumbled from its UK apogee of Number 16 long ago in spring 1958 - 'Beautiful Delilah', 'Carol' and all the rest of them - and even some of their B-sides and his LP tracks - 'Around And Around', 'Little Queenie', 'You Can't Catch Me' and so forth - were to be prominent in the repertoires of virtually all British beat groups that counted and that Berry items would often be the redeeming features of many that didn't?

The Cliftons spared a lot of on-stage time for Berry already, but not many outfits known to Alan, Dick, Mike, Robert, Keith Richards and other victims of the same passion bothered. 'Dick and I used to go and watch Bern Elliott and his Fenmen,' recollected Phil May, 'but we would wait for them to play their two Chuck Berry numbers. The best English R&B band was Johnny Kidd and the Pirates. I remember going with Dick to Blackheath purely to see them because they were one of few English ballroom bands to actually have R&B roots.'

For all their overriding interest in music, May's and Taylor's lecture notebooks at Sidcup were as conscientiously full as Keith Richards' were empty. When written or practical assessment was pending, he'd cadge assistance just as he would a cigarette. His tutors couldn't help but imagine that Keith did very little of the mandated reading, and that, when drawn from deep silence, he prevaricated his way through prolonged discussion on art. His bluff was called sometimes by graphics lecturer John Sturgess, whose strategies would be unorthodox even now. Phil May's recollections leave little doubt that in a more strait-laced cultural era, Sturgess's methodology may have been seen as verging on lunacy: 'I remember one life-drawing class. I was a very naive fifteen-year-old, standing there, looking at this naked person, and I couldn't put a mark down. John gave me ten bob and told me to go down the pub, have half a pint and come back when I had something to say. He was fantastic like that.'

Sturgess was also either unaware or turned a blind eye to the use of stimulants other than beer to, say, steady nerves for sketching a nude. Benzedrine from nasal inhalers would turn out to be the thin end of the wedge for his most apathetic and unpromising student, who, nevertheless, would blame his profound dependency in later life on narcotics, not on nasty habits picked up at Sidcup, but on their being 'passed from one generation of musicians to the next'. [5]

Keith Richards was to be the college's most notorious Old Boy. As it had at Dartford Technical School, failure seemed inevitable from the start. By the middle of his second year on the graphics course, he, his parents and the teaching staff acknowledged tacitly that his higher education studies were unofficially over and that the ugly moment was approaching when, as his father reminded him, he'd have to find a job to keep alive.

For Brian Jones, such a notion was almost a cheering thought as long as it entailed leaving 'Ravenswood', where an unremittingly ugly mood had intensified to near-breaking point. Much of it was centred on deciding Brian's future. There was nothing as yet to indicate possibilities other than in well-paid but, to Brian, suffocatingly humdrum jobs like his Dad's at an aeronautical engineering works - with a gold watch at sixty-five to tick away the seconds before you went underground. Attempts to discuss a different life plan with his father would prove pointless. The same maxims about hard work, common sense and religion that were, to Lewis's mind, unanswerable, would just come up over and over again and end, as likely as not, with a blazing row. Trying to elicit his mother's sympathy only brought to the fore how little she ever considered not only what his ambitions might be, but whether he even had any. Eventually, hardly a word would pass between parents and child that wasn't a domestic imperative, and by the time Brian reached the Upper Sixth, he was almost permanently out of the house.

To Lewis and Louisa's mingled delight and exasperation, he had passed with flying colours his 'A' levels in chemistry and physics. This was an excellent result, all things considered - for Brian's heart had been heavy with fear and guilt in the weeks leading up to those days of days. His courtship of Valerie, a schoolgirl three years his junior, had led to the most ruinous of all British social disgraces. As far as the Jones family's parish circle of bring-and-buy sales, nativity plays and tombolas was concerned, Brian could blow Weber's clarinet concerto and gain 'A' levels for the next thousand years and yet never wipe out the stain of Valerie's pregnancy.

The baby was taken away from her as soon as he was born, and delivered as arranged to a infertile couple. Both Valerie and Brian were then sent on respective 'holidays' before the vapourings of the town's scandalmongers reached the ears of the muck-raking *News*

*Of The World*, who commissioned a nicotine-fingered doorstepper to investigate this rare instance of moral indiscretion that lurked in refined Cheltenham.

Though going at as full a gallop, Mike Jagger's jousting for the downfall of knickers in Dartford would never take such a serious and abandoned turn. In the Sixth Form common room he was above detailing any previous evening's carnal shenanigans - though his habit of bringing a given discussion, however unlinked, round to his favourite records could be just as yawnsome. 'Skiffle' had become a vile word amongst Mike and his blues evangelists now that an over-publicised *Skiffle Mass* by a curate in The Cliftons' London stamping ground had made a cheerful noise unto the God of Jacob, and barren booking schedules had forced many a still-functioning skiffle outfit back to Church-organised 'young people's clubs', where part of the deal might be that their set was to be interrupted by a 'spontaneous' on-mike dialogue between the vicar - exclaiming 'too much', 'squaresville' and other Transatlantic expressions he believed teenagers still used - and one of his juvenile flock. They'd chat about sin. His Reverence would be against it.

So would the rabbi saying grace at the Jewish wedding reception in Wembley that marked Charlie Watts's first cash-in-hand outing as a drummer with a semi-professional unit. 'I just used to play with anyone really,' he shrugged, 'which was mostly jazz people, but not on a very high musical level, not the best - though some of them turned out to be the best as time passed.' [6]

Unlike Eva Jagger and Mr. and Mrs. Jones, Charles and Lilian Watts weren't the sort to gripe about their only son mucking about with music instead of devoting more of his energies to homework. 'I don't know if they were supportive of jazz,' he'd recall, 'but they were certainly supportive of me playing. My dad used to take me to gigs in the car and pick me up. I used to spend everything on taxis because I don't drive. David Green and I used to go on the 'bus sometimes. We joined a swing band together, and David went on to work at Ronnie Scott's. At the age of eighteen, he was in the house band.' [7]

Charlie was pleased for his bass-playing friend as Ronnie Scott's was defying all comers as London's foremost jazz venue since its opening in 1959 in Soho, the closest the city came to a recognised red-light district. Its back-alleys proliferated with striptease joints, illicit gambling hells and clandestine brothels - as Mike Jagger gleaned when, with 'A' levels in history and English literature, he had been persuaded to apply for a course focused principally on economics and political science at the London School of Economics within walking distance of this cosmopolitan island of sin in a sea of bustling consumers' paradises centred on Oxford Street.

For lads from Kingsbury too, this quarter of the capital was quite exotic with its aroma of percolated coffee and mega-tar French cigarettes - and, of course, wanton perfume. It was flattery of a kind that Charlie Watts and Dave Green were accepted, not as suburban striplings, but as just two of the crowd, when they first ventured into the open-all-night Flamingo where prototype Mods, even back in 1959, would recognise each other by their short-haired pseudo-suavity and classless, whim-conscious dress sense.

The headlining act that night was Georgie Fame and the Blue Flames, but Charlie was more captivated by the jazzier supporting quintet who were led by a certain Phil Seaman, 'the best drummer in England. He used to play timpani style - very unusual in those days - but he played with his fingers like a real timpanist. I learnt to play by watching Phil Seaman play a bass drum or Red Reece, in Georgie Fame's band, play a backbeat. [7]

Another inspired by Seaman was Peter 'Ginger' Baker, from the same part of west London as Charlie and Dave, and rated as 'bloody good' by the former, who'd discovered Baker in 'one of the best - well, the most exciting, if not the best - jazz groups in London.' [8]

The Johnny Burch Octet also contained tenor saxophonist Dick Heckstall-Smith, by day an X-ray technician at St. Bartholemew's Hospital, with Graham Bond on alto sax and keyboards, and bass player Jack Bruce was on the boards the night that Alexis Korner, the former BFN broadcaster, turned up. A singing guitarist too, he was in the process of forming Britain's first electric blues band with mouth-organist and Chicago-style blues shouter Cyril Davies, also in his thirties and an ex-member of Chris Barber's New Orleans Jazz Band. They'd already given it a name: Blues Incorporated.

A principal reason why Barber had asked Davis and Korner to leave his own Band was their ceaseless and unsolicited attempts to impose a surfeit of their own stylistic determination upon the established trad status quo. Yet Chris wasn't anti-blues, very much the opposite in his pre-emption of Jimi Hendrix's perspective on jazz: 'A lot of horns and top-speed bass lines. Most of those cats are playing nothing but blues' [9], itself unknowingly reiterating skiffle scribe Brian Bird's 'blues, then, may be looked upon as the main content of jazz'. [10]

Barber was actually as major a catalyst in the development of British blues as Davis and Korner - for, unlike others who merely acted as agents for tours, he financed the conservation of the form, and ensured in the most pragmatic way that British experience of *bona fide* black American blues needn't be limited to mere records. In the teeth of much advice to the contrary from the National Jazz Federation, he was ready to suffer monetary losses on such as that hour and a quarter of Muddy Waters in October, 1958 at St. Pancras Town Hall that Mike Jagger's father wouldn't permit him to attend. In the West End at the Federation's own venue, the Marquee, Barber had also underwritten visits by other leading US blues - and gospel - artists including Little Walter, Sister Rosetta Tharpe, Roosevelt Sykes and Brownie McGhee's multi-instrumental duo with Sonny Terry, who Mike Cooper, as committed a fan as Jagger, Taylor, Jones *et al*, saw at Reading Town Hall as 'special guests' of the New Orleans Jazz Band.

That night, blues was sung too by either Barber's then-wife Ottilie Patterson and Alexis Korner who had been Lonnie Donegan's deputy and then his replacement with the band, having first supplied appositely toiling grunts on Ken Colyer-as-skiffler's 78 rpm crack at Leadbelly's 'Take This Hammer'. Under Barber, Korner was probably the first professional British vocalist to try Muddy Waters' 'I Got My Mojo Working', which was to become the British blues movement's anthem - though among close seconds were Ma Rainey's 'See See Rider' (recorded by Barber in 1957), 'Hoochie Coochie Man', John Lee Hooker's 'Boom Boom', and 'Baby Please Don't Go', erroneously credited to Ottilie Patterson on disc and augmented by a visiting Sonny Boy Williamson's harmonica. Another contender was Bobby Troupe's '(Get Your Kicks On) Route 66'.

It was when Korner performed these in the context of a Donegan-length interval spot of maybe four numbers that he wondered if a show consisting entirely of blues was feasible. With Davis, he'd already tried to establish a 'Blues and Barrelhouse' club in a Soho pub, and, in September, 1960, had raised a derisive eyebrow on learning details about a Church hall in Putney hosting the inauguration of a 'blues society'. It turned out that 'opening night' meant 'final meeting' as, aided by discs, its patrons had discussed how 'interesting' it all was, this Twisted Voice of the Underdog. Then, in a knowing, nodding kind of way, they'd sat through what was billed as 'the debut of a fabulous new group, Benny Green's Rhythm And Blues All Stars', whilst blocking out the impure thought in the unspoken question, 'How could anyone like this stuff?' Perhaps the greater the effort required to appreciate it, the more 'ethnic' it must be, even if white, British Benny and his accompanists had never toiled on a chain gang or dwelt in the ghettos of southside Chicago, and played and sang the blues as if it was a series of quotations from a language so archaic as to seem slightly foreign.

Alexis knew all about Benny. He'd been on tenor sax in Lord Rockingham's XI, the house band on *Oh Boy!* - the less pious ITV successor to *Six-Five Special* - and functioned now as a music critic who, biting the hand that had fed him, was especially scathing about rock 'n' roll. He was also a BBC radio 'personality' of Steve Race ilk, and one of a self-contained caste with first refusal on more or less all London studio dates.

Likewise, the Dartford and Cheltenham wings of the movement could imagine that Green's transitory Rhythm And Blues All Stars hadn't been very good. They opined too that Blues Incorporated, if it ever became quorate, might be - even if Alexis Korner's principal income came from numerous un-bluesy voice-overs for ITV commercials in his BFN announcer's mahogany husk. He and Cyril Davies were also mainstays of the London session crowd with the likes of Green, drummer Andy White from the Vic Lewis Orchestra, and Brian Poole and the Tremeloes, the group its leader consolidated after seeing Buddy Holly. They'd been signed initially by Decca as a backing vocal group.

Mike Jagger had as much chance of a stake in that world as he had of being knighted. Feeling the chill of reality, especially in the light of 'A' level grades that weren't brilliant, was it time now to cast aside adolescent follies? Blues and rhythm-and-blues was the most exciting music ever, but maybe he'd grow out of it, apart from immersing himself in it as other men did in their spare time in do-it-yourself, photography or football.

In his office as careers advisor, headmaster Lofty Hudson had laid on the London School of Economics with a trowel. Puzzled because his passes were in History and English, Mike did not know then that, over the years, Lofty had worked up some influence with the interviewing panel.

If modelled on L'Ecole Libre Des Sciences Politiques in Paris, the LSE was a British university by any other name. Nevertheless, while it wasn't yet the New Left furnace it would become, Trotskyists looked down on Leninists there, and words like 'materialism', 'bourgeoisie' and 'existential' filtered around the corridors. As it was everywhere else on the further education map, other than lecturers and mature students, everyone occupied that awkward stage where you were deciding whether to grow up or not. Most obviously, clothes polarised each social group.

Grey flannel trousers, twinsets and 'chunky' hair glaciated with spray or brilliantine stated that either you hadn't yet escaped the clutches of parents who expected you to be a 'credit' to them - or that you accepted with hardly a murmur the promise of jam tomorrow if you beavered away, sidestepped the more tempting of extra-mural distractions, and attained your degree. On the other side of the sartorial coin were 'beatnik' girls wearing either no make-up at all or a detergent-white mask relieved by black eyeshade and lipstick; conducting themselves as if in a trance, and hiding their figures inside baggy jumpers annexed from 'existentialist' boyfriends, who either contrived to keep a day away from a shave or went more of the whole hog with bumfluff beards like half-plucked Fidel Castros. Their manner of dressing said - wrongly - that they were not aware of the clothes they had flung on after rising that day.

Mike Jagger walked an uncomfortable line between the two extremes. If anything, he could be classed demeaningly as a 'Millet' in his nylon pullover and yet-unfaded jeans from the Dartford branch of the 'outdoors' clothing and camping equipment store of the same name. The LSE's official broad and striped scarf was draped round his neck. Gilding an indeterminate image too was that, to his father's disappointment, he had started smoking.

His first cigarette of the day was generally when waiting among the bowler hats and furled umbrellas for the commuter train at Dartford railway station. Lighting up and inhaling nonchalantly but deeply, he was trying to impress waiting girls who might have been making circuitous enquiries about him as he'd been about them. Yet, while the daily ride to and from Holborn via British Rail and the London underground system was still novel, Mike wasn't regarding it and his subsequent hours at the LSE entirely as a forum for initiating carnal adventures. Indeed, he appear to be devoting himself to his studies as if he almost meant to become a middle-weight financial executive in five years time, on the board of directors in ten, and chairman by the time he was forty. After a fashion, this was to come true after everything changed, albeit with majestic slowness, via a deceptively casual encounter - as casual and, in retrospect, as momentous, as that of John Lennon and Paul McCartney at a church fete just over four years earlier.

On the platform for the London stopping train, the sun peeped through gaps in 1961's cloudy October sky as Keith Richards slouched past the newspaper stand with its chalked headline from the *Kentish Times*. The locomotive was just pulling in, and it was by the merest chance that Richards was to slide open the door of the same dusty second-class compartment where Mike Jagger had just seated himself.

Paths had crossed fleetingly since Wentworth Primary - most memorably when one of Mike's holiday jobs had entailed selling ice-creams outside the public library - and so they granted each other an irresolute nod and exchanged desultory platitudes as increasing sunshine gleamed where it could through the grime-encrusted window. Under normal circumstances, each might have then lost himself in his thoughts for the remainder of the the stop-start journey, gazing at without seeing the over-familiar shopping precincts, recreation grounds and waste-piped backs of buildings hurtling by after the sluggish embarkations from Crayford, Albany Park, Barnehurst and the other Kentish London boroughs that preceded Sidcup.

Richards was the first to be roused from the train-rhythm lethargy, not by babble penetrating from outside at the next station, but on spying Chuck Berry's *Rocking At The Hop* on top of a pile of five LPs that Mick had on his lap. He almost shouted with astonishment, forgetting both the other passengers and a natural shyness, because that particular vinyl black beauty was freshly available only on import, and he could understand perfectly why someone might give up five years of his life to own it.

Of ensuing remarks that weren't directly to do with *Rocking At The Hop*, *The Best Of Muddy Waters* and Mick's other albums, Keith spoke with quiet pride of his new Hofner Futurama 'cutaway', which, compared to his first guitar, was as a fountain pen to a stub of pencil. Then Dick Taylor's name cropped up. When Mike waved from the window at Sidcup and went back to his peace, it had been agreed that Keith was to attend the next blues session round Dick's place.

Notes

1. *Old Gods Almost Dead* by S. Davis (Aurum, 2002)
2. *Record Collector*, No. 231, November, 1998
3. *Our Own Story By The Rolling Stones* by P. Goodman (Bantam, 1964)
4. *New Musical Express*, 1st November, 1957
5. *Keith Richards In His Own Words* ed. M. St. Michael (Omnibus, 1994)
6. *The Rolling Stones In Their Own Words* ed. D. Dalton and M. Farren (Omnibus, 1980)
7. *Rhythm* June, 2001
8. *Best Of Guitar Player* (Rolling Stones special), November, 1994
9. *Jimi Hendrix* by S. Mann (Orion, 1994)
10. *Skiffle* by B. Bird (Robert Hale, 1958)

*Chapter Four*
**Incorporated And Disconnected**

*'Brian was a reformed traddie, and, although he despised them, he was really one of them' - Mick Jagger* [1]

It had been on another train journey along the same route that Keith and Mike took as students, that Rick Huxley had seen a scuffed page of Melody Maker on the carriage floor. It contained the 'musicians wanted' column and Dave Clark's advertisement for like-minded players to join what would be his Five. Rick had already passed through the ranks of Kentish Town's Riverside Blues Boys, less specialist than cousin Mike's nascent outfit, and sporting a stage costume of blue suits with white ties. Next, Huxley had been one of The Spon Valley Stompers, walking a line between blues and trad, now a nationwide pop phenomenon, having developed into such a skiffle-sized fad that many of its practitioners, most of them very unlikely-looking teen icons, had made the Top Twenty.

The period was to be bracketed roughly by 1959's international best-seller, 'Petite Fleur' by Chris Barber and his Jazz Band - with 'New Orleans now hacked from its name - and the same combo framing the ebullient soprano of Ottilie Patterson over the closing credits of 1962's expedient It's Trad Dad movie. Yet it was not London but Bristol, where clarinettist Bernard 'Acker' Bilk was king, from which the pestilence had begun ravaging the kingdom in earnest. Soon it had gone beyond the collegiate intellectual fringe to a proletariat with 'ACKER' studded on the backs of leather jackets where 'ELVIS' once was. Towards the end of 1961, Bilk's 'Stranger On The Shore' was the longest reigning single in the UK hit parade thus far, and was racing to the top in the USA. Moreover, despite 'economic' acting abilities, Acker's Paramount Jazz Band were about to star in a film, *A Band Of Thieves*.

Attempting to cash in quick too, *Trad Tavern* filled the air-time once occupied by *Six-Five Special* and *Oh Boy!*, booking bands in matching Donegal tweeds, horned 'Viking' helmets, Confederate army uniforms, Roman togas, barrister wigs and similarly ridiculous variations on the striped waistcoats and bowlers worn by Bilk and his Band. Off-screen, the trad network spread seemingly overnight to venues that had once been the exclusive domain of skifflers and rock 'n' rollers.

All the bands were different, all of them were the same: a plinking banjo, a confusion of horns to the fore, and an especially extrovert 'dad' who imagined that a hoarse monotone was all you needed to sing like Louis Armstrong.

After an absence of two years in the merchant navy, John Keen, another Cheltenham Grammar old boy, had been astonished to find that the local trad scene had exploded: 'You could go and hear it every night of the week. Rock-and-roll and rhythm-and-blues weren't considered important at all.' That was sad news for The Ramrods as home-reared trad performers began to monopolise dates in village institutes, pub function rooms, sports pavilions and whenever the Alstone Baths was boarded over for dancing. In town centre coffee bars too, trad rather than rock bands were being hired as a change from the juke-box.

Brian Jones had been a regular at Club 66, a suburban jazz stronghold, since its 1958 opening, eventually becoming its appointed secretary. Generally, a given bill was top-heavy with trad nowadays, but one evening, a headlining outfit led by John Keen deviated from ordained Dixieland precedent by including saxophonists and committing the more cardinal sin of amplification to the disgruntlement of watching devotees likely to know more about the music's history than the musicians - so much so that the 'jazz' content in numbers by certain local outfits was frequently negligible because, if some black dotard from New Orleans had recorded a particularly definitive solo, it was often thought prudent to learn it note-for-note for regurgitation at every public performance.

The more incensed purists might boo, but Keen not sticking to the rules was a point in his favour to Jones - who said as much when introduced to the trumpeter at 38, Priory Street, the family home of Jane Philby, who, with a team of helpers, had spent most of the summer of 1958 converting the basement into a cafe-*cum*-party venue for Cheltenham musicians and their retinues. 'Then a stage was set up,' recalled John Keen, 'and the place flourished. It was a gathering of like-minded people in their late teens and early twenties.'

Soundproofing was so inadequate that the high Cs from Keen's horn would stab the night air in surrounding streets. More insidious was the muffle of Brian Jones's guitar fed through an amplifier that John had bought for his use: 'a Vox AC15 for thirty pounds from Ray Electrical in the Lower High Street. Brian put his acoustic guitar fitted with a pick-up through it. He never paid me back by the way. My hero was Louis Armstrong - whom I'd met and got his autograph. He had used a guitar in his band in the 1920s, and on a 1957 LP, *Louis Armstrong's Musical Biography* - so I liked the idea of having a guitar in my band instead of a banjo. Therefore, Brian was welcome. He was very keen on the way Freddie Green, the guitarist with Count Basie, played. Very tasteful. Brian was a good jazz rhythm guitarist, and used to sit in with us, Bill Nile and visitors from London such as The Alex Welsh Band.

'Brian despised certain aspects of the jazz scene. On a personal level, he could certainly charm people, but he was a jazz snob in some ways, and could be unco-operative. When we were on stage, he just wouldn't play some numbers if he thought they were old hat. He was also unreliable and just didn't turn up for gigs if he couldn't be bothered.'

When circumstances were favourable, Jones's chord-strumming and *obligatos* were controlled but lively, and his relocation, via Freddie Green, of eight-to-the-bar banjo to electric rhythm guitar was to be lasting and beneficial. [2] Yet, while playing trad Cheltenham-style could, indeed, take up every evening of the week, Brian was fundamentally of 'modern' bent. Most conspicuously, he was a fan of alto and soprano saxophonist Julian Edwin 'Cannonball' Adderley.

On instant replay for weeks at a time was Brian's swiftly dog-eared 1958 album, *Somethin' Else* by Adderley and assembled hard boppers that included Miles Davis and drummer Art Blakey. At its worst, some of the textural complexities of *Somethin' Else* and later Adderley LPs either reminded you of that 'party sequence' music that dates 'modern times' continental movies made over and over again since the late 1950s, or else came over very Light Programme, as on the 1963 single, 'The Sidewalks Of New York', dominated by the too-pure tone of a vibraphone. Otherwise, it bordered on that jazzy pop that was acceptable to the hipper patrons of Club 66 and 38, Priory Street, chiefly through Adderley's mingling of state-of-the-art jazz with elements of Louis Jordan, Cab Calloway and other pre-Presley executants of a jovial and danceable hybrid of trad and jump blues. In parenthesis, Adderley's composition, 'Sack O' Woe', was to emerge as a British rhythm-and-blues 'standard', being recorded by Manfred Mann, Van Morrison and The Rats, a beat group from Hull led by the late Mick Ronson, later guitarist with David Bowie's backing outfit, The Spiders From Mars.

No less an authority than Paul McCartney was to concur with his biographer - who happened to be Barry Miles - that, for all his intense pre-occupation with Cannonball Adderley, Brian Jones was 'a really ropey sax player'. [3] The fellow himself found it convenient to accept that if he wasn't to be an Adderley in a wider world, he could be distinctive in, ostensibly, a simpler option than jazz. While he continued to fret guitar behind the toot-tooting of John Keen and other local jazzers, 'he saw it,' elucidated Keen, 'as a crusade to play blues.

However, unless you pulled some chartbusting stroke like Bilk - or Dave Brubeck - you couldn't live on jazz alone, and much less by more nakedly 'starvation music' like blues. Among Brian's various and fleeting jobs after leaving school under the darkest cloud possible - and, soon afterwards, leaving home too - was counter assistant at Curry's Record Shop. This had been more socially acceptable to Louise and Lewis than that of his new girlfriend, fifteen-year-old Patricia Andrews, a 'shop girl', shortly to move from part-time at the Aztec coffee bar to full-time at Boots, the chemist's. Brian might have argued that he was a 'shop boy', but he had long become used to keeping his opinions to himself at 'Ravenswood'.

More distressing to Louisa and Lewis were his stints as a coalman, on the night shift in an ice-cream factory and in the uniform of a bus conductor after he'd been found wanting as an office junior in the architectural department of Cheltenham District Council. Into the bargain, Brian was turning into a spendthrift with a lackadaisical attitude towards the accumulation of debt. A month's wages had been blown on a down-payment for an electric guitar to be powered by the amplifier he'd acquired via John Keen. Almost as a matter of course too, he still owed rent for previous dwellings when he moved into the first-floor flat of 73, Prestbury Road, five minutes dawdle from the High Street, early in 1960.

He shared the double bedroom there with a certain Richard Hattrell. Five years Brian's senior, Richard's immediate family were from the legal and military professions. His had been a privileged upbringing, albeit one that had been as bleak after its fashion as Brian's. Enduring the rigours of expensive boarding schools before finishing his education at Tewkesbury Secondary Modern, he was also saddled with an

Army colonel martinet of a father who, groaned Richard, 'went berserk when he found out I was a jazz fan'.

Indeed, Richard had noticed Brian Jones one Thursday during a show starring Kenny Ball's Jazzmen - shortly to all but top the charts with 'Midnight In Moscow' - at the Rotunda, a venue along the Promenade. The two first spoke at length, however, at Club 66 after Brian endorsed Richard's membership card. He signed it 'L.B. Jones', although he was toying with the notion of giving himself the stage alias 'Elmore Lewis' or, less obvious a salaam to a hero second only to Adderley, 'Elmo Lewis'.

Jones was never to see Elmore James - who was to die in 1963 - in person, but he and Hattrell hitch-hiked to London to catch Muddy Waters at the Marquee. With regular pianist Otis Spann plus Chris Barber's drummer and bass player, Waters had ambled onto the boards with a Fender Telecaster round his neck. On this first occasion when Brian had ever heard a solid-body electric guitar in such a context, his path became clear. He wandered into an autumn night afterwards, lost in dreams and already half-formed ambition. He was, he said, going to teach himself to play just like that, and one day either form his own blues - no, make that 'R&B' - group or insinuate his way into whatever existing unit, anywhere in Britain, was closest to one.

Big time aspirations had not yet entered the equation of the nameless Dartford group, still larking about round each other's houses. Nonetheless, for an audible if private gauge of how they sounded with Keith in the ranks, a Grundig tape recorder had been rigged up in the most acoustically sympathetic corner of a bedroom or shed, and, after much fiddling with microphone positioning as the valves warmed up, the lads had committed fifteen pieces to reel-to-reel, among them no less than six Chuck Berry items plus 'You're Right I'm Left She's Gone', Bo Diddley's 'You Can't Judge A Book By The Cover' and other pieces regarded as harsh throwbacks in the Bobby age. [4]

Mike, Dick, Keith, Alan and Robert wondered for who else they'd recorded this music. Perhaps in some remote, amateur way, they were carrying an Olympic torch for it to their vicinity of England. No-one else was listening other than an involuntary audience of their own families and neighbours, but the ultimate aim was 'to turn people onto the blues,' outlined Richards, 'If we could turn them onto

Muddy, Jimmy Reed, Howlin' Wolf and John Lee Hooker, then our job was done.' [5]

Without being pushy or showing off, Keith Richards was playing an increasingly more noticeable part in the proceedings as a close friendship with Mike took hold. Without purposely snubbing anyone, the two were seeking each other's particular company, and evolving a restricted code that few outsiders could crack, not even Dick Taylor. The personal dynamic and interaction between them was to intensify to the degree that Jagger would joke, 'He was born my brother by accident by different parents!' [6]

Mrs. Jagger's disapproval of Keith's relatively loutish demeanour and attire didn't count against him, even though this was just when she and Joe had imagined that Mike was over the developmental stage known as 'rebellious adolescence' - expressed most overtly in an inverted snobbery - and was changing, not with a lightning conversion, it was true, but slowly, into a serious, thoughtful young adult, applying himself industriously to his degree studies.

It was, therefore, worrying to witness outlines dissolving between Mike and his dubious new best friend. They started to copy each other's idiosyncracies, and style their hair and dress similarly - Mike, for example, exchanging 'sensible shoes' for winkle-pickers and drain-piping his jeans so tightly that it looked as if his legs had been dipped in ink. As a further act of class betrayal, he was now styling himself 'Mick' as if he was the by-blow of some London-Irish navvy.

Brian Jones's more tight-lipped parents were still deluding themselves that his 'better self' could be reclaimed, even though he was in the throes of a new - or, perhaps, not so new - public disgrace. Pat Andrews, so Brian had confided to Richard Hattrell and then others, was 'up the duff' - and she was too far gone to do anything other than have the nineteen-year-old's second son, who arrived on 23rd October, 1961.

Brian insisted the boy be called Julian after Cannonball Adderley, but, from the cradle, he was known by his middle name, Mark. The mother's family did not, as yet, put financial pressure on Brian, knowing as they did that here was a man of straw who regarded the present turmoil as regrettable rather than disastrous, and who strove to keep a concrete decision about the future at arm's length.

With indecent haste, he had left one obligatory call on a heavily pregnant Pat to rush across town to St. Luke's Hall where Alexis Korner, Cyril Davies, Dick Heckstall-Smith and singer Long John Baldry - the nucleus of what would be Blues Incorporated - had been among a jazz amalgam under the aegis of trumpeter Ken Sims. Catching only the 'I Got My Mojo Working' finale, Brian was, nonetheless, placated when the Londoners joined him and Richard for a few after-hours drinks back at Prestbury Road.

In the kitchen, Alexis and an amazing young man talked blues and picked at guitars. Had Brian ever enjoyed a more interesting conversation? The feeling seemed to be reciprocal because Jones was the first British bottleneck player ever heard by Korner, who, just prior to the long drive home that night, mentioned that he'd be appearing in the locality again very soon at the Town Hall in his still-tolerated office as featured vocalist with Chris Barber. Could Brian, Richard and their pals get along to that one?

They could. What's more, they'd serve as Korner's wildly applauding *claque* during his brief solo spot. Afterwards - and backstage at a Sonny Terry and Brownie McGhee appearance in Cheltenham a few days later - Brian nattered with proud familiarity to Alexis, who was in two minds about whether to counsel him to take his chances in the capital - where a now fully-mobilised Blues Incorporated were searching for premises in which to establish a weekly club - but it was the advice that Jones wished to hear.

Within weeks, Brian's search for like-minded musicians took him halfway there when Alexis put him in touch with an entity in Oxford called Thunder Odin and his Big Secret, fronted by an acne-pitted singing mouth-organist named Paul Pond, and with a repertoire that embraced a wide range of blues forms, particularly Chicago. With delight - and a little amusement - Jones gathered that Pond was endeavouring to copy the energetic wailing of Muddy Waters' sometime harmonica players, Little Walter and Junior Wells: 'I don't know what I sounded like then, but it was Brian who said to me one day, "If you want to sound like Little Walter, then you have to take that C harp and play it in the key of G." Since then, I've found that to be not exactly true. Lots of harp players play it in the regular key - including Little Walter.

'Brian and I did briefly have a band together. He would stop off at Oxford and stay overnight at my place. By this time, I'd been sent down from university. It must have been late 1961 or the beginning of 1962. There was always a party going on. If my band was playing one, Brian would often sit in with us.' [7] A University of Oxford-derived blues band might have seemed a contradiction in terms, and its transient nature precluded anything beyond rehearsal. In any case, Pond - who was to adopt the stage name 'P.P. Jones' and then just plain 'Paul Jones' - was about to seek his fortune in London, and thought it would make sense for Brian to do the same.

As well as the much increased opportunity to find artistic kinship, a spell outside his usual orbit seemed a fine notion to Brian for other reasons too. For a start, the Cheltenham jazz crowd - or that section of it containing his cronies - had all but broken up, most of them departing to the world of work, the marriage bed or, in the case of Richard Hattrell, as one of the last young Britons to endure National Service. While Jones didn't envy Hattrell, there were dismissed moments when he imagined he would have preferred the orderliness of military life to the close and guilt-inducing smell of soiled nappies around Pat and Mark and the potential complications of further parochial romantic pursuits.

Yet, to affect an easier escape to London, Brian, ever cunning and mendacious, reappeared on the doorstep of 'Ravenswood', thinking aloud about a steady job, a mortgage, maybe wedding bells. He didn't go so far as to suggest to a bemused Lewis and Louisa that he'd flushed that music nonsense out of his system, but he wanted, so he emphasized, to disengage himself from his frivolous Cheltenham acquaintances like Shakespeare's Henry V had Falstaff, and the only way to do so was to leave not only the flat to where he'd just moved on Bath Road - smaller than that on Prestbury Road, too small for parties anyway - but Cheltenham altogether.

Thrusting aside well-founded doubts about these fine words, his parents, shackled by invisible and, in the death, unbreakable chains to the most wayward of their offspring, got on with what needed to be done with whatever tools were available. Among these were the science 'A' levels, a favourable referee in Dr. Bell, and Brian's unsettling acquiescence when vocational decisions boiled down to him writing off for details of a course at the London College of Applied Optics, beginning in the New Year. Lewis's reasoning behind this was, though it wasn't university, if Brian stuck at it, he'd be well-placed to gain a post with a decent salary - and in a suit rather than overalls. What more could he want?

There was a hint of Brian's hidden agenda less than an hour after the subsequent interview - to which he was accompanied by his father. While they were waiting for the train home at Paddington station, Brian decided on the apparent spur of the moment that nothing would do but he had to sample some of the West End jazz clubs. Then he strode off, intending to get up to Lewis knew not what.

What Brian was not intending to do was become an optician - or a dentist, pedicure, tree-surgeon or any other of his father's suggestions of how to make most use of his qualifications. To all intents and purposes, he'd quit the London College of Applied Optics after a solitary term of skipped lectures, overall passive disinterest and a non-collegiate objective with which none of the other students could have either sympathised with nor understood. As it had been in Cheltenham, he was soon establishing a pattern of job-hopping, doing a runner whenever landlords pressed for perhaps weeks of unpaid rent and searching constantly for prospective members of the R&B outfit that, in reveries, he was convinced would make enough to get by.

Though nothing was going to deflect Brian from his iron purpose, 'Mick' Jagger mightn't have been especially upset if the Dartford blues collective had fallen apart. 'I don't take anything seriously,' he grinned, 'Since the age of fourteen, I haven't taken anything seriously, whatever I do.' [6] He was unbothered that there were cracks appearing with regard to musical direction such as his advocacy of, say, 'La Bamba' and items by The Coasters, a black US vocal combo, with a 'fool' bass singer and gimmick records like 'Yakety Yak' and 'Charlie Brown'. He - and Keith - also favoured adapting songs by black American girl groups to a different set of hormones - say, 'Boys', B-side of The Shirelles' 1961 million-seller, 'Will You Love Me Tomorrow'.

Yet, if not everyone in the group was of like mind, there remained a sufficient sense of unity for Mick, Keith, Dick and the other two to undertake, when the time came, a crowded journey in Mick's father's car to the far west of London when blues hit the suburb of Ealing after Alexis Korner and Cyril Davies found a home at last for Blues Incorporated.

Their drummer was Charlie Watts, who, during 1960's exceptionally rainy summer, had switched smoothly from the art school in Harrow to a lowly post at Charles Hobson and Gray, one of numerous London advertising agencies that had sprung up since the war. The wage was sufficient - after his mother's housekeeping cut - to pay for clothes, records and drum accessories. Furthermore, after he'd been shown the ropes, Charlie's flair as a commercial artist pushed him up the ladder within months from tea boy to 'visualiser' in the design studio. He was even to be trusted with an assignment that was to take him to Denmark for a few winter weeks as 1961 mutated into 1962.

Outside office hours, he still tinkered with cartoons, and was in the process of creating *Ode To A High-Flying Bird*, an articulation of sorts of his veneration for Charlie Parker. Yet he had no particular desire to see the *Ode* published, even if any commissioning editor was interested in, at first glance, a children's picture book, albeit with 'all of Parker's life in it, all wrapped round this fictitious bird'. [8]

The rest of his spare time was dominated by drumming. During that trip to Scandinavia, he'd 'sit in' one evening at an unfamiliar kit behind fast US saxophonist Don Byas, who bridged swing and bebop. Back home, Watts had moved on already from parochial Jewish wedding celebrations to a unit that played regular Saturday nights at the Troubadour, an Earl's Court coffee bar that presented both folk and jazz.

One summer night, Alexis Korner had insinuated his way onto the stage with the group, 'wearing Rupert Bear trousers and carrying an amplifier, which he put above my head,' grimaced Charlie, 'It was only six inches square, hardly an amp at all, but I still hated it. I thought, bloody hell - noise!' [9] Yet, irritated as he was, Watts was willing not to dismiss the proposal out of hand when Alexis approached him afterwards about joining Blues Incorporated. 'I was all for modern jazz,' ventured Charlie, 'but I suppose I had a theory that R&B was going to be a big part of the scene.' [10]

Watts promised to think about what Korner had had to say - and had appeared to have done so a fortnight later when he flew to Denmark, where 'I sort of lost touch with things.' [10] Nonetheless several written and verbal messages from Korner, requesting his services, reached the Watts family home. On returning, Charlie sought the learned advice of a local musician, Andy Webb, pianist intermittently with the notorious Screaming Lord Sutch and his Horde of Savages.

Wren, who, modelling himself on Ray Charles, also sang with the embryonic Blues Incorporated, prevailed upon Watts to take up Korner's standing offer. Another deciding factor was that members of the formidable Johnny Burch Octet had also been enlisted to assist Alexis and his rather rancorously subordinate co-founder. Cyril Davies' definition of blues, see, was far more rigid than that of Korner, who also blew the mouth-organ, an instrument Charlie had hitherto associated more with the theme to the BBC television police series, *Dixon Of Dock Green.*

Nevertheless, Watts was to perceive that Cyril's 'God-given talent' [10] was at least equal to that of the less versatile Korner. He learnt too that both of them cut familiar figures as session musicians in metropolitan studios - at least, when Davies was not attending to his panel-beating business in South Harrow. It may have occurred to Charlie then that Blues Incorporated could be a useful shop window for a talented drummer too - particularly as a recording deal for the band with Decca was a foregone conclusion, according to Alexis.

Dick Heckstall-Smith's argument for quitting Johnny Burch for Blues Incorporated, however, had little to do with financial gain: 'I was getting fed up with the pale imitation and copying that went on in the British bebop scene. For me, it just wasn't exciting - too timorous, too polite. I was happy to play in a blues band because there was much more to do. I felt that much greater use of the saxophone could be made rather than in the limited and repressed way in which they were being used in American blues bands.' [11]

When Dick arrived in the back room of Soho's Round House pub for Charlie Watts's first rehearsal with Blues Incorporated late in January, 1962, the newcomer's kit had been assembled already and a desultory jam session was underway with pianist Keith Scott and, on double-bass, a teacher called Andy Hoogenboom, who'd brought along a spectator, twenty-one-year-old Shirley Ann Shepherd, then in her final year at Hornsey School of Art. She looked a little like a blonde edition of Juliette Greco, all cheekbones and pale lipstick, the thinking man's monochrome French actress and spectral high priestess of popular existentialism.

Shirley's humorous and intelligent eyes would sometimes catch Charlie at his drums half-looking at her, half turning away. Unknowingly, a shy courtship had begun, but the spell was broken when 'the door burst open, and closed again with a huge slam,' chuckled Heckstall-Smith, 'It was Cyril carrying a bulging old briefcase. He doesn't even say hello or anything, just grunts. Whilst wildly wrestling with the buckle of his briefcase, he roundly curses, and up-ends the contents - a liquid mass of harmonicas - out on the piano.' [11]

As Blues Incorporated continued to jolt into quivering life, Keith Scott was to be superseded by Graham Bond as Andy Hoogenboom was by a Spike Heatley, and then the more suitable Jack Bruce. 'It sounded like rock 'n' roll to me,' Bruce confessed, 'but working with Alexis was the most formative, important time of my life'. [9]

While Charlie was taken aback that Cyril Davies was leery of jazz - with which Heckstall-Smith's saxophone was inseparable - his rapport, and fascination, with the more bohemian Korner was such that he became a frequent visitor to the Bayswater flat where Alexis resided with his wife Bobbie and children, who were more steeped in the detours of culture than most, what with hanging prints of Cezanne, Matisse and Chagall, first editions on the bookshelves, and lodgers such as Bill Colyer and Charles Fox, a *Melody Maker* jazz columnist.

Of more import to Charlie Watts was that, thanks in no small part to his visits to the Korners, the blues no longer meant just titles for jazz tracks like 'West End Blues' by Louis Armstrong, and the underlying thrust of, say, 'Chips Boogie Woogie' by Woody Herman or Parker's 'Now's The Time'. It helped that Alexis, as a music media personality, had been receiving review copies of the latest releases, blues and otherwise, via virtually every post for years. 'The walls were full of records,' gasped Charlie, 'The hip thing was to have them on the floor as well. They'd been sent in by record companies, and I thought it was the hippest thing in the world. The whole Alexis set-up was very glamorous to me, something I wanted to be a part of, whether it was musicians, painters or whatever.' [10]

Sometimes, Brian Jones would pop in for tea and biscuits with Bobbie and Alexis after he'd sir'd and madam'd from nine till half-past-five, firstly, at the Civil Service Stores along the Strand, and then in Whiteley's, a department store just round the corner from the Bayswater apartment. It wasn't exactly showbusiness, even on blues terms, but it would do while he bounced ideas off Alexis about a yet undimmed vision of getting something started, maybe with Paul Jones - with whom he'd continued to practice - as lead singer, and Alexis was still in touch with two guitarists, former seaman Geoff Bradford - who also blew harmonica - and Brian Knight, one of Cyril's panel-beating colleagues. Each was a veteran of the ill-starred Blues and Barrelhouse Club. Another keeper of the faith known to Korner was a thick-set Scottish-born pianist from the East End named Ian Stewart, seen by day as a desk-bound clerk at Imperial Chemical Industries, a stone's throw from Buckingham Palace. On auto pilot, twenty-four-year-old Ian's left hand could roll a fast and circular boogie-woogie bass while the right skipped up and down the higher notes in incorrigibly 'barrel-house' fashion. Would Brian like his telephone number?

The rearing up of family commitments, however, was to brake progress towards any vocational goal. His latest abode was a bedsit along a forlorn side-road a stone's throw from Hampstead Cemetary, and, one Saturday lunchtime, Pat Andrews had turned up suddenly, pushing Mark's pram with one hand, and clasping a too-full suitcase in the other. The place was too small for two adults and a baby that cried and cried, so, leaving no forwarding address, Brian moved everyone to more adequate furnished accommodation in Notting Hill, where the corresponding rent increase was met via Pat working in a laundry and his pay-packet from Whiteleys - which he was supplementing with petty-cash pilferings.

In the flat below dwelt Billie Davis, a singer from Woking, who was then making exploratory recordings with freelance console boffin Joe Meek. Sometimes, she'd pass the time of day with a besuited Brian as he shuffled off to work, fish-paste sandwiches in the Oxo gravy tin that served as a lunch-box. Yet, as his child began to pick up a west London accent, Jones began to drift gradually further and further away from paternal responsibilities. Wistfully *chez* Korner, he'd drink in accounts of Alexis's pot-boiling one-nighters with this famous trad band, his fraternizing with that wizened Delta legend, and the time that would surely be when Blues Incorporated made the stage debut that would precipitate comparable renown.

It came sooner rather than later. Despite past altercations with Alexis, Chris Barber couldn't help liking him, and had permitted the new group, fresh from rehearsing at the Round House, to fill an unbilled support spot for his Jazz Band at the Marquee, then in a cellar below a cinema in Oxford Street. Similar sporadic engagements followed as a result of 'loving self-destruction on his part,' deduced Korner, 'because Chris must have realised that a major R&B boom would kill the trad boom, but he still did it. Chris was the only person who liked us playing electric guitar, but there was only a limited amount of work with him, possibly on Thursday or Wednesday at the Marquee, maybe once a month.

'Then Blues Incorporated played its first couple of concerts as a band, supporting Acker Bilk. The second was at the Civic Centre in Croydon. It was a riot. Acker did a set, and then we went on and did one, and then Acker came back on. The Bilk fans loathed us to destruction because we were the first loud - by the standards of the day - electric blues band. The Acker concert attracted a certain amount of press, but not much. The odd folk or jazz club which had given us gigs immediately withdrew their patronage as soon as we appeared with amplifiers, so we had to get a club of our own together in another way.' [12]

Thus Blues Incorporated became the self-appointed resident combo in a downstairs room between a jeweller's and the ABC teashop along Ealing Broadway. A former trad jazz hang-out, it was to be known variously as the G Club, the Moist Hoist - a nickname coined for the dripping condensation that had necessitated the hauling of a tarpaulin over the stage to render overloaded amplifiers with naked wires less lethal - and simply the Ealing Blues Club. The opening at 7.30 pm on St. Patrick's Day 1962 had been heralded in a *Melody Maker* notice with a captioned endorsement from Chris Barber that wished 'the first R&B club [*sic*] in the country every possible success'. [13]

Unlike the ill-fated Blues and Barrelhouse night five years earlier and Benny Green's effort in Putney, the Ealing club was patronised immediately by fire regulation-breaking zealots from London, Middlesex, Surrey and as far distant as Eric Burdon's Newcastle, all as devout about blues as other cliques were about yachting, numismatics, animal welfare and Freemasonry. Most of them were students, weekend dropouts or middle-class bohemians who might have 'dressed down' - frayed jeans, Jesus sandals, holey pullover, carefully tousled hair and CND badge - for the occasion while *Jimmy Reed At Carnegie Hall* or the plaintive debut album by Bob Dylan span tinnily on the Dansette.

If in more highbrow mood, they'd dry their hair to Coltrane, Parker or Adderley.

Some were players themselves - or thought they were. So it was that, rather than merge into the shadows, spiritual and artistic descendants of the Great McGonagall became responsible for a number of musical assassinations, having got up from the audience to pitch in - thrashing guitars, more often than not - with the loose collective over which Korner and Davies presided. Moreover, because Blues Incorporated was primarily an instrumental unit reliant on much improvisation, any singers there, even those with self-conscious voices that hadn't quite broken, were welcome in theory to step up onto the bandstand - though you'd be received more gladly if you'd nurtured a connection with the inner sanctum centred on Cyril and Alexis.

One of the most promising vocalists from the throng was Art Wood, who Cyril had heard leading The Art Wood Combo at the Blue Circle in Ruislip. 'We were a nine-piece Count Basie-type swing band,' elucidated Art, 'in which I tried to sing like Joe Turner. One night in 1962, Cyril asked me to attend a rehearsal with the outfit he was forming with Alexis Korner, who came round my house to take me through one particular number he wanted to do - 'Forty Days And Forty Nights' by Muddy Waters - because he felt I wasn't singing dirty enough, *nastily* enough to be a blues singer, and that I should put more feeling into it by accentuating certain words. I learned a lot from Alexis both before and after I joined Blues Incorporated as their first - and then only - lead vocalist.'

More prominent physically than Wood was Blues Incorporated's second incumbent singer, the imposing Long John Baldry, whose clean-shaven light complexion beneath a neat, blonde crop made you think of Himmler's Aryan exemplar. Later on, the microphone would be lowered for a fifteen-year-old Cockney named Steve Marriott, once in the cast of the West End musical, *Oliver!*, and now contracted to record two flop Buddy Holly-ish singles for Decca. Yet Marriott put up a surprisingly good show as a black soul in a white skin. The genuine North American article would be represented by two black US servicemen awaiting imminent demobilisation. Urged by both Korner and customer reaction, Ronnie Jones and Herbie Goins decided to stay on in Britain; Goins forming a backing unit, The Night Timers, for himself and second-string vocalist Jones.

Yet passers-by along Ealing's main thoroughfare on any given Saturday night were brought up short not by leakage of the amplified voices from below the pavement, but the underpinning four-in-a-bar rhythm. 'What struck me was the beat of the drums,' confirmed Keith Richards, 'Before you saw the band, you heard it.' [9]

Temporary brake failure had had Keith and his Kentish contingent accelerating down a hill towards a level crossing on the way to West London where, in the first instance anyway, it was enough that Blues Incorporated and its stamping ground even existed. However, it seemed to be better to travel, no matter how hazardously, than to arrive, because it was already over somehow as the party from Dartford trooped across the opaque paving windows and down the worn stairwell into the enveloping fug and sticky heat. Only a miracle could have stopped them feeling a sense of anti-climax. It was like expecting a drop-handlebarred racing bike for your birthday but getting a huffpuff sit-up-and-beg with no gears.

Cyril Davies, balding, obese and baggy-trousered, was centrestage at the beginning of a typical open-ended set that flitted fitfully from 'How Long How Long', a skiffle stand-by originated in Mississippi during the 1930s, to 'Blue Monk', an opus of heart-sinking dreariness in the wrong hands, that stretched to the limit the envelope of what Cyril deemed to be blues - a disagreement with moustachioed, seated Alexis, that wasn't yet out in the open.

Yet, while Blues Incorporated didn't consist entirely of hoary and factional old troupers, 'it was young guys among a bigger bunch of old jazzers,' remembered Don Craine, then studying at Acton Hotel And Catering College, 'Though in reality, they were probably only in their thirties at most, Blues Incorporated's take on R&B didn't impress me, and I couldn't see a future for it outside the jazz clubs.' The honeymoon was over quickly for the lads from Dartford too. 'We reckoned Alexis Korner's band was fantastic the first week,' summarised Dick Taylor, 'quite good the second, but by the third week, we thought it was really a bit off.' It was as if serious British blues wasn't going to be workable in any other way or by any other musicians than the self-contained core of what amounted to not so much an R&B group as an *R&B revivalist* group, just as Acker Bilk *et al* were trad revivalists; too pat, too dovetailed, too English.

While familiarity didn't breed anywhere near complete contempt, having accertained the situation, Jagger - and then the less assertive Richards and Taylor - pondered tentatively whether to join the queue of guest musicians from the crowd, groping for reasons why they would or wouldn't be either laughed off stage or be granted a mingling of amused cheers and prolonged clapping for their youthful cheek. Either way, it might mean having to flee the place, pride smarting and heads exploding, never to go there again.

A hard yardstick for any of the hopeful, the hopeless and just plain starstruck, had been a floor spot by Brian Jones and his Thunder Odin namesake on 7th April, 1962. While Paul Jones's delivery of Elmore James's *magnum opus*, 'Dust My Broom' - as 'Dust My *Blues*' - from behind huge sunglasses was competent, the careen of a seated and neatly attired Brian's unprecedented bottleneck was what most transfixed Dick Taylor: 'Paul sang well, but Brian was absolutely brilliant. He was probably at the height of his powers then, playing that blues stuff.'

After 'Dust My Blues' ended to a thunderous huzzah, Dick and a similarly overwhelmed Keith and Mick threaded across the club to flock round Brian like friendly, if over-attentive, wolfhounds. Most round-eyed of all was the usually reticent Richards, combining rapturous exclamation and appearing coolly well-informed about Elmo-Brian's methodology. 'Brian used open G tuning,' exemplified Taylor, 'which Keith was aware of, but didn't use himself.'

In retrospect, this was as crucial an opening exchange as that of Keith and Mick on the rails to Sidcup the previous year. It was also the Jones boys' valedictory recital as a duo, although, with Brian at the helm, they were to muddle through a loose handful of indifferently-received jam sessions with Ian Stewart and Geoff Bradford in a couple of Soho pubs before Paul chose to mark time - as 'Paul Petersen' - belting out assembly-line pop with Slough's Gordon Reece and the Adelphians, prior to enrolment in what was to become Manfred Mann. As for Brian, he was now, through his concord with Alexis Korner and his observations at the Ealing club every Saturday night, short-listing potential members for that long-mooted R&B group.

Notes

1. *Melody Maker*, 23rd November, 1969
2. Leaving its mark on, for instance, 'It's All Over Now', 'You Can't Catch Me' and '19th Nervous Breakdown' by The Rolling Stones.
3. *Paul McCartney: Many Years From Now* by B. Miles (Vintage, 1998)
4. This tape was to fetch a huge amount when auctioned at Sotheby's in 1995.
5. *Blues Guitar* ed. J. Obrecht (Miller Freeman, 1993)
6. *The Rolling Stones In Their Own Words* ed. D. Dalton and M. Farren (Omnibus, 1985)
7. *Talk To Me Baby: The Story Of The Blues Band* by R. Bainton (Firebird, 1994)
8. *Downbeat*, February, 1987
9. *Alexis Korner: The Biography* by H. Shapiro (Bloomsbury, 1996)
10. *The Rolling Stones: The First Twenty Years* by D. Dalton (Thames & Hudson, 1981)
11. *Rhythm*, June, 2001
12. *Rolling Stones '76* (Second Foundation, 1976)
13. *Melody Maker*, 11th March, 1962

*Chapter Five*
**Follow My Leader**

*'I got up and sang. Before I knew it, I was one of the band's featured vocalists. Then Keith would come up and we'd do a couple of Chuck Berry things' - Mick Jagger* [1]

Oblivious to the mild sub-cultural commotion in Ealing, The Cliftons had been tussling with The Wranglers over bookings at St Michael's Youth Club in Lower Sydenham before compromising with alternating weeks. Nevertheless, The Cliftons seemed to be forging ahead of all parochial rivals, what with the broadening of a work spectrum that now embraced a riverboat 'shuffle' on the Thames, several consecutive wild nights in the unlikely location of a cavern within Bromley's man-made Chislehurst Caves - a mushroom farm lately converted to a music venue - and a penetration into the college circuit, namely the London School of Economics.

As well as their hard-won musical proficiency, The Cliftons were distinctive for a sharp corporate persona epitomised by matching jeans, white shirts, slim-jim ties and black mohair pullovers. As a further indication that Bill Perks, at least, meant business was his purchase of a spare amplifier - a Vox AC30 - as insurance against it being needed should the Watkins Westminster fall silent midway through a song on, say, that night-of-nights in June, 1962 when the group supported the similarly costumed Paramounts at Greenwich Town Hall. The headlining act, though only semi-professional too, had become both a reliable draw in the ballrooms and an all-purpose backing unit whenever stars of the modest chart magnitude of Tommy Bruce, Dickie Pride and Lance Fortune visited The Paramounts' native Southend.

Any competitiveness in front of the promenading audience deferred to easy camaraderie off-stage. During the long chat that preceded the loading of equipment and subsequent departure in respective vans, Bill complimented the other outfit on an ability to perform black R&B - some of it quite obscure - without losing any of the overriding passion.

It had been a learning experience for all The Cliftons, who, while keeping a weather eye on whatever was shaking up the Top Twenty, took the opportunity to insert a little more Paramount-esque music into their repertoire during the turnovers of personnel that punctuated a year of mixed fortunes. A new guitarist, Brian Cade, seemed to be there for the duration, but a saxophonist whose heart was in jazz, lasted only a month. When Dave Harvey had quit too in July, the group tried out another singer before opting for the simpler expedient of continuing as a quintet with Steve Carroll and Bill sharing lead vocals.

However accomplished they'd become, The Cliftons remained the sort of group to which folk jived rather than surged stagewards to watch within a few bars of the opening number. This may be why Mick Jagger would have remembered nothing about their appearance at the LSE - that is, if he'd bothered to go to a function involving uniformed perpetrators of 'white rock 'n' roll' - Bill's own description [2] - rather than the darker stuff that only the finest minds could appreciate.

It was also becoming ever clearer to Mick that those concurrent Ealing club denizens with notions of personal talent were trying, but mostly failing, to emulate the Jimmy Reeds, Slim Harpos, Muddy Waters and Howlin Wolves of black America - especially vocally. 'Alexis sang these funny blues interpretations in what seemed to us a very upper-class English accent,' he scoffed, 'We used to hoot with laughter about this. I saw people my own age getting up, and I thought to myself, "They're not that brilliant". That's how it started.' [1]

'It' was prefaced by a tape of 'La Bamba', Jimmy Reed's 'Bright Lights Big City' and a couple of inevitable Berry items, labelled 'Little Boy Blue and the Blue Boys', an arbitrarily-chosen name, and mailed from Dick Taylor's address towards the end of April, 1962 to Korner who, while not as unimpressed with it as he'd been by a like offering from Brian Jones, Paul Jones and the Thunder Odin group, returned it without comment. [3] This rejection had not, however, blurred Jagger's understanding that there was no artistic force field surrounding Blues Incorporated like there'd been round The Southerners and Danny Rogers and his Realms back at Dartford Grammar.

If he could gather the nerve to finally mount a public stage for the first time, why, therefore, shouldn't he volunteer to give 'em one or more of the items on the tape the following Saturday? As he had when Jones and Jones had asked three weeks earlier, Alexis raised no objections, so Mick stubbed out a cigarette, cleared his throat and stood before the microphone, motionless bar trembling knees. Behind him, Dick and Keith - now, with Jagger, all that was left of the Dartford blues brotherhood - plugged in, and Taylor informed anyone in the house band who wanted to play along that the key to the standard twelve-bar chord structure of 'Around And Around', the B-side of Chuck's million selling 'Johnny B. Goode' from 1958, was A major.

The hubbub subdued to frozen faces staring up at Mick. He nearly felt sick, but a deep breath later, he was into the opening line, 'Well, the joint was rockin'...'. There'd be a little self-conscious head-shaking - as if trying to slough off the onlookers' hushed attention - but that was the only indication of the trademark caperings of Mick Jagger, the future rock star. As the number died away, Mick-Mike Jagger, callow LSE student, blinked at his feet while a spatter of applause for his courage as much as his singing ensued. So began the flight of Jagger - and Richards and, to a more qualified degree, Taylor - to the very peaks of pop - though it didn't seem like it as the three heaved guitars and amplifiers onto the late train back to Kent.

While reliving an eventful evening, they debated whether it would or would not be presumptuous to drop in on Alexis during the afternoon before the next Ealing session. Though he was jovial, open-handed and blessed with a gift for rousing undying affection with a mere look or gesture, the liberty hall that was Korner's flat was not for anyone. There was nothing to prevent any finger calloused by guitar strings from pressing its bell, but you had to decide for yourself, with the help of friends equally perplexed, when the position you had attained within the British blues firmament entitled you to pay your respects to the Grand Old Man, then aged thirty-four. It was a super-lative test of democracy because the challenge had to be met by the individual. Unless specifically invited, you'd never dare ask Alexis or Bobbie if the moment was right for you to take tea in Bayswater.

Jagger was to find that moment over the next few weeks when, with and without Richards and Taylor for musical and moral support, he slipped into less inert gear during subsequent G Club performances - such as a duet of Jimmy Reed's 'I Ain't Got You' with Eric Burdon - quite tickled when anyone cried encouragement to him. He even haz-arded blowing tyro harmonica in the teeth of Cyril Davies's grouchy 'Get a pair of pliers' when he sought directives on how to bend notes.

Mick's teenage spots rose through the lacto-calamine lotion and turned red as concentration on every phrase lit his face. He was proba-bly nothing then without the public-address system, but each utterance he dredged up was like a brush stroke on a sound-painting. Learning all the time, when he wasn't trying consciously to mimic someone, he sounded like a cross between Slim Harpo and the obscure and stentorian Boogie Bill Webb, maker of just one single, 1952's 'I Ain't For It' on Imperial, a disc of which Jagger, expert though he'd become, was probably unaware then, let alone ever heard.

Yet there was also an near-intangible something else about Mick's overall effect on listeners. If his pitching of high notes was a bit hit-or-miss then, a pimply herbert in his second year at the LSE, barely the Mannish Boy that Muddy Waters bragged about being, he demonstrated that you didn't have to come from the chain gang or the ghettos of southside Chicago to sound world-weary, cynical and knowing beyond your years. If you half-closed your eyes, with delicate suspension of logic, this stripling's bashed-about rasp would seem believable as, from a reserve of inner fire, however unsubstantiated, he would be putting on the agony three nights a week with Blues Incorporated either at the Marquee - the National Jazz Federation's main London venue - or the Moist Hoist. One such appearance brought Jagger his earliest mention - and that's all it was - in the British music press.

Mick regarded this as an extremely minor breakthrough for the R&B movement rather than a sea-mark on the voyage to his own fame. It was sufficient for now that he and his pals had their feet under the table in the captain's cabin. Immersed in the traditions and lodged conventions of British showbusiness as he was, Alexis tried on these occasions to instil 'professionalism' into the ramshackle Dartford trio, but succeeded chiefly in entertaining them with his name-dropping and endless anecdotes about the old days, laced with the inner history of each event or person. More to the point, when he spoke in his affable way of the here and how, there were shrewd judgements about contemporaries, and sound reasons why any given musician was popular, disliked or just ignored.

So began a lifelong amity exemplified by Alexis nurturing an almost paternal pride in Mick, Keith and Dick's later achievements, and the phonetically pliant Keith's tongue slipping easily into Korner's hip, pseudo-transatlantic vocabulary, inserting 'man' into sentences where 'mate' had once been. Richards also got used to referring to females as 'chicks' and men as 'cats'. As appealing to him was Korner's speaking voice, a smoky drawl with a seasoning of the officer-and-gentleman. Within a couple of years, Taylor would be amused when, on meeting

Richards for the first time in ages, 'he'd gone all la-di-da: "How fabulous! Lovely to see you!" - just like Alexis Korner rather than Keith, the barrow-boy-type I knew of old.'

The shy and ponderous youth of 1962, however, was more inclined to draw on a cigarette and nod in smiling agreement with whoever had spoken last during those Bayswater afternoons. 'At first, you got the impression that he was just trailing around with Mick,' considered Alexis, 'but it didn't take long to realise that Keith wasn't trailing around at all. He just happened to be quieter.' [4]

As far as Korner was concerned too, Richards - and Taylor - were occasional parts of the package and Jagger the drawing card every Saturday night as, to the disgust of blues diehards, the loudest ovations were saved for the numbers that teetered on rock 'n' roll, a fact not lost on Mick: 'When we got up and did our two numbers, the crowd went bananas, It was quite obvious they liked that kind of music'. [5]

Hence, it wasn't entirely by coincidence that Jagger was not singled out as a particularly integral part of the set-up, often taking a literal back seat while waiting his turn as one lower in the vocal hierarchy than Long John Baldry and Art Wood. 'Alexis didn't really want a singer who would take over the front line,' summised Mick, 'It was like the old big bands where you had the singer who would croon a couple of numbers and then the "real thing" would happen, and the band leader would take over'. [5]

This policy was echoed in Bluesville in faraway Sheffield, which had its own Blues Incorporated in The Chuck Fowler R and B Band. Other provincial venues were also to turn into blues strongholds on off-peak evenings. Random examples are the R&B Club on Tuesday nights above Andover's Copper Kettle restaurant, where The Troggs came into being; Club Rado - which cradled Van Morrison's Them - in The Old Sailors' Maritime Dance Hall in Belfast; the Gamp in Edinburgh; the Downbeat in Newcastle's dockland, where Eric Burdon hollered with what would metamorphose into The Animals and, in a hostelry beneath the shadow of Birmingham Town Hall, Rhythm Unlimited, birthplace of The Spencer Davis Group, where, within an hour of its 7.30 start, over eighty latecomers had been turned away. 'The packed crowd at the opening session and subsequent evenings make it quite clear,' co-promoter Brian Allen would crow, 'that there is a tremendous following for R&B in the city.' [6]

Rhythm Unlimited's inaugural evening would incorporate a bash by The Renegades who, with peroxided hair and an all-electric front line, looked and sounded dangerously like a pop group. That would never have passed muster in Ealing in 1962 where it was expedient for Mick Jagger, in his office as Wood's & Baldry's second understudy, to deny that he sang anything other than strict R&B. Nevertheless, a few weeks after their maiden blow at the G Club debut, he, Dick and Keith began investigating possibilities of putting together a group with a freer attitude within a more fixed set-up than either the 'Little Boy Blue' bedroom band or Blues Incorporated. It would remain more eagerly abreast of the latest genre developments than former 'trad dad' Alexis - and Cyril, sweating over his harmonica while glooming at Heckstall-Smith's too-jazzy sax and Graham Bond's aberrant electric organ.

What was this Brian Jones bloke intending to do? Would he be prepared to give Reed, Berry, Diddley and so forth a go? There'd been little evidence of that when Keith had watched Brian jamming in the Bricklayer's Arms in Soho with Paul Jones, Geoff Bradford and Ian Stewart, a stylistic hostage to Jelly Roll Morton, Little Brother Montgomery, Pinetop Smith and other ancient black masters of boogie-woogie. Yet, intrigued, Messrs. Richards, Taylor and Jagger turned up when Brian booked consecutive midweek afternoons in the Bricklayers' functions room, having advertised in *Jazz News*, a London periodical bought mainly for its venue information, features such as a column by Manfred Mann and job opportunities.

His unboxed three lines indicated that Brian too was after musicians of like mind to the Dartford three. As it wasn't all smiles between Blues Incorporated and Long John Baldry - who sided with Cyril Davies over the true Chicago blues issue - Jones, with his ear to the ground, had been on Long John's case with the promptness of a vulture. Art Wood was another possibility until it transpired that he was thinking aloud about the formation of another Art Wood Combo with organist Jon Lord - later a charter member of Deep Purple - and other members of the alarmingly-named Red Bludd's Bluesicians.

Jones was also rubbing his chin over Tony McPhee and Peter Cruikshank, respectively a guitarist and bass player, who'd been on the periphery of those surrounding him and Paul after their Ealing club triumph. Tony and Peter, however, had been charged with finding a drummer for a trio, The Groundhogs, to accompany John Lee Hooker on a forthcoming tour of Europe. Geoff Bradford and Brian Knight - though now members of Blues By Six, containing personnel from Blues Incorporated, past, present and future - were less busy. Brian also spoke to singing guitarist Mike Cooper, who commuted virtually every Saturday from Reading to Ealing.

Though it hadn't occurred to Brian to approach Keith Richards and Dick Taylor or the fractionally more illustrious G Club bluesman, Mick Jagger, they were on the spot anyway on the first of those unseasonably cold afternoons at the Bricklayer's. It'd do no harm, he supposed, for them to join in, even if he - and Ian Stewart, also present - had already judged Bradford and Knight to be head-and-shoulders above Chuck Berry enthusiasts from Kent as more 'authentic' blues instrumentalists.

With a bass player whose name has been lost in the mists of time, and 'a drummer with only half a kit', so a sniffy Geoff Bradford noted [7], the session got underway - and its participants were at loggerheads almost immediately. 'Geoff Bradford and Brian Knight thought Keith was too rock 'n' roll,' remembered Dick Taylor, 'and stomped off in a purist huff. The bass player, whoever he was, went with the general stampede as well.'

To the discerning Mike Cooper too, 'when Mick and Keith turned up, suddenly it all sounded too commercial. In retrospect, I also perhaps didn't like Jagger and Richards. It was nothing to do with them really. I was always very anti-social with certain "up-front" personality types - and those two were, or at least Mick was. I didn't like Chuck Berry then either, and I couldn't see a group with them in it going in a way that would lead down a jazz-R&B road.'

After more than a month of further try-outs at the Bricklayer's and other licensed premises, jamming became formal rehearsal, and antagonistic youths milling around whittled down to Ian and Brian plus the Kentish knot. The five of them were a motley crew whose extremes were represented by Jones, whose assumed reposeful 'cool', coupled with a girly lisp and camp mannerisms, belied both ruthless ambition and his self-promoted reputation as a devil with women, and Stewart, as ostensibly manly as Jones wasn't. A sweaty aptitude for athletics had wrought in Ian a sturdy rather than slim physique. He also had a rugged, lantern-jawed face on which craggy eyebrows jutted from a forehead topped by a slicked-back smarm of an ICI pen-pusher's hair-cut. Yet, even on the most worn-out pub piano, his beefy mitts had an intuitive feel for the melodic and lyrical intent of a given number, employing the utmost delicacy or muscle-bound force as required.

There wasn't room for three six-string guitarists, so Dick Taylor was to succumb eventually to constant overtures from Jones to invest in an 'Emperor' bass. Among a movable feast of drummers were Tony Chapman from The Cliftons, who'd responded to Brian's 'wanted' ad in *Melody Maker*, and the more satisfactory Carlo Little, a former Royal Fusilier who now served Lord Sutch's Savages - for whom he was also what might be described as 'musical director' in that, as Tony Dangerfield, Sutch's bass player, would observe, 'He drilled me through the act. He'd been in the army, and was like a sergeant-major'. While Brian was keen on retaining the exacting Carlo, Mick Avory, a painter-and-decorator from East Moseley, Surrey, was tolerated for just two rehearsals in the light of his meandering tempo and a near-total ignorance then of even Chuck Berry, let alone Muddy Waters. [8]

Dick Taylor's reflections on these first exploratory weeks are worth quoting at length: 'Brian regarded himself as leader because he'd invited Mick, Keith and I to join, whereas we thought it was a logical development of what we'd been doing with Robert Beckwith and Alan Etherington. It was really a hybrid of that and Brian's band - which was on the way to being fully formed by him and Ian Stewart.

'They liked the idea of having Mick as a singer, having seen his potential at the Ealing Club, and they thought he could transform their band - and wherever Mick went, Keith came too - and they invited me along as well. Brian was very complimentary about my bass playing, though when I first started learning, I didn't have many problems because it was just a case of figuring out a few riffs through listening to what seemed to be the bass lines on disc. These were often more a presence than a sound on domestic record players in those days.

'Depending on where was free, we convened either at the Brick-layers', the White Bear behind Leicester Square or the Wetherby Arms in King's Road, mid-afternoon to mid-evening to allow time to catch the last train back to Dartford. Brian was sometimes late because he was still working at Whiteley's. He seemed more of a grown-up than us, but he was capable of being pretty damned moody, mostly about how things were going with the group. He didn't want us necessarily to be rich and famous then, but he did want us to find work. I think he was introverted and maybe insecure, but, although he'd despair and get out of his head a bit, he had an acute sense of humour in those days, a highly amusing fellow. In the beginning, everyone was great mates, and we used to have lots of laughs.'

There had been, for instance, hilarity rather than annoyance when rehearsals at the White Bear were terminated after the landlord caught Jones clambering over the unattended bar in the upstairs room to pilfer cartons of cigarettes. The discord, intrigues and general unpleasantnesses that make pop groups what they are did not become overt, though they might have done had the others known that Brian would be taking 'agency commissions' from the meagre payments the group received for the intermittent engagements that disrupted the working week, college timetables and recreational sloth during the latter half of 1962.

As self-designated 'leader' too, Jones had also given the group a name. When the myth gripped harder, it was said that he'd chosen it from 'Rollin' Stone Blues', the title of the first single - a 1953 seventy-eight - by Muddy Waters to be issued in Britain. The expression 'rollin' stone' was also contained in a throwaway phrase on a field recording made by Waters prior to his migration to Chicago. Other of its mixed and disparate precedents include a 1957 Lonnie Donegan B-side, 'I'm Just A Rollin' Stone', and just plain 'Rollin' Stone', a minor hit in 1958 for The Marigolds (formerly The Prisonaires). Into the bargain, The Rolling Stones were a cartoon circus family in a pre-teen comic called *Robin*, and it was also the name of a group operational in Bristol, who'd been known to The Ramrods - and possibly Jones too before he left Cheltenham.

Ian Stewart had been especially disgruntled with 'The Rollin' Stones', but accepted Brian's assurance that it would be altered once they'd got a stage debut at the Marquee on a Thursday in July out of the way. What amounted to a mere interval spot had come about through Blues Incorporated, despite its rapid turnover of musicians, continuing to go from strength to strength. Most recently, they'd snared a bold weekly residency at the Flamingo, patronised principally by hip West Indians, GIs on a pass and prototype Mods, who preferred what was becoming known as 'soul music', stretching from smooth Motown to James Brown call-and-response panic, nearly all of it infused with horns and female chorale. The Flamingo's principally male clientele considered themselves more sophisticated than the middle class bohemians heading for darkest Ealing on Saturdays - 'Because they weren't jazzers,' opined club regular John Baldwin, who had now assumed the stage alias John Paul Jones, 'There was this little white R&B movement, which grew up quite separately. We were into Otis Redding, and they were all into Chuck Berry and the Chess people, blues twits really. As a musical scene, they just didn't rate.' [9]

While merely going the distance at the Flamingo, Blues Incorporated had proved an on-going and profitable market exercise at the six hundred-plus-capacity Marquee since that first recital in May - so much so that the place inspired the title of the long-awaited debut LP, scheduled for release in autumn, though, admittedly on Decca's budget subsidiary, Ace of Clubs. Nonetheless, *R&B From The Marquee* had been realised not 'live', but in the studio under the supervision of Jack Good, the brains behind *Six-Five Special* and *Oh Boy!*.

One of Good's final productions before emigrating to the States, the album did not feature Charlie Watts, but Graham Burbidge, a Chris Barber Jazz Bandsman. He had taken the trouble to buttonhole a visiting Muddy Waters' drummer, Francis Clay, for a few pointers, and, with a pound-sign over every crochet, in Decca's West Hampstead studios, 'Alexis asked me to do it,' said Burbidge, 'because, in his exact words, he didn't think Charlie was up to it.' [5]

Though disappointed, Charlie too thought that Graham was more equal than he to this ultimate litmus-test of musical competence, especially at such an important juncture in Blues Incorporated's career. Just as attractively in his selfless and matter-of-fact candour, he also suggested that, for future stage performances, they might be better off with Ginger Baker, still with The Johnny Burch Octet. In any case, implied Charlie, a double life as a Charles Hobson and Gray employee and Blues Incorporated drummer was burning the candle to the middle. 'During the course of the summer, the band was working more and more,' confirmed Alexis Korner, 'and Charlie had decided that he didn't want to be a professional musician because it was too uncertain an existence.' [10]

Watts had pledged himself already to the less demanding Blues By Six, whose workload was concentrated more conveniently on weekends, embracing Fridays and Sundays at Studio 51 in a basement off

Covent Garden, which, starting life nine years earlier, was England's oldest jazz club, and alternate Saturdays at the Piccadilly Jazz Club and the Six Bells in Chelsea. As these bookings were within comparatively easy reach, the group relied on buses and either Brian Knight's father's Ford Anglia or Mr. Watts's Humber until the transport of Charlie's kit was eased by leaving it when convenient at the left-luggage office at Leicester Square underground station.

It was also easier for Watts to drum non-committally with other groups. These still included Blues Incorporated whenever Ginger Baker was indisposed, which he wasn't when a streamlined Blues Incorporated, with 'very suspect tuning and internal balance', [11] were booked to reach across the Empire on the Light Programme's *Jazz Club*.

The BBC was prepared to pay only for five musicians, necessitating such cost-cutting expedients as Korner doubling on lead vocals, and dispensing with the services of Long John Baldry, who was in any case keeping his options open by singing with both Blues Incorporated and the newly-formed Cyril Davis All-Stars. 'Blues Incorporated had split in two,' elucidated Art Wood, 'There was now Alexis Korner's Blues Incorporated and The Cyril Davies All-Stars, who I took my brother Ronnie, who was music mad, to see at the Railway in Ruislip.'

In the light of the forthcoming broadcast, it was decided that, to keep the light burning at the Marquee that Thursday, Long John Baldry and an ad-hoc ensemble, The Hoochie Coochie Men - with Geoff Bradford on lead guitar - were to be the main attraction, and Brian Jones was to be asked by Korner if his untried group could support.

Though Mick Avory's name had been prominent in what little publicity preceded it, Dick Taylor is certain that Charlie Watts was a temporary Rollin' Stone on that night when, just as far too many would profess to have been at Belfast's Club Rado to listen to Them, at the Cavern for The Beatles or to have danced at The Sex Pistols' early fiascos, there would be a profound lack of retrospective honesty about the first manifestation of The Rolling Stones. Hundreds more than can actually have been there were to remember a set that walked an uncomfortable line between reassuringly familiar G Club crowd-pleasers and Chuck Berry.

Some pop historians have portrayed it erroneously as an ignition point for extreme reaction and, while it didn't provoke an actual riot, discontented murmurings from pockets among the onlookers became shouted statements about the impudence of imposing rock 'n' roll on the blues grid - as instanced by Dick Taylor thrumming his electric bass guitar rather than an acoustic double-bass like that which underpinned Blues Incorporated. 'The audience was like Christianity versus Islam,' he recalled, 'The scene was dominated by trad jazz so you can imagine what it was like when a bunch of amateur blues players stepped up. We were the wrong colour to play the blues. We did Muddy Waters, Jimmy Reed... It wasn't wall-to-wall Chuck Berry by any means, but neither was it the stuff Blues Incorporated did.'

It might not have appealed to everyone, but the overall feeling, as the neon twilight struck the departing music-lovers, was that the new outfit had provided stimulating entertainment. Their unbottled exuberance - just enough then to not upset the majority of conservative palates - was certainly a key to further stints at the Marquee until the weight of unfavourable opinions about their 'authenticity' - one from no less an authority than Chris Barber - caused Harold Pendleton, the venue's manager, to stop engaging them. 'That's because they mucked about with things and played them faster, not like the records.' suggested Phil May, 'They didn't have the reverence for the form that Alexis Korner and all that high church of the Ealing club blues potentates had.'

Yet, for every door slammed on The Rollin' Stones, others creaked pedantically ajar, and *Jazz News* was to name - to Brian's chagrin, no doubt - 'Mick Jagger's Rollin' Stones' among London's 'eight R&B bands now in business'. They were, it continued, 'touring the local clubs to appreciative audiences.'[12] The journal did not stress that some of these 'local clubs' had been convened for one night only at the Stones' own expense, usually in parish institutes used more frequently for amateur dramatics and table tennis. On one occasion, a hall was empty for the entire four hours booked, apart from the five Stones and a stand-in drummer, but it was decided that the show must go on regardless.

**Notes**

1. *London Live* by T. Bacon (Balafon, 1999)
2. *Stone Alone* by B. Wyman and R. Coleman (Viking, 1990)
3. With an awesome contempt for historical and cultural context, one of

Dick Taylor's then-flatmates erased the tape in 1965.

4. *Keith Richards In His Own Words* ed. M. St. Michael (Omnibus, 1994)

5. *Alexis Korner: The Biography* by H. Shapiro (Bloomsbury, 1996)

6. *Midland Beat*, October, 1963

7. *Blues In Britain* by B. Brunning (Blandford, 1995)

8. The following year, Avory was to join The Kinks.

9. *Stoned* by A. L. Oldham (Vintage, 2000)

10. *Rolling Stones '76* (Second Foundation, 1976)

11. *Melody Maker*, 19th July, 1962

12. *Jazz News*, 21st November, 1962

## Chapter Six
## Room At The Top?

*'Brian and Keith never spoke to me until they found out I had some cigarettes' - Bill Wyman* [1]

Having read Nietzsche, Brian - then the only Stone with, I suppose, a family to support - might have stumbled upon and agreed with the German philosopher of irrationalism's personal credo: that domesticity is incompatible with a life of constant creativity. For him and Pat, therefore, there had never been much hope.

It was, perhaps, an emotional release for both sides when the Notting Hill household split in two, and Pat and the baby fled back to Cheltenham. From a purely financial perspective, this left Brian with nothing. His thieving of what was, cumulatively, a huge amount of money from the till had brought him the sack at Whiteley's and would have come to court too if not for a convincingly contrite routine and associated sob-story about marital breakdown that was worthy of an Oscar.

He'd certainly looked and behaved like a hard-working husband and father driven to crime by domestic problems, instanced by the wearied indifference towards any customer pausing at his counter, and the cash register receipts swimming before budgerigar eyes. Fortunately for Jones, the slow-witted manager who'd third-degreed him had not gathered from the store grapevine that Brian's aura of depressed forbearance had less to do with a troubled personal life than him getting to bed as the small hours chimed after making a row at some Teddy Boys' gala.

Once again, Brian was out of the soup, but, without Pat's wage from the laundry, he was soon being hounded by an irate rent-collector. By late summer, room had been made for him in a two-bedroom flat, situated in World's End, a few streets too far from the more fashionable heart of Chelsea, and about to be occupied by Mick and Keith too, partly because it was handy for the Wetherby Arms, now The Rollin' Stones' principal gathering point.

Jagger had had to jump the highest hurdle of parental opposition, but eventually Joe and Eva had supposed it was fair enough for him to fly the nest in August, 1962, just before his second academic year at the LSE. If nothing else, living at 102, Edith Grove would lessen the chances of him being late for morning lectures.

Dick Taylor preferred to remain in Bexleyheath, confessing that he was 'slightly appalled by Edith Grove. It didn't exactly inspire me to want to leave home'. Once it might have been the acme of elegance with its bay windows and the pillars supporting the front porches, but No. 102's present state of disrepair was expressed to passers-by in peeling paintwork, leaky guttering, ledges off-white with pigeon droppings, and rubbish sogging behind railings. Inside, there was no adequate sanitation or central heating. The entire terrace in which it stood seemed to quiver as underground trains within close proximity clattered along the three Circle and District line tracks that connected at Earl's Court.

Each visit brought another detail to dingy light for Dick Taylor, whether the soiled tissue in the stinking and frequently unflushable communal lavatory; a fresh avalanche of plaster that the knocker's rapping thunder had dislodged from the hallway wall, and a puddle of congealing vomit on the stairwell, now giving life to some sort of fungus. Well, it would have revolted pigs.

In the bedsit that an estate agent might have described as 'compact' was a ravenous slot electricity meter, neglected household chores, body odour, undisguised greed at meal times and general unconcern about the condition of the place. It was understood by Jagger, Jones and Richards that as long as you didn't fall behind with the rent, you could get carried home drunk at seven in the morning, lie in until the street lights came on, leave crockery unwashed in the sink for days, and entertain persons of a different set of hormones behind the closed door of a bedroom so untidy that it looked as if someone had chucked a hand-grenade into it.

This was Keith and Mick's first taste of roughing it and the full horror of No. 102 reared up during their very first night there. They jerked in and out of the uneasiest of slumbers, waking to open-mouthed snores. As daybreak pierced the sock-smelling gloom, they perceived the grey-green of mildew, bare light-bulbs coated with dust, and the frowziness of duffel-bags for pillows, coats for supplementary blankets, a frayed sofa, a cigarette-holed table cloth, screwed-up fish-and-chip paper in the fireplace, Brian breaking wind and a most singular fellow named James Phelge hacking a phlegmy cough on his way to the toilet.

He was the apartment's fourth tenant. A printer by trade, Jimmy Phelge was, like Beckett's Mr. Knott, inclined to dress inappropriately for any given time of day, and, in common with Barry Miles, he liked to be addressed by his surname. The Dartford boys wondered again what they were doing there with this peculiar Phelge and Brian, who, on closer acquaintance, they weren't sure they liked that much either, even if, according to Pat Andrews, 'Keith idolised Brian then because his own repertoire was very limited - more or less just Chuck Berry.'

The partitioned house became even more loathsome when the seasons turned from vapoured gold to chill marble. As it had been in Bill Perks' Penge in 1948, windows iced up and goose-flesh rose during an especially cheerless winter of low temperatures, seething east winds and snow on snow still on the ground at the end of March.

Most of the rent came from Phelge's earnings and Jagger's grant cheque because, although the jobless Richards had acquired a Harmony Meteor semi-acoustic - an improvement on the Hofner - an individual Stone's income on aggregate was a fraction of that of the counter assistant at the cafe near Notting Hill Gate tube station where they used to congregate before Jones moved into No. 102. 'One day, Brian and I met Mick and Keith there,' remembered Pat Andrews, 'Mick, whose student money had just come in, bought us all a mixed grill, and Brian's and my budget did not extend to that.'

In the pantheon of Blues Incorporated splinter groups, The Rollin' Stones, for all the *Jazz News* hyperbole, weren't yet also-rans, let alone pop-stars-in-waiting. Nonetheless, the very idea of becoming one wasn't so much of an afterthought for such as stout, pipe-smoking Graham Bond - who was contemplating whether to sound out Jack Bruce about forming another breakaway unit - or Cyril Davies who, as Alexis Korner alone did at the G Club now, ruled a venue in Harrow-on-the-Hill, fronting his All-Stars, bereft of the hated saxophone and organ and with musicians from Lord Sutch's Savages and West Drayton's Cliff Bennett and the Rebel Rousers, among them sixteen-year-old *wunderkind* Nicky Hopkins on piano, and Carlo Little on drums before his overwhelming obligations to Sutch necessitated the recruitment of a Bill Eyden.

That ruled out Carlo as more than a stop-gap measure during a vexing search for a drummer by a Rollin' Stones for whom prospects seemed to be fractionally rosier of late. A date schedule that had once signified a month's work became a fortnight's when, guffawed Keith, 'We thought the absolute pinnacle of success would be maybe three or four regular gigs in London.' [2] As well as the Marquee - soon to move to Wardour Street - among further suitable outlets in the inner city were the Booker T Club within Shoreditch Town Hall and South Kensington's Crypt Youth Club, while the 100 Club, the Piccadilly Jazz Club, Ken Colyer's Studio 51 and other jazz strongholds had capitulated to new guidelines that would allow guitar groups to defile their stages.

The pestilence was spreading to the most far-flung suburbs, especially towards the south-west. Dotted in and round Richmond, Kingston and Twickenham, venues that regularly clasped across-the-board pop to their bosoms began engaging the Stones, notably Eel Pie Island hotel auditorium - 'a place to dance to the music of a locomotive band,' Dickens called it in 1832. After the Great War, it hosted tea dances, but in the 1950s, a sociologist named Arthur Chisnall launched a jazz club, not merely to provide entertainment, but to bring its young patrons Living In The Shadow Of The Bomb into contact with radical thought.

Yet, while Putney's St. Mary's Hall - location of Benny Green's 1961 bash - Richmond's Station Hotel and L'Auberge - where Brian Jones gazumped the promoter into paying £2 10s over the £10 agreed originally - Sandover Hall and the Crown all transformed themselves into R&B haunts at least once a week, the Stones supported parochial heroes Ricky Tyrrell and his Presidents at the Red Lion in Sutton for successive Friday evenings. 'Music was just music in 1962 and 1963,' explained Brian Poole, 'A club might have the Tremeloes and me one night, a trad band the next, and Blues Incorporated the night after that. We all appeared on the same nights sometimes.'

After maybe days of inactivity, Brian, Keith and Mick would stumble from the fug of No. 102 into the rainy autumn, lugging amplifiers and guitars, for a jolting journey to the other side of London where, with Dick, direct from downing his paint-brush at Sidcup Art College, and whatever drummer could be persuaded to forsake an evening's cosy television, they were going to be paid in coins rather than banknotes for taking the stage before a small audience, mostly with only the vaguest notion about the music they had come to hear.

The following afternoon, you might Mick see cutting lectures to mooch around Denmark Street with the other two Edith Grove scapegraces, calculating what the one-shilling-and-sevenpence-halfpenny between them would do. A plate of beans-on-toast might be washed down with a cup of liquid smoke from a snack bar on the Embankment before they traipsed back to the flat where, as a middle-aged Keith would reminisce fondly, 'we just starved and listened to the blues, and played all day.' [2]

As it had been with Keith and Dick at Sidcup, guitars were the common denominator between Keith and Brian. From the beginning, the concept of one cementing the other's runs with subordinate chord-slashing hadn't been a natural consideration. Indeed, the often compulsively exquisite instrumental passages over Taylor's low throb on stage were as much duets as solos with less emphasis on improvising over chord patterns than predetermined construction. Like Scotty Moore's 'You're Right I'm Left She's Gone' break, certain transcendental moments on the boards would look impossible if transcribed on manuscript paper after they'd learned to anticipate and attend to each other's idiosyncrasies and clichés. 'Brian and I really got into the essence of this two guitar thing,' recounted Richards, 'Of trying to get them to go into each other - and you wouldn't care particularly who suddenly flew out and did a little line, and that you could almost read each other's mind.' [3]

Depending on your point of view, Keith and Brian's fingered concord seemed either bland or attractively unfussed against would-be guitar virtuosi like high-speed Alvin Dean [4] of Nottingham's Jaybirds, Stan Webb of Kidderminster's Shades Five or Frank White, the first British owner of a twin-necked Gibson, in Jimmy Crawford and the Ravens, one of Sheffield's leading groups. At the opposite extreme of their grimacing flash was the grinning vibrancy of The Remo Four's Colin Manley, Paddy Chambers of The Big Three and other strikers of fretboard lightning in the faraway maelstrom of Merseybeat.

'We had no idea about what was going on in Liverpool,' smiled Keith Richards [5] - though he was nowhere as amused by the memory of that record-breaking winter chill striking Edith Grove like a hammer, accompanied initially by a windy downfall that was almost but not quite a gale. During a particularly severe spell of blizzards in the dying days of 1962, Richards woke up so headachy and fevered that he went home to mother.

'Keith was to portray himself as a street-wise bad boy,' scoffed Pat Andrews, 'but he came across as exactly the opposite. He was a mummy's boy.' Yet, it has to be said that, despite Doris's worry, Richards dragged himself from a huddle of bedclothes to honour the next evening's date at the Piccadilly Jazz Club where The Rollin' Stones were third on the bill to Blues Incorporated.

If hardly able to say boo to a goose then, Keith was determined that nothing was going to show him up for less than the hard case he'd never really been. He was wary to the point of terror of the more sinister of narcotics, understanding as he did that skeletal Ginger Baker was a registered heroin addict whose 'junk' and the hypodermic syringe needed to pump it into exhausted veins had become, according to hearsay, as essential to him as drum sticks when he set off for a booking. Keith had heard too about the uncontrollable shivering, convulsive fits and nightmare hallucinations that could be demanded as payment in kind for the 'high' of heroin.

Yet, now and then, Richards - and, more so, Jones - would dip into surreptitious pockets for a black or blue-ish capsule. Not long after they'd left Kent or Gloucestershire, they'd graduated from the fiddly job of extracting benzadrine from nasal sprays to 'Purple Hearts', 'Black Bombers' and other outlawed pep-pills. Dick Taylor had come to know them well too - and that a cloak-and-dagger supply could be obtained with ease in London, what with the Government's net-closing Bill 'to penalise the possession and restrict the import of drugs of certain kinds' over a year away. It was, therefore, no hanging matter then if you were caught.

Jagger's attitude towards artificial stimulants was as cautious as you'd expect from the son of a physical education specialist, for whom sit-ups, press-ups and similar exercises had been a daily habit since childhood. Furthermore, there was always the bolt-hole of Wilmington - where the sugar was in its bowl, the milk in its jug and the cups unchipped on their saucers and set on an embroidered tablecloth - whenever it made abrupt sense for Mick to look homeward again in order to get his nerve back for another few weeks of revelling in romantic squalor - well, squalor anyway. Within hours, Mick could be back home, wolfing down the hot meal prepared for him by Mum. Then he might get lost in a cowboy film on television prior to lowering himself into the hot, scented water of the citrus-coloured bath before going to sleep in his own little room again.

Yet there as much as Chelsea, snow thickened, on and off, from December until the following so-called spring. At the dirty heart of the Stones' operation, the triumvirate of Jagger, Jones and Richards continued to pool loose change and argue about whose turn it was to brave the icy walk to the convenience store for food that, if cheap and dull, could, when fried in a perpetually greasy pan and washed down with a grubby glass of tap water, make you feel full. Bickering helped pass the time, and so did poking ruthless fun at whoever seemed likelier to rise to it - usually Brian, who was prone to bouts of sulking.

They utilised time more constructively with hours of practice - into which a new instrumental dimension had been incorporated. During one Edith Grove afternoon, Brian had by accident bent a note on a harmonica. Thus he stumbled upon Cyril Davies's great secret of how, say, Little Walter obtained the sound that complemented the singing on the *Muddy Waters At Newport* LP. Brian repeated what was technically an error for its tonal impurity, and was able to greet an enthralled Keith, returned from the tobacconist's, with a blues-wailing improvisation from the top of the stairs.

Brian's mastery of harmonica was to be on a par with that of self-protecting Davies, while Mick too became able to wail along more credibly than before when, perhaps *Folk Festival Of The Blues* - from a concert the previous summer showcasing the cream of Chicago bluesmen - heated up No. 102's record-player. Indeed, other players, like Rod Stewart, then a West End busker, learned what they could of his or Brian's technique from below the lip of the stage.

It wasn't hard to get sufficiently close to make out whether Jagger and Jones were blowing or sucking, and, though attendance figures for non-support engagements had risen of late, The Rollin' Stones amassed audiences so small that Dick Taylor was disquieted when the others suggested 'going professional'. The notion of making a living in showbusiness generally, let alone as an R&B musician, was taken seriously by few arty bohemians. Nevertheless, Dick - as dexterous on a six-string fretboard as either Jones or Richards - continued to pluck wistfully the prescribed simple riffs on his Emperor until 'I got so fed up playing bass rather than guitar'. Finally, with a scholarship at St Martin's Central College of Art beckoning for September, he tendered his resignation, but agreed to help out until a replacement was procured. 'They were sorry to see me go,' he recalled, 'and we remained on good terms.'

Taylor's departure might have presented an opportunity to change the name, but, as no-one other than Ian Stewart objected much, the group remained The Rollin' or Rolling Stones. The 'g' came and went and eventually stayed forever, although, as 1963 crept nearer, the future still held little outside the orbit of specified metropolitan blues nights, albeit one growing in impetus and cohesion.

Moreover, with Dick Taylor's waning availability, the situation regarding a bass player for a suddenly more amorphous Rolling Stones had become so desperate that Brian cajoled his old Cheltenham pal, Richard Hattrell, to both move into 102, Edith Grove and take rudimentary lessons on an instrument borrowed from Jack Bruce. Three sessions at the Hampstead flat he shared with Graham Bond were sufficient for Bruce to report to Jones that the group was barking up the wrong tree with Richard.

Then someone at Edith Grove uttered the phrase 'road manager'. Richard's chief qualification for this post was that he didn't mind being unpaid and unrecompensed, buoyed as he was by a lump sum for a recent sojourn with the Territorial Army.

Physically, there wasn't much for Hattrell to do as the equipment was portable enough to be carried via public transport. 'We used to take the guitars and amplifiers on the bus,' said Richard, 'When it stopped at a T-junction or slowed down, we'd avoid the fare by jumping off.' It hadn't occurred to Richard who was going to pay whenever this wasn't possible, but he quickly got the message – and having to shell out for six or seven came a bit pricey, especially as, so he lamented, 'We were all struggling to survive at Edith Grove. Well, Brian and I were. Mick and Keith were getting money and food from their parents, while I was on National Assistance, which was peanuts. My health was cracking up, and it was inevitable, I suppose, that I'd eventually go back to Cheltenham.'

Two major tactical difficulties were eased when Ian Stewart gained access to a pink Volkswagen van and the group a full-time bass guitarist in Bill Wyman, who, through Jones supplicating Tony Chap-

Top; Blues Incorporated 1961 at the Marquee Club (left to right): Dave Stevens, Dick Heckstall-Smith, Alexis Korner, Jack Bruce, Cyril Davies, Charlie Watts (obscured on drums)
Bottom; 1963, with Ian Stewart still in the line-up

The early progression

Clockwise from top left; Carlo Little, Ian Stewart,
Mick Taylor, a proud Andrew Loog Oldham

Clockwise from top; The Pretty Things, The Birds,
The Bluebreakrs, The Creation

Richmond and Twickenham Times, Saturday, April 13, 1963    13

# Barry May writes about the 'new' rhythm and blues

# JAZZ

## Nowadays it means the music that goes round and around—or the Rollin' Stones are gathering them in

The line-up of the Rollin' Stones, with vocalist Mick Jagger, guitarist Keith Richards, and extreme left, guitarist Brian Jones.

A MUSICAL magnet is drawing the jazz beat-niks away from Eel Pie Island, Twickenham, to a new mecca in Richmond.

The attraction is the new Craw-Daddy Rhythm and blues Club at the Station hotel, Kew Road—the first club of its kind in an area of flourishing modern a n d traditional jazz haunts.

Rhythm a n d blues, gaining more popularity every week, is replacing "traddypop" all over the country, and even per-suading the more sedate modernists to leave their plush clubs. The deep, earthy sound produced at the hotel on Sunday even-ings is typical of the best of rhythm and blues that gives all who hear it an irrisistible urge to "stand up and move."

Akin to both rock 'n' roll and the skiffle music that raced up and down the charts of three and four years

blues as "pe "origin pop-m also t leanin from s used rhythn

Trac comme played jazz h to com ences i

One the ja as it i tempts traditic jazz i Arthur that " quiet." nights on the to only end

Rhyt claim t

resident group, the Rollin' Stones.

From a meagre 50 or so on the club's first night, less than two months ago, attendances have rocketed by an average of 50 a week to last Sunday's record of 320. And the membership book lists more than 700 names of rhythm a n d blues devotees from all parts of London and West Surrey

Club promoter, bearded Italian film director, Giorgio Gomelsky, is

Economics student Mick Jagger, vocal a n d har-monica. He is backed by architect Brian J o n e s (guitar, harmonica, mara-cas), guitarist K e i t h Richards, an art student, bass guitarist Bill Wyman, a representative, drummer Charles Watts, a designer, and on piano, Ian Stewart.

Although "pop" num-bers are sometimes played, songs written and recorded by the American rhythm and blues guitarist Bo Diddley are the Rollin'

backing for the blues of the harmonicas and lead guitars.

Save for the swaying forms of the group on the spotlit stage, the room is in darkness. A patch of light from the entrance doors catches the sweat-ing dancers and those who are slumped on the floor where chairs h a v e not been provided.

Outside in the bar the long hair, suede jackets, goucho trousers and Chel-sea boots rub shoulders

man, had been lending his brand-new Vox Phantom model every so often to Dick Taylor - when he was still wavering about the purchase of the Emperor - and then Richard Hattrell.

Now a travelling salesman, Chapman's time as even an occasional Rolling Stone had been running out. 'We were getting very fed up with Tony not turning up,' groaned Dick Taylor, 'He couldn't keep time either. I remember us making this little cartoon - I think it was Brian Jones's drawing - me with my beard, Brian and his big guitar, Keith with his little dotty eyes, Mick another stick figure and an arrow pointing off the page to Tony who was in Liverpool at the time he should have been at a rehearsal.'

The writing was on the wall for The Cliftons too now that they were becoming more and more embroiled in cash-flow problems, and were talking more and more about the tailing off of bookings and the bad faith of certain promoters. It was nothing very tangible, just a steady gnawing away with little peaks and troughs, but it seemed fanciful to imagine much of a future when you'd come across groups of their ilk in virtually any town in the country. Yet from this, The Cliftons' darkest hour, the slow pageant of sunrise was about to begin for their bass player.

Shortly before Christmas, Tony Chapman called on Bill Perks - now defiantly using the stage surname 'Wyman - to tell him that the bunch who'd been borrowing his instrument needed a bass player too. Ideally, this person would be one who could reproduce lines like those on the tape of Jimmy Reed tracks that Tony threaded onto the machine he'd brought with him. Tomorrow night, he and a couple of the Stones were going to the Red Lion in Sutton where Ricky Tyrrell and the Presidents were still going strong. Bill could come along too. As it happened, the Stones were represented in the pub only by Ian Stewart, who invited Wyman to a Wetherby Arms session two evenings later.

Brushing non-existent specks from the suit he wore to work, Bill stalked into the functions room to be introduced to Mick Jagger, who seemed amiable enough, certainly more amiable than the two scruffy guitarists who all but ignored the newcomer. Bill thought Brian and Keith were posers; they thought he was a yob - or was it *vice-versa*? The ice melted slightly when he lugged in both of his pristine, state-of-the-art amplifiers. Even the spare one was more splendid than either of theirs. After Bill proffered cigarettes and bought drinks, Jones and

Richards remained borderline civil throughout the subsequent music-making, agreeing tacitly that, while there was nothing to intimate that this Bill whatever-his-name-was was the *beau ideal*, he coped well enough with numbers that were largely unfamiliar to him. He was all right, they supposed and, for his part, Bill wasn't entirely convinced about the Stones, but he still left his equipment at Edith Grove, as did Tony Chapman, so that he could travel independently to the next rehearsal by tube rather than endure a stop-start drive through the tail-end of the rush-hour.

If markedly older than his new acquaintants, Bill did not impose immediate unsolicited ideas upon the musical status quo or impinge upon the oligarchy of Jagger, Jones and Richards that had replaced the democracy of old. Like Scullion of Tom Sharpe's *Porterhouse Blue*, he knew his place: 'I was only the bass player. I was replaceable.' [6] Peripheral to the Stones socially too, 'Bill didn't make waves,' noticed Phil May later, 'He accepted that he wasn't in the inner sanctum and was OK about it.'

Wyman stayed on even as, sooner rather than later, Chapman was squeezed out after one particularly uncohesive Stones performance at Windsor's Ricky Tick Jazz Club. Honouring bookings as far a-field as Epsom School of Art and The Boy Blue Club in Woking's Atlanta Ballroom, they muddled on with a Steve Harris or, when there were gaps in his Lord Sutch itinerary, Carlo Little, who, at Brian Jones's request, had biro-ed Charlie Watts's current telephone number onto an empty cigarette packet.

Charlie had already been lending an intrigued ear to the Stones to the point of being present at several Wetherby Arms rehearsals where Dick Taylor had observed 'that the same chemistry wasn't there when Charlie was with Alexis Korner as when he was with the Stones.'

This was so most of the time. A glaring exception had been when Dick, Brian, Ian, Keith and Mick with Charlie shared a bill in a Harrow church hall with what was now The Graham Bond Trio - with Jack Bruce and Ginger Baker. In order to speed up the equipment changeover between acts, Watts agreed to use Baker's home-made kit of perspex plus *bona-fide* African 'talking' drums of thick, shaved animal skins - 'but I couldn't play it. Nothing would happen. I broke three pairs of sticks. He had them set up so that the angle was all wrong for me.' [7]

130

As this incident - and the Graham Burbidge business and the subsequent gradual parting from Blues Incorporated - had not diminished Charlie in their eyes, so he recognised that the Stones were not marking time like Blues By Six or Alexis and Cyril, living evidence that you could have the most extensive R&B repertoire in the world, sing like a nightingale or make a guitar talk, but if you suffered from middle age, obesity or baldness, you'd never amass more than a cult following. Whatever your popularity, booking fees would remain at best static because then, as now, most promoters took no account of inflation.

Not that this bothered The Rolling Stones, who, felt Watts, could offer both R&B credibility *and* teen appeal with Jagger's grotesque beauty and Jones's blond androgyny. Moreover, though Charlie was aware that 'they were working a lot of dates without getting paid or even worrying about it', [8] incomings were such that Bill Wyman was able to hold in his heart the exciting hope that one day he might be able to pack in his day job.

All Charlie had to do was ask and this would be his too. The Stones lacked only the recording deal that would either turn them into more of a commercial proposition or nullify them if the slicker exactitudes of the studio sterilized their *au naturel* impact. Still Charlie Watts waited and pondered, though one night, he telephoned Bobbie Korner for an unbiased opinion. 'She asked Charlie if he liked the Stones, and he said yes,' remembered her husband, 'She asked if she liked Blues By Six, and he said yes. So she said, "Which group has the most work?" He said the Stones, so she said, "Well, I advise you to join the Stones then, if you like them equally".' [9]

Were the Stones too rock 'n' roll? Geoff Bradford and Brian Knight thought so, but Charlie didn't dislike it on principal as they did, despite outlines dissolving between the Stones and the lurid theatrics of Screaming Lord Sutch via, say, the incorporations of The Coasters' 'I'm A Hog For You Baby' and any number of Chuck Berry items into their respective sets. It had, Watts theorised, an opaque connection to jazz, but was controlled by a more stilted discipline. 'Rock 'n' roll is restricting,' he surmised, not disparagingly, 'Jazz breathes - or improvised music breathes. It's got an elasticity to it, which is very hard to do well. There's different volumes you play. Most rock 'n' roll is totally on top. It's just volume the whole time. There's no budging. If you budge, it's wrong. It doesn't work.' [9]

As poker-faced playing rock 'n' roll as when he did jazz or blues, Watts looked neither as if he wanted to crawl away and hide nor condescendingly superior, smirking at jazz cronies at the back, demonstrating to all the world his contempt for this simplistic drivel, as a bass guitarist who shall be nameless had by pumping Buddy Holly's 'Peggy Sue' with one hand in his pocket, an attitude intolerable to The Zombies, who were glad to see the back of him. They held the Market Hall in St. Alban's as The Beatles did the Cavern and Eric Burdon's outfit did the Club-A-Go-Go on Tyneside.

In the offices and factories of Britain today, how many are the fifty- and sixty-somethings who took the then wise course of abandoning early 1960s groups later to Hit the Big Time? In some parallel dimension, perhaps it's Charlie Watts, not Carlo Little, who turned his back on the Stones, returning to Straightsville after years spent crisscrossing Europe in draughty, overloaded vans with David Sutch, the most famous British pop singer who never had a hit. After all, as Charlie would tell you himself, 'I was a bit used to rock 'n' roll. I knew most of the rock 'n' roll guys, people like Screaming Lord Sutch and Nicky Hopkins. I was quite used to Chuck Berry and that.' [1]

Instead, with a face like the Edith Grove winter, he continued to react instinctively to Blues By Six's twelve-bar set-works, smacking that endless, changeless backbeat on the snare drum, a backbeat not even a half-wit could lose. Some stretches on the boards went by as complete blurs. Charlie's disenchantment with the Blues By Six routine as opposed to his fascination with both the Stones' angle on R&B and their personalities was kindled in particular by a growing rapport with Keith Richards, 'the classic naughty boy. He's the sort of guy I knew at school who hated the head boy.' [3]

While he could sense the crouched force in Keith, Charlie recognised too that, while Mick hogged the central microphone, it was Brian who mapped out most of the musical direction and was, agreed Bill Wyman, 'the business manager too in those formative days'. [10] Little might have been achieved without him emerging from the blistered front door on days when, despite every water-pipe at No. 102 being frozen, he'd somehow washed, shaved, shampooed and booted-and-suited himself for another round of pavement-tramping to venues that might be coaxed into hiring him and his fabulous Rolling Stones. The most willing to picket on the group's behalf, Jones would also lay on a silver-tongued guile with a metaphorical trowel when negotiating with this quizzical pub landlord or that uninterested social secretary. Introducing himself as 'manager', he would weigh every word of his supplicatory letters and calls made from a kiosk now that he could no longer make illicit use of the telephone at Whiteley's where he used to glance over his shoulder for nosier members of staff, and do something 'normal' whenever one hoved into view.

A later girlfriend, Anita Pallenberg, would aver that 'Brian was the one who did all the hustling, getting the band together and believing in it.' [11] Who could blame him for imagining that he had the same all-powerful hold over the rest as drummer-manager Dave Clark had over his Dave Clark Five, who then ruled Tottenham Royal Ballroom, and were forever working the Home Counties palais circuit. On the evidence of a maiden single, 'Chaquita', late in 1961, the Five might have developed into one of the great English instrumental acts like The Tornados or Shadows, but, sniffing the wind, they were in the process of shifting their stylistic emphasis to vocals.

Seeing what was coming too, countless other locally produced alternatives to hit parade pop across the realm were either making the switch too or starting from scratch with the concept that the Group could be a plausible and self-contained means of both instrumental *and* vocal expression without having to skulk beyond a main spotlight occupied by a singer who wasn't an integral part of the set-up as Cliff Richard wasn't of The Shadows. By 1963, nearly all of them would exemplify the two guitars-bass-drums that was to be the archetype of the British beat explosion, whether The Cherokees, resident at Ventnor's 69 Club on the Isle of Wight or The Golden Crusaders at the Plaza in Belfast.

The Stones' name was not quite yet synonymous with a particular venue, despite their headlining at the Marquee on 10th January, 1963 and the following three Thursdays. While anything approaching a capacity audience couldn't yet be guaranteed, they were hitting their hard-won stride as one of the capital's six most active R&B outfits. The others were Blues By Six, The Wes Minster Five - house band at the Flamingo - those led by Cyril Davies and Alexis Korner and Dave Hunt's Rhythm & Blues Band.

Trombonist Hunt and his boys had brought their take on rhythm-and-blues to Surrey when presiding over Sunday evenings in the club in the back of Richmond's Station Hotel, that would be as vague in name as the one in Ealing for months until its promoter, Georgio Gomelsky, a White Russian who'd lived in Germany, Italy and Switzerland, was pressed for one by a local journalist and responded with an off-the-cuff 'Crawdaddy', possibly in vague recall of a Bo Diddley lyric.

Specialised in Louis Jordan-style jump-blues, Dave Hunt had been disdainful in *Jazz News* about interpretations of Diddley, Waters, Harpo *et al* by guitar-based white R&B outfits, principally via the telling sentence: 'It's what the rockers call jazz, and the jazzmen call rock 'n' roll'. [12] He also denigrated the Stones as 'a glorified skiffle group' [13] - and was rather disconcerted when they took over at the yet-unchristened Crawdaddy in late January.

'The young Brian Jones was always bending my ear,' grinned Georgio Gomelsky, 'He'd say with his lisp, "You *mutht* help *uth*. We have the *betht blueth* band in the land."' [14] Therefore, on the snow-flecked afternoon of Sunday 27th January, 1963 when Dave Hunt rang to say that he and his boys couldn't make it, Gomelsky, clutching at straws, commenced a wild-eyed search for Brian's scribbled contact number. The consequent call was answered by a receptionist at Ian Stewart's place of work. Georgio told Ian that, as long as the Stones didn't turn up with only half their equipment or a player short, the gig was theirs.

Notes

1. *The Rolling Stones In Their Own Words* ed. D. Dalton and M. Farren (Omnibus, 1985)
2. *Q*, October, 1988
3. *Keith Richards In His Own Words* ed. M. St. Michael (Omnibus, 1994)
4. Later, Alvin *Lee* of Ten Years After
5. *The Sunday Times*, 10 August, 2003
6. *Record Collector*, November, 1998
7. *The Big Beat* by M. Weinberg (Billboard, 1991)
8. *The Rolling Stones Chronicle* by M. Bonanno (Plexus, 1995)
9. *Alexis Korner: The Biography* by H. Shapiro (Bloomsbury, 1996)

10. *Record Collector*, April, 2001

11. *The Rolling Stones: Best Of Guitar Player* ed. J. Obrecht (Miller Freeman, 1995)

12. *Jazz News*, 21 November, 1962

13. *X-Ray* by R. Davies (Viking, 1994)

14. *London Live* by T. Bacon (Balafon, 1999)

*Chapter Seven*
## The Threshold Of Eminence

*'The politics of everything changed after I left' - Dick Taylor*

Replaced in Blues By Six by a drumming train driver named Derek Manfredi, Charlie Watts became an official Stone at the Flamingo Jazz Club on a Monday night during 1963's severe January. In spite of all his friends could say, he also gave notice at Charles Hobson and Gray: 'They thought I'd gone raving mad. There was me, earning a comfortable living, which obviously was going to nosedive if I got involved with The Rolling Stones'. [1]

While he wasn't immune to twinges of conscience as the enormity of what he had done sank in, Charlie's boats were only half-burned as the firm implied that, like it had been with Bill Wyman and National Service, his old job *might* be waiting for him when he got back. He also made ends meet as a freelance commercial artist while roughing it for a while in Jagger, Jones and Richards' horrible Chelsea flat.

As it was for Mick and Keith, Charlie could fall into the safety net of Mum's home cooking and clean sheets whenever he became too nauseated by smeared coffee cups, overflowing makeshift ashtrays and pooling loose change for a trip up the off-licence to see him and the other tenants through record-playing sessions and other indoor pursuits that turned afternoon into gone midnight.

'I'd get up in the morning,' he'd remember, 'and Brian and Keith would be snoring away, and I'd think, "I'm not going to that interview today. We're playing tonight anyway". I was out of work at the time, and I just used to hang about with them, waiting for jobs to come up, daytime work, just listening to Little Walter and all that. It was actually through sitting around endlessly with Keith and Brian that it got ground in. I learned the blues in general through Cyril Davies and Alexis Korner, and Brian and Keith taught me Jimmy Reed. They also taught me to enjoy Elvis Presley through DJ Fontana, who I think is a wonderful player. Before that, there was only one record I liked by Elvis.' [2]

Yet, while not to the same degree as Bill Wyman and Ian Stewart, Watts became less and less involved with the Stones socially. 'He was very much a man of few words,' observed Pat Andrews, 'Just getting on with what he was supposed to do and then going back to his parents' house.' Nevertheless, he and Wyman were solidly at the music's heart, providing a sturdy and fully interlocking rhythmic skeleton which the others were able to veil in musical flesh. There were fringe benefits too. Charlie made a valuable offstage contribution to the group by designing most of the rather prosaic posters and flyers whenever they were either on a percentage or hiring a venue themselves, while Bill had a baritone loud and tuneful enough for harmonies and responses behind Jagger.

Possessing a lighter tone than Bill, Brian joined in too, but, in the first instance, Keith shied away from singing with the group. He'd been finicky about pitch from earliest youth during 'musical evenings' at his grandfather's. 'If I didn't sing a *grace* note,' reminisced his mother, 'Keith would tell me to do it properly. He'd know it was wrong. It's something that's just built into him.' [3]

It wasn't worth being too fussy about negligently-strewn vocal mistakes in the Stones. 'Harmonies were always a problem with us,' shrugged Mick, 'Keith tried to get them off the ground, but they always seemed messy.'[3] The choirboy in Richards was dejected further by having to virtually gulp the microphone when straining to hear himself through puny PA systems and amateur dramatic society acoustics in the days before on-stage monitors, and at venues yet unused to the new breed of amplified combos that went in for a lot of vocals, not to mention the idea that someone like Mick was an integral part of the group rather than singled out as a separate entity as Cliff Richard was with The Shadows or Bern Elliott with The Fenmen.

Another aspect of these emergent blues/R&B outfits - especially the Stones - was an unbottled and uncool enthusiasm and an absence of both a stage uniform - no Acker Bilk waistcoats and bowler hats there - and even a defined presentation - none of that intricately synchronised footwork with which The Shadows iced their instrumentals. Moreover, unlike most established UK pop stars as well as every other trad band, the Stones *et al* aped their North American cousins only semi-consciously. Rather than mechanical mimicking, the gathering intention was to make 'Money', 'Poison Ivy', 'Fortune Teller', 'Do You Love Me', 'Walking The Dog', 'Boys', 'If You Gotta Make A Fool Of Somebody' and other fresh pickings from the R&B motherlode sound different from not only the US templates, but also any other domestic outfit's arrangement.

Attempting to get a handle on it, Joe Boyd, an expatriate New Yorker, contended, 'Americans, if they sang blues, were obsessed with sounding like black men, whereas Mick Jagger showed them how to sing blues and be unashamed of being white and being a kind of tarty little English schoolboy. There wasn't the same awkwardness. It was a much more relaxed position towards shopping in different cultures among the English'. [4]

As well as its weakening bond with jazz, such a take on blues and R&B was so dissimilar to anything pop on television that a metropolitan jazz club felt that it would be culturally acceptable - and profitable - to follow the example of Studio 51, still a 'home of purist traditional jazz'[5], as founder Ken Colyer had designated it way back when, but with a new guideline that enabled trad bands and the likes of the Stones - who gained a Sunday afternoon residency from the beginning of 1963 to the late spring - to share the same bill.

Once as impenetrable a bastion as Studio 51, Oxford Street's 100 Club - opened in 1942 as The Feldman Swing Club - capitulated too, and, by the end of the year, both had hosted all-R&B events. Elsewhere, similar establishments would be putting the last vestiges of their jazz dignity into booking trad acts to warm up for R&B outfits, and, at one such evening, Chris Jagger - now a Dartford Grammar sixth-former like his brother before him - had been amused that the token trad ensemble had hedged its bets by crowbarring 'R&B' into its name.

Not bothering with any trad, pure or transitional, the Crawdaddy had been doing brisk business since the midwinter arrival of the Stones. From that unpromising first night - when Georgio Gomelsky tried to supplement the mere handful watching by barking the show to drinkers in the public bar - the place was two-thirds full by the third of the group's sessions. The following week, customers were spilling out onto the pavement, chattering excitedly after what amounted to a sweatbath with musical accompaniment. Even without the relatively capacious Station Hotel back room's obstructing chairs and tables, it was too tightly packed to dance unless you rooted yourself to one spot. 'Soon, it really was an amazing night out,' reminisced Jane Relf, whose art student brother Keith was in something called The Metropolitan Blues Quartet, 'It was a regular thing to go down and watch the Stones, queuing for hours to get in, then you just couldn't move in there, bodies just squashed together. The Shake came in then. It sort of evolved because people couldn't move. You used to just stand there and just, well, shake.' [6]

'Boys would take off their shirts,' added Bill Wyman, 'and wave them round their heads.' [7] The more exhibitionist began doing so on table tops as the multitudes being turned away grew with every passing Sunday. Descending on the Crawdaddy in droves were 'youths' and, half a class up, 'young adults', whose liberal-minded parents might collect them afterwards in estate cars. Ever-tighter clusters of females in fishnet, suede and leather would block the view too for the dismayed R&B devotee with memories of the dodgy Blues Incorporated offshoot that had supported Long John Baldry at the Marquee only a few months earlier.

The Stones were also luring aesthetes whose record collections might once have advertised a pseudo-sophistication that ran from Stravinsky to the most limp and 'tasteful' modern jazz, and whose skip-read Genet, Nietzsche, Camus and Sartre looked well on university hostel bookshelves. Such an intellectual, generally male, detected a certain Neanderthal *epater la bourgeoisie* in the group, and came to understand that this rugged type of pop music was 'uncommercial', and thus an antidote to the contrived splendour of television pop idols. He'd tell his mates where he'd been, describing what happened at the Crawdaddy in awestruck detail, and delighting in the faint revulsion that chased across their faces. However, not wishing to appear prudish, they'd go with him - with toffee noses asking to be punched - on his next jaunt to this low-life spectacle.

Yet, when the initial shock was over, they'd feel what he'd felt. Losing a little of their cultivated *sang-froid*, they even began to have fun or, at least, via some complex inner debate, gave in to an observed conviviality as they tuned in to the situation's epic vulgarity.

These Rolling Stones got to be quite addictive. Much of the Crawdaddy's attraction too was being studied, not always surreptitiously, by not just blue-stockings in glasses, but gaggles of short-skirted 'town girls', jabbering incessantly until the Stones sauntered onto the boards, downright uncouth in their verbal retaliations to yelled comments from the massed humanity bobbing up and down in the blackness. Hitting all their instruments at once at a staccato 'Right!' from the blond exquisite to the right of the singer, they'd barge into a glorious onslaught of pulsating bass, dranging guitars, crashing drums and ranted vocals, walking what seemed to be a taut artistic tightrope without a safety net.

A kind of committed gaiety from an increasingly more uproarious crowd lent an inspirational framework to performances that covered a waterfront from country blues to the latest from Chuck Berry, about to make a comeback as a UK chart contender. In between lay works by Elmore James, Muddy Waters, Jimmy Reed, Rufus Thomas and Bo Diddley, and ventures into rock 'n' roll and that seam of North American R&B known more universally now as 'soul'.

A galvanising squiggle of guitar might plunge the Stones into Chuck's 'Back In The USA', or possibly his 'Roll Over Beethoven' or 'Beautiful Delilah'. The spooning out of a just-sufficiently ramshackle lucidity would continue as Jones, Richards, Stewart, Wyman and Watts advanced with the grace of fencing masters on 'Hoochie Coochie Man' in which a suspensory hissing hi-hat beneath the stop-start five-note riff, played over and over again, stoked the prickly heat to a simmer for Jagger's 'Well, the gypsy woman told my mama' entry, and boiled over just as the chord rose finally to a shuffling sub-dominant and a tension-breaking first chorus.

Then Brian might abandon guitar to emote on his recently-mastered harmonica the exquisite dirge that is 'Soon Forgotten' from *Muddy Waters At Newport*. Next, he'd be wielding maracas like a man possessed on a sure-footed 'Baby What's Wrong', and be back on guitar for Mick's audience-participation number - its title lost in the mists of time - that involved bawling 'five-ten-fifteen-twenty...'

Riding roughshod over tempo refinements, complicated dynamic shifts or, indeed, anything that needed too much thought, a few verse-chorus transitions would be cluttered, and certain numbers a fraction too bombastic - but so what? Haphazardly-strewn errors were brushed aside like matchsticks and, by the time the Stones resolved into the finale - maybe 'Diddley Daddy', 'Big Boss Man', 'Ride 'Em On Down' or 'Let It Rock' - they'd long been home and dry.

In the hallowed G Club as much as the Crawdaddy, the first screams had already reverberated for Brian with his firm jawline, Norse cheekbones and thick fringe - and, more so, for lead singer Mick. Exuding all the breathy sentience of a man who has been sprinting, his sylph-like athlete's physique drew cow-eyed efforts to grab his attention from libidinous front-row females. 'If they couldn't get him, they'd go for the others,' observed Richard Hattrell, still hanging on as 'road manager', 'Surprisingly, many of them were aristocratic birds, kicking up against their titled backgrounds and looking for excitement. It was sex for the sake of sex.'

'My whole act is made up from different girls I've been with,' the lad himself would joke later, 'I took the pout from Chrissie Shrimpton.' [8]

This was a reference to the seventeen-year-old younger sister of Jean Shrimpton, an up-and-coming fashion model. An acquaintance of Rod Stewart, it had been Chrissie who'd told the struggling entertainer about the Stones after she and Mick had started walking out together. She'd have a blink-and-you'll-miss-her role in a promotional film of the London R&B scene in all its sweaty intensity being formulated by Giorgio Gomelsky, who, as far as he was concerned, was the Stones' manager in all but name. From the stage, he'd be observed at the table to the immediate right of the door, eyeing a biscuit-tin half-full of coins, and then the group, fingering his moustache with crafty satisfaction.

The Stones' casually cataclysmic effect on the Crawdaddy crowds was food for thought too for other onlookers towards the back, some awaiting destinies in groups that would enter the British Top Fifty within a year. Running in the same pack, the less fortunate Downliners Sect's career trajectory would be more typical of legion other units in and around Teddington Lock that would owe much to the Stones. They were traceable to a Twickenham outfit trading as just plain 'Downliners' in the late 1950s, and operating simultaneously as Geronimo and the Apaches with Calamity Jane, complete with war-paint and feather bonnets.

'Late in 1962, a friend recommended that I see this group playing the Station Hotel in Richmond,' recollected Sect mainstay Don Craine, 'It turned out to be the Stones. Within a couple of songs, I experienced a road-to-Damascus moment. I thought, "That's it! This is what I want to do." They were doing all the stuff Blues Incorporated and The Cyril Davis All-Stars were doing, but it was, to all intents and purposes, a rock band of young people playing rhythm-and-blues. They were our age; they were in-yer-face; they were behaving like rock stars and, unlike Blues Incorporated, it boiled down to electric guitars. It was clear that the Stones were going to Make It as pop stars on those terms, and The Downliners Sect's forty per cent R&B went up to one hundred percent R&B, and Geronimo and the Apaches petered out.'

Charlie Watts had noticed the difference too: 'Suddenly, I was in this band where everybody was clapping. Alexis Korner's was a big band to be in, but the Stones had such a mad following, and it got bigger every week. Then The Beatles happened, and it became the thing to be in a beat group.' [9]

While 1962 was shuddering to a halt, The Beatles' debut release, 'Love Me Do', had fallen from its high of Number 17. They had done well for first timers, but few assumed that they'd amount to much more and that they'd soon be back on their old treadmill of Merseyside engagements - with side-trips to Hamburg clubland - by this time next year. However, the rip-tide from the north-west that was to flood British pop washed nearer with the New Year. A second Beatles single, 'Please Please Me', touched an apotheosis of Number Two, checkmated by C&W balladeer Frank Ifield's 'The Wayward Wind'.

By April, 'How Do You Do It' by Gerry and the Pacemakers would be the first disc by a Liverpool group to top the charts. Yet what was now seemingly discernable as the 'Mersey Sound' or 'Liverpool Beat' would be in sharper focus the following month when The Beatles' 'From Me To You' eased 'How Do You Do It' from pole position. Seven weeks later, Gerry's next offering, 'I Like It', would bring down The Beatles. After The Searchers - from the same region - did similar damage to Elvis Presley in August, they, Gerry, The Beatles and, yet another Scouser, Billy J. Kramer were to slug it out for hit parade supremacy for the rest of the year, interrupted only by 'Do You Love Me' from Brian Poole and the Tremeloes, who, partly through implications in Brian's surname, would be promoted - as Bern Elliott and the Fenmen were - as a southern wing of the movement.

Just as some English history primers start with the Battle of Hastings, the year that divided the Dark Ages from the mediaeval period of UK pop was, therefore, 1963 when Liverpool, where nothing used to happen apart from dock strikes, became the most romantic corner of the kingdom and Scouse the most seductive dialect with the coming of Merseybeat, spearheaded - and soon dominated - by the Beatles. After an all-Liverpool edition of ITV's *Thank Your Lucky Stars*, commercial expediency sent all but the most dim-witted London talent scout up to the Holy City to plunder the musical gold. Accordingly, having been gutted of all its major talents, Liverpool was left to rot as, like pillaging Vikings of old, the contract-waving host swept eastwards to alight on Manchester where there were also guitar groups that had mastered 'Twist And Shout', 'Fortune Teller', 'Money' and other numbers that became British beat standards.

When it was decided that the Manchester scene had 'finished', the metropolitan invaders fanned out to other territories now that every one of them had been deemed to have a 'sound' or a 'beat' peculiar to itself - though somehow a lot of the two-guitars-bass-drums outfits over which chins were rubbed, looked and sounded just like The Beatles, even down to tortuous faux-Scouse accents for onstage announcements.

In the middle of 1963, however, Brian Poole and his Tremeloes' arrangement of 'Twist And Shout' penetrated the Top Five as a harbinger of the greater triumph of the 'Do You Love Me' follow-up. While this was the most convincing sign that the search was rebounding more conveniently to the capital, thus signalling a finish to journalists traipsing up north for pop news, The Dave Clark Five, in the midst of their residency at Tottenham's Royal Ballroom, were, bragged drummer-leader Clark, 'packing 'em in six thousand a night, four nights a week. We even got a gold cup for pulling in the biggest amount of business in the chain of dance halls we worked.' [10] As a result, though three Five singles had flopped when issued by other labels, an EMI subsidiary was not only offering a huge advance for the group's services, but was also willing to allow Clark, a most astute businessman, more studio freedom than any other pop artist of the time.

More to the point, in the context of this discussion, Cyril Davies of all people had been signed to Pye, who were to release a single, 'Country Line Special', by him and his All-Stars in May. Moreover the *Richmond And Twickenham Times* had, on 13th April, 1963, made passing reference to The Rolling Stones - their first ever mention in the press - when devoting a page to an evening at the Crawdaddy.

In microcosm, the Stones in Richmond paralleled The Dave Clark Five in Tottenham as potentially hot pop property even as the first tinges of autumn gold were yet to signal the end of Merseybeat's high summer. The craze was already streamlining itself into the more enduring 'Beatlemania' when Gerry and the Pacemakers as well as The Beatles represented Liverpool at the *New Musical Express* Pollwinners concert at Wembley Pool on 21st April. With indecent haste, they and the other new sensations were to condemn to qualified degrees of obsolescence most of the remaining acts on a bill that included The Springfields, Frank Ifield, Adam Faith, Mark Wynter, The Tornados, The Brook Brothers ('Britain's *ace* vocal group', according to a 1962 press hand-out), Billy Fury and Cliff Richard and the Shadows. The last named and, to a lesser extent, Adam and Billy would weather the deluge, and Dusty, The Springfields' panda-eyed glamour puss, would achieve spectacular solo success, but, within eighteen months, the rest would be performing in venues where current chart standing had no meaning.

Seeing what was coming, Georgio Gomelsky - for whom it was still a foregone conclusion that the Stones would melt into his managerial caress - had been doing whatever willingness and energy would do to advance their cause. Crucially, he had pulled strings so that IBC, a central London studio suggested by Ian Stewart, would waive charging the group by the hour in exchange for first refusal on the rights to whatever tracks were completed. Over the road from BBC Broadcasting House, it had housed Radio Normandy during the Second World War, and, during a break in Frankie Laine's European tour itinerary in 1959, had been booked for the recording of his final UK Top Ten strike, clippety-clop 'Rawhide'.

Though IBC was one of the most sophisticated and well-equipped complexes in the country during this mediaeval period of recording methodology, it's not much of a exaggeration to say that the order of the day then was sticking a microphone in front of a group and hoping for the best. Moreover, obligatory neckties and white laboratory jackets for IBC's technical department weren't too distant a memory, even if the wearing of jeans to work had become a matter of choice.

Thus, like old millstones, the next chapter in the story of the Stones quivered, stirred and groaned reluctantly into its first Tippex-drenched paragraph with an off-peak IBC session on a Monday in March, 1963, arranged via Glyn Johns, a twenty-two-year-old sound technician, approached mainly because he was no regimented clock-watcher, and because he'd also heard and liked the Stones at the Crawdaddy. He had also said as much to IBC proprietor Eric Robinson, a sort of British Mantovani, whose string-laden, middle-aged musak oozed regularly from the Light Programme. 'I was thrilled!' exclaimed

Charlie Watts, 'Glyn did it when they stopped work at 5.30. We did eight tracks in about ten minutes. [*sic*], and then went off and played at a club.' [9]

From being a mere trainee on the Frankie Laine date, Johns had become so console-literate by 1963 that he was more at ease with IBC's two-track analogue desk, with its limiters, equalisers and other attendant state-of-the-art gizmos, than most older employees, however much he protested that he was 'far more interested in playing and singing than anything else.' [11] Indeed, he had been moonlighting as one of Ricky Tyrell and the Presidents, the combo that the Stones had supported in a Sutton pub before ignition-point at the Crawdaddy.

It wasn't Jagger, Jones, Richards and Stewart's first corporate essay as recording artistes. With Tony Chapman, they'd taped 'Soon Forgotten' plus two items from the respective portfolios of Diddley and Reed in a studio in North London the previous October. Though a copy was packaged and mailed by registered post, without much hope, to EMI, it served chiefly as an audible but private gauge of their efforts and, when absolutely necessary, as a bartering tool for engagements, few and far between then.

Now that a calendar that had once indicated a month's worth of bookings had become a week's, the purpose of the *five* numbers finished at IBC - two Diddleys, two Reeds and a Muddy Waters - was so that Georgio could play it to any interested parties they passed on the road to a recording deal. If just turned thirty himself, Gomelsky didn't expect one such as Eric Robinson to go ape over the Stones, but he had high hopes of Albert Hand, editor of *Teenbeat Monthly*, who was invited to one of the newly-instigated lunchtime sessions so he could see for himself that something incredible was taking place at the Station Hotel.

Struggling through the crowd afterwards, Hand spoke to Jones and Jagger, but 'the sum total of their conversation was that they were pulling in big crowds at the pub, that they couldn't get a recording contract, and what a big old wicked world it was. They were strange characters, and they had a sort of built-in resentment of the general attitude of showbusiness.' [12]

As a power on the National Jazz Federation, Gomelsky had cultivated all manner of further vital connections, most recently with Brian Epstein, The Beatles' manager, now uprooted from Liverpool to London. This manifested itself most tangibly when Georgio engineered a trip to the Crawdaddy by The Beatles after they'd plugged 'From Me To You', on *Thank Your Lucky Stars* at ITV's Teddington studios on 21st April, 1963. It would be a fillip for the Stones if they impressed an act who were already as big as Frank Ifield. Yet, though John Lennon, Paul McCartney, George Harrison and Ringo Starr attracted a small cluster of tongue-tied fans, they were not yet so well known around London's southernmost extremities that they couldn't be steered safely by Gomelsky through the crowded Crawdaddy to the side of the stage.

As Georgio had foreseen, their more revered peers took a shine to the Stones. Lennon's dockside mouth-organ on The Beatles' first three smashes had had hardly a trace of Little Walter *et al*, but he loved the blues, and was keen to pick up tips from Brian - and Mick - on how to improve what he dismissed as his 'blowing and sucking'. The cordiality between the two outfits after the customers left the Crawdaddy concluded with the Stones receiving complimentary tickets and 'access all areas' passes for 'Swinging '63', an all-styles-served-here pop extravaganza, headlined by The Beatles, at London's Royal Albert Hall the following Thursday.

'Brian wanted to be a pop star the minute he saw The Beatles,' sneered Keith Richards [2] - for, in the Kensington dusk afterwards, Jones had liked the taste of a morsel of ersatz-Beatlemania when, because of the backcombed moptop he was sporting now, some girls mistook him for George Harrison and asked for his autograph.

Noting Brian's peculiar exaltation at this incident, Georgio pressed home the point that he was at least acquainted with the manoeuvres necessary to give the Stones extra pushes up the ladder, maybe all the way up if the time came. The king of the Crawdaddy considered too that he had also amassed the experience to sidestep most quagmires of the music business. But in coaxing not so much The Beatles as the less illustrious Albert Hand and other journalists to the club, how could Gomelsky have known that he'd set in motion a chain of events whereby The Rolling Stones would slip through his fingers?

The weekend after 'Swinging '63', he began grooming the group for Beatles-sized stardom in earnest by immortalising on film - as the centrepiece of his intended twenty-minute short about London R&B - another Stones recording session, this time at RG Jones Studio in Morden. Next he had them miming to one of them - Bo Diddley's 'Pretty Thing' - in the Crawdaddy before the customers assembled. The tracks found their way to Decca and possibly other companies, accompanied by a covering letter promising to send on request an edit of the Stones' contribution to the documentary.

It may have been expected that the tape would fall on stony ground, though it mightn't have done had it been heard by a certain Mike Vernon, then Decca's 'general runaround, making tea' [13], but aiming to declare his independence as a freelance producer. Among his first essays as such were items by Texas-born pianist Curtis Jones and - another US bluesman who made England his home - Champion Jack Dupree. Later, Vernon would found Blue Horizon, the most popular blues label in Britain, but in 1963, his ambition was of a smaller scale. With his brother, he was thinking aloud about the publication of *R&B Monthly*, perhaps the first fanzine of its kind in Britain. He also had his ear to the ground for UK talent of that persuasion. Among his earliest discoveries was Art Wood, then functioning both as one of Blues Incorporated's incumbent vocalists and as front man of The Art Wood Combo. [14]

Nineteen-year-old Mike's recommendations about possible signings had, however, the impact of a feather on concrete for most of the older hands at Decca - and so did Georgio Gomelsky's Stones tape, even though Billy Fury, the company's 'answer' to EMI's accursed Cliff Richard, had been giving 'em Jimmy Reed's 'Baby What You Want Me To Do' on the boards of late. [15] Yes, we agree, Mr. Gomelsky, that these Rolling Stones of yours probably go down a storm in that little club in Richmond, but, on the evidence of this reel-to-reel, they'll sound thuggish and dull on a gramophone record in comparison to the Merseybeat combos with their appealing harmonies and anglicizing of rounded songs by black vocal groups like The Isley Brothers, The Shirelles and The Miracles rather than what we hear as the extemporized gutbucket grunting of these Chicago performers, 1950s backdates the lot of them. Revivals are all very well, but that stuff isn't right for today's teenagers. We know these things...

Georgio's documentary was never released either. Yet, for all it signified rather than what it actually was, it was something big for the Stones - still treated with amused contempt by the more bigoted Ealing club connoisseurs - to tell people like Art Wood, who was to recall: 'One morning, Jagger rang me at work to ask, "Art, can you do Studio 51 this Sunday because we're filming." I thought, "Wow! They've made it!", although they hadn't yet had a hit.'

Further crestfallen headway was made through a mid-week audition before a panel of seven at the BBC's Maida Vale complex. Reined by both nerves and Ricky Brown and Carlo Little - deputising for Wyman and Watts, fearful for their current day jobs - Jones, Jagger, Stewart and Richards delivered the goods with cautious accuracy.

No radio broadcast was forthcoming from this try-out, and, though the Stones were welcomed back to the Crawdaddy and Studio 51 with the anticipated warmth the next Sunday, the consolation of a crowded workload near home was wearing rather thin. Nevertheless, it was gratifying, they supposed, that new groups were being formed in their image, and existing ones were copying their repertoire and off-hand stage craft. Old confrere Tony Chapman, for instance, had lasted a few months with a Croydon outfit dealing in Top Twenty covers, before he and Steve Carroll started The Preachers - strictly R&B with perhaps even more Chuck Berry than the Stones.

What was slightly worrying was that, from other regions, R&B groups, if not as electrifying as they, were breaking free of parochial orbits and were even invading metropolitan clubland. Praise indeed for Birmingham's Jimmy Powell and the Five Dimensions was annotated in Mike Cooper's diary after their inaugural evening at the 100 Club: 'Powell is a reasonable harmonica player and vocalist. His rhythm guitarist is quite good too. The rest of the group are mediocre but produce a competent sound which does at least sound like R and B and not rock.' Slightly more impressed, Georgio Gomelsky hired them as the Stones' intermission act at the Crawdaddy.

Before he became a solo singer in an age of groups, Decca had already taken a chance with Powell's 'Sugar Babe', a cover of a minor US hit by Buster Brown, and regarded in retrospect as the first 'Brumbeat' disc. Yet what the label was after now was either a new Beatles - or an *anti*-Beatles, because, after waving a cheery goodbye on ventriloquist dummy Lenny The Lion's show on BBC TV's *Children's Hour*, it wouldn't have seemed all that peculiar if the 'Fab Four' had been soft-shoe-shuffling next. 'It registered subconsciously,' ruminated Andrew Loog Oldham, one of Epstein's publicists, 'That when they made it, another section of the public was going to want the opposite.' [16]

As his Rolling Stones were far from being fun for all the family, Georgio Gomelsky's thoughts ran on similar lines. Could his rough diamonds be marketed to a wider world as devils to The Beatles' angels? All the essential elements were in place now and countdown to lift-off was underway, courtesy of Norman Jopling of *Record Mirror* who, through Georgio's prodding, had penned a glowing review. 'The paper's policy was only to write about people who had records out,' Jopling elucidated, 'But there was such a buzz about them, Peter Jones, the editor, told me to go ahead. What amazed me - because I was a huge Bo Diddley fan - was that they could replicate his raw sound. I'd never seen a British band that came anywhere near that. My feature appeared on May the 11th 1963, but *Record Mirror* was on the streets three days earlier, and immediately, three of the four major British record labels, Philips, Decca and EMI, were on the 'phone to me. They all wanted to know where they could contact The Rolling Stones.' [17]

Notes

1. *The Rolling Stones Chronicle* by M. Bonanno (Plexus, 1995)
2. *The Rolling Stones In Their Own Words* ed. D. Dalton and M. Farren (Omnibus, 1980)
3. *Keith Richards In His Own Words* ed. M. St. Michael (Omnibus, 1994)
4. *Days In The Life* ed. J. Green (Heinemann, 1988)
5. *London Live* by T. Bacon (Balafon, 1999)
6. *Yardbirds World* ed. R. Mackay and M. Ober (privately published, 1989)
7. *Mature Times*, December, 2004
8. *Rock Explosion* by H. Bronson (Blandford, 1986)
9. *Rhythm*, June, 2001
10. Worldwide Dave Clark Fan Club newsletter, No. 58, December, 1984
11. *The Record Producers* by J. Tobler and S. Grundy (BBC, 1982)
12. *Teenbeat Annual 1968* ed. A. Hand (World Distributors, 1967)
13. *Beat Instrumental*, August, 1968
14. Who were to mutate during 1964 into The Artwoods with a line-up that included not only organist Jon Lord, future mainstay of Deep Purple, but also Keith Hartley, who drummed with John Mayall's Bluesbreakers and then his own Keith Hartley Band. 'The Mann-Hugg Blues Brothers started calling

themselves Manfred Mann,' noticed Art, 'So our agent suggested that we re-name ourselves The Artwoods.'

15. It was to B-side 1964's 'It's Only Make Believe', Fury's penultimate Top Ten entry.

16. *The British Invasion* by B. Harry (Chrome Dreams, 2004)

17. *Q*, May, 1995

### Chapter Eight
## New Messiahs

*'During the discussions, they didn't mention Gomelsky. Really, I think they were stringing him along'* - Andrew Loog Oldham [1]

Towards the end of April, 1963, every recording manager outside EMI was alighting with nitpicking hope on the remotest indication of The Beatles' fall. On a recent round-Britain package tour headlined in theory by Tommy Roe and Chris Montez, Bobby-ish Yanks both with singles currently in the UK Top Twenty, the running order had had to be reshuffled so that the group played last. Yet, though Beatles one-nighters too caused scenes as uninhibited and contagious as those that had accompanied concerts by Johnnie Ray back in the 1950s, there was gleeful speculation that they had got into a rut with the just-released 'From Me To You' having much the same overall sound as 'Please Please Me'.

Even The Beatles themselves weren't so dazzled as to think that pop stars were immortal. 'It's been fun, but it won't last long,' avowed John Lennon, 'Anyway, I'd hate to be an old Beatle.' [2] Nevertheless, for the time being, they were 'good copy' for pop columnists on national newspapers: plain speaking laced with quirky wit delivered in thickened Scouse. They'd be ideal for pantomime, charity soccer matches and children's television when they were overtaken - as they surely would be - by a fresher sensation.

The Rolling Stones weren't yet the talk of the hour, but the *Record Mirror* feature had created a mild buzz. However, the telephone number passed onto interested parties by Norman Jopling and Peter Jones was not Georgio Gomelsky's but that of Andrew Loog Oldham, who'd seized the reins of the Stones' management while the hapless Georgio was at his father's funeral in Switzerland. Though, with the benefit of hindsight, Albert Hand would be another one of many claiming to have been the first to mention the Stones to Oldham, soon to be one of about half-a-dozen pop starmakers in Britain who truly counted for anything.

There remains bitter division about Andrew Oldham. Was he one of the cleanest new brooms ever to sweep the pop industry; an English edition of conniving and manipulative 'Sergeant Bilko', living on his wits in BBC television's *The Phil Silvers Show*, or an imaginative and overgrown boy sucked into a vortex of circumstances he was unable to resist?

In 1963, he was only just nineteen and younger than any of the Stones. Following the rigours of expensive boarding schools, he had been taken on as a general assistant-cum-window dresser in Bazaar, a Knightsbridge boutique owned by Mary Quant, Jean Shrimpton's *haute couture* Diaghilev. Since early 1962, however, he had been hovering round the music industry in mostly menial capacities in preparation for a grander but yet unknown purpose. Though he toyed fleetingly with trying to be a pop singer himself, he elected instead to shadow comprehensively the methodology of, initially, those from the old regime of showbusiness administration. Most pointedly, he began modelling himself on fictitious 'Johnny Jackson', the fast-talking and irrepressibly confident Soho agent, who was the central character of Wolf Mankowitz's quasi-satirical play, *Expresso Bongo*, and based on Larry Parnes, the 1950s impresario and inspired generator of correlated publicity. In a 1959 movie adaptation, Jackson was played by Laurence Harvey. The thrust of the plot was the metamorphosis of 'Bert Rudge' - Cliff Richard's second big screen role - into a overnight Presley-esque sensation via much browbeating hyperbole and media manipulation.

Adhering to lodged conventions, Jackson was not, however, quite as impressive to Andrew as Bob Crewe and Bob Gaudio, the brains behind The Four Seasons, former New Jersey session singers, whose first million-seller, 1962's 'Sherry' - with a trademark shrill falsetto to the fore - paved the way for further such chartbusters of the same persuasion.

Then there was Phil Spector, into whose orbit Oldham drifted when the US producer was on a business trip to London in 1962. Styled 'the Svengali of Sound', Spector's was then a fashionable name to drop in record industry circles for his spatial 'wall of sound' technique, whereby he'd multi-track an apocalyptic *melange* - replete with everything but the proverbial kitchen sink - behind acts who'd submitted to his master plan, notably two beehive-and-net-petticoat female vocal groups, The Crystals and The Ronettes, whose lead vocalist, Veronica 'Ronnie' Bennett, he was to marry.

Oldham was amazed at how privileged he felt to have gained access to Phil's hotel suite, almost as off-limits as Howard Hugues's Las Vegas penthouse. There, the rather weedy young New Yorker gave informal and guarded lectures on the tricks of the trade. The gist of these was that Spector had won respect within the trade because, while advised by payroll courtiers, he was not a corporation marionette in an age when many other pop illuminati - in the States and, by implication, everywhere else - seemed devoid of independent opinion about career development. Although he'd made doubtful decisions since achieving back room fame, Spector alone accepted responsibility for them. Indeed, he maintained an intense and often unwelcome interest in every part of the process from studio to pressing plant to market place.

In the limousine that carried him even the shortest distance, he continued holding forth to Oldham and, Andrew noticed, a flanking of burly retainers, all distinguished by dark glasses that hid fathomless glares at intruders. Resembling a convention for the blind, they hushed when Phil spoke, exchanged knowing smirks at Mr. Spector's witticisms, laughed when Mr. Spector laughed, fetched him drinks, and learned quickly to leave him alone and field all outside interference when he was in a ponderingly creative mood.

Oldham also made myriad private observations of Joe Meek, a British producer who many - I for one - would rate far higher than Phil Spector for inventiveness and originality in his striking juxtaposition of funfair vulgarity and outer space aetheria. He commanded terrified admiration from Andrew, who, in autumn 1962, was present in the alarming Meek's RGM Sound, a set-up above a shop on Holloway Road, one of North London's busiest thoroughfares, during the recording of a vocal version by Geoff Goddard, RGM's in-house songwriter, of 'Telstar' [3], the quintessential British instrumental by The Tornados. Astonishingly, it had topped the US *Hot 100* where, Aker Bilk's band apart, no Limey group - not even The Shadows - had made much headway. Though a capitalising tour of North America by The Tornados was to be cancelled at the eleventh hour, 'Telstar' played Eric the Red to the so-called 'British Invasion' of the sub-continent's charts in 1964.

Astonishing too had been the Heath Robinson conditions under which 'Telstar' was made. 'I was no expert on electrical gear,' recalled Geoff Goddard, 'But the equipment at RGM looked like odds and ends

Joe had picked up from a junk shop, wired them all up and made something of them. He didn't have the capital for much else.' Yet, though a backroom functionary, Meek - like Spector too - had become a pop personality in his own right, granting interviews to relevant media organs, and eliciting headlines when his suicide in 1967 confirmed his status as a rock 'n' roll legend.

'Meek really scared me!' gasped Andrew, 'He looked like a real mean-queen Teddy Boy and his eyes were riveting.' [4] Oldham's, however, weren't, so he covered them in public with sunglasses, even in a midnight black-out, just like Phil Spector and his men.

After listening hard as one of Spector's surrounding cortege, Oldham, according to Joe Meek, next spent 'a couple of months with RGM as a public relations officer, but got bitten by the recording bug and buzzed off.' [4] His subsequent and brief spell as a cog in Brian Epstein's publicity machine had a lasting beneficial effect too - in an understanding that was deeper than many a more battle-hardened talent scout, that Epstein's manipulation of The Beatles and his other acts was the tip of an iceberg that would make more fortunes than had ever been known in the history of recorded sound.

Oldham seemed content, nonetheless, to continue as a freelance publicist: 'Contrary to popular opinion, I wasn't looking for something else to do. I was a very happy man. One day, I went to see Peter Jones of *Record Mirror*. He kept talking about this group called The Rolling Stones, playing around London'. [1] Thinking it over, Oldham felt he might be ready to go for the jugular as Brian Epstein had done - if it turned out that the outfit Jones had mentioned were a viable means by which to do so. Unlike Epstein, however, he intended also to produce its records and, like Meek and Spector, be more than an *eminence grise* behind merchandising ballyhoo. He didn't know much about rhythm-and-blues, but he did know what he'd like to exploit - and The Rolling Stones seemed as likely to be the next titans of teen as any other in this new breed of guitar outfits.

He was convinced that he may have struck lucky - and was a nose ahead of an oncoming rush - when, a week after The Beatles had been spared the giggling indignity of queuing for admission to the Crawdaddy, Oldham merged into the middle distance between the nodding 'appreciation' at the back and the massed females positioned stage-front to better gawk at Mick, Brian - 'an incredible blond, hulking hunk' [4] - and, in less demonstrative fashion, the other four, even Ian.

Then Andrew suffered days of private anxiety. As he had neither the cash to launch the Stones nationally nor the clout to enchant record company representatives or James Grant, producer of *Saturday Club*, to listen to him, he was accompanied by someone with both these assets to another Crawdaddy session the following Sunday, 28th April.

Outwardly, Eric Easton wasn't an obvious person to solicit to be co-manager. If the generally dapper Oldham had heeded the advice of Percy Dickins, co-founder of the *New Musical Express*, to dress down a bit if he was to effuse credibility as would-be manager of The Rolling Stones, Eric turned up in his usual suit and tie. As mild-mannered as Oldham wasn't, he was also receding and nearing his forties. He had framed photographs of his wife and children on his office desk, and was a self-confessed 'square'.[5] The depths of depravity for Eric were twenty filter-tips a day. He ran a cautious West End booking agency, and was respected and liked by his many prestigious artistes, not least because he had once been one himself, chiefly as a cinema organist. Prior to accepting that his time in this qualified limelight was up, he'd amassed enough connections in the music industry to make a living behind the scenes with an organisation that was concerned more than others might have been with the long term maintenance of clients that veered towards the middle-of-the-road, including as they did, guitarist Bert Weedon and sing-along pub pianist Mrs. Mills - for whom Easton had secured respective residencies on ITV's *Five O' Clock Club* children's series and BBC television's weekly *Billy Cotton Band Show*.

He also represented Brian Matthew, presenter now of not only *Saturday Club* but also *Thank Your Lucky Stars* for which, pullovered and *sans* tie, he was as casually dressed as he could be without being reprimanded by the staider ITV programme planners - or Eric Easton, who hadn't let personal dislike of the more transient pop stars and their teenage devotees prevent him from turning a hard-nosed penny or two when the opportunity knocked. Indeed, he behaved like a stereotypical pop group manager from a monochrome Ealing film such as 1959's *Idle On Parade* with Anthony Newley as a rock 'n' roller conscripted into the army. In common with Sid James, Newley's on-screen man-of-affairs, Easton seemed as if all he liked about his pop charges was the money they could generate, selling them like tins of beans - with no money back if they tasted funny.

Yet Eric, if sticking out like a sore thumb among the Shakers at the Crawdaddy, hadn't behaved as either a stone-faced pedant or as if visiting another planet. He knew showbusiness forwards as well as backwards, and was perfectly aware, thank you, Andrew, that the hunt was up for beat groups with sheepdog fringes who, if required, could crank out 'Money', 'Poison Ivy', 'Boys' and the rest of the Merseybeat stand-bys plus a good half of the Chuck Berry songbook. One of these could be recorded in a few takes and released as a single. As Oldham suggested, why shouldn't another variation on the format of two guitars-bass-drums catch on like others of its kind? Neither did he eliminate the Stones from the running as a New Beatles, far from it: 'They were producing this fantastic sound that was obviously exactly right for the kids'.[1]

Before it ended in a shower of writs long before the decade was out - with Eric very much the 'Colonel Hall' to Andrew's 'Bilko' - , there'd be, therefore, sufficient common ground between the bombastic *parvenu* and the traditionalist who preferred hard cash to the acclaim of the Great British Public, for each to be prone to both thrift and extravagance when introducing The Rolling Stones to the nation.

As Eric saw it, their first task would be to transform the group into altogether smoother 'entertainers'. They had to be compelled to wear uniform stage costumes and direct Beatle-esque grins at the audience. Each one of those smiles had to be diffused to the general populace, not just, well, a certain sort of girl. Had they ever come across the term 'back projection'? Something else: continuity between numbers was not to include swearing. That front man muttered something off-mike with 'bloody hell' in it. 'Bloody hell, you don't say!' exclaimed Andrew.

They had to realise, Eric went on calmly, that, beyond scuffy jive hives like the Crawdaddy, there were strict limits of 'decent' behaviour in a naturally prudish Britain that had obliged Billy Fury to moderate his sub-Elvis gyrations before he could be allowed on television. Another thing was that producers could insist that male performers with unacceptably long hair go post-haste to the barber's upon pain of not appearing on *Cool For Cats, Wham!, For Teenagers Only* and other of the sub-*Oh Boy!* programmes that still surfaced and sank.

Even liberal-minded Jack Good had demanded and got that from Vince Taylor, as wild in his way as Lord Sutch.

There were more specific hurdles that might need to be jumped too, perhaps involving some very serious structural tampering. Easton wasn't sure how someone like Jimmy Grant, Norrie Paramor - Cliff and the Shadows' producer at EMI - or Dick Rowe at Decca would react to that funny-looking lead vocalist and his half-caste nasalings. Another principal gripe about the group was also centred on Jagger, because one of the main reasons why Georgio Gomelsky was about to receive an 'I regret to inform you...' letter about that BBC audition was because Mick had, indeed, sounded 'too coloured'. Easton went further: although Jagger had 'image', in that he was just the sort of loutish show-off that you'd teach your children to despise, he 'couldn't sing' - not 'real singing' like Roy Orbison's cowboy operatics or Presley on his 'religious' albums. Why didn't Andrew think that that mattered?

Easton was, however, in total agreement with Oldham that some way would have to be found to tell Ian Stewart that he couldn't be a visible member of the Stones any more. Neither of them questioned his piano- playing, but, to put it bluntly, Stewart's face didn't fit. To drummer Jim McCarty, two months away from joining The Yardbirds, 'Ian always reminded me of "Hoss Cartwright" in *Bonanza*'. A comparison to the obese and figure of fun in the 1960s cowboy series is unkind, but another reservation was Oldham's 'I didn't know a really successful group with six people in it. Peter Jay and the Jaywalkers? Cliff Bennett and the Rebel Rousers? The public can't count up to six.' [4]

It was, nonetheless, thought prudent to thrust such misgivings aside during the conclusion of the joint visit to the Crawdaddy. After the performance, Eric and Andrew spoke at first to a nonchalantly indifferent Charlie Watts, who continued dismantling his kit on calling over the Stone they'd heard addressed as 'Brian' to see what these two geezers wanted. 'Brian was the one we had to negotiate with,' [1] remembered Oldham, noting that Jones at least had the good manners to be civil to him and Easton when the latter bought a round of drinks and suggested a formal meeting at the agency office. Shall we say two o' clock on Tuesday?

Jones arrived with Jagger in tow, and did most of the talking on his own and the group's behalf, hearing fine words when Andrew put them on a par with The Beatles. For Brian, the principal outcome was that he could wash his hands of the begging letters, cold telephone calls and ensuring that musicians and equipment were in the same place at the same time. The offstage machinations that were as crucial as his playing were no longer his responsibility. Something may have warned him that loss of responsibility equalled loss of power, that he was conceding a defeat in his acceptance of a subordinate administrative role in the new situation, but the overall feeling was one of relief. It was a moment, seemingly, of open-handed affability that stuck in Andrew Loog Oldham's memory: 'Brian sat across from Eric Easton and began the long goodbye'. [4]

Jones's *de facto* leadership of the Stones might have been tacitly over that day, but it would appear as if nothing was amiss at the beginning of May when it was he who signed the official agreement, permitting Oldham and Easton's newly-founded Impact Sound management company to take official charge of his Rolling Stones' professional lives for the next three years.

The only tangible fly in the ointment was Georgio Gomelsky, harmlessly across the Channel, attending to his family bereavement, when Oldham and Easton had pounced. Yet Georgio didn't make token legal threats, bar them from the Crawdaddy or create any trouble whatsoever. Perhaps he was too saddened by what he saw as the group's disloyalty in reneging on 'a verbal understanding, I felt tremendously let down.' Nevertheless, he couldn't be blamed for hurling a metaphorical stone at the departing back of the one he had no serious doubt had been the deception's principal advocate: 'I never like to work with monsters, no matter how talented. Jones should have had treatment. His responses were never those of a normal person.' [1]

Following any signpost that pointed in the direction of fame and wealth, Brian was quite prepared, if needs must, to sacrifice Jagger and Stewart too, as he was when Eric Easton voiced an uncertainty on an occasion when the singer - if that's what you call him - was out of earshot. 'Easton said to Brian, "I don't think Jagger is any good",' snarled Ian, 'and so Brian said, "OK, we'll just get rid of him." I felt sure Brian would have done it. I said to him, "Don't be so bloody daft".' [1]

Like a cat who has tried and failed to catch a mouse, Jones walked haughtily away from the discussion, pretending that he had never had any such idea. Given to shaking a head to signify his wisdom, Easton let the matter drop too, while continuing to try to instil into the ramshackle Stones the 'professionalism' he'd perceived in others on his books. A Professor Higgins job on them proved, however, too Herculean an effort. After a while, he supposed that presenting their Crawdaddy fans - and, indeed, teenagers everywhere else - with a smartened-up Stones would be akin to feeding a pig strawberries.

That record companies wouldn't see it like that was a consideration when he and Andrew were mulling over a means to an end that was, to Keith Richards, 'Almost as remote as God talking to you when you've been working backwater clubs for a year.'[4] However, he was confident that if anyone could work such magic, Andrew could: 'He was a fantastic hustler. Although he didn't have much to offer, he did get people interested in what he was doing.' [4]

Easton, nevertheless, felt that his sidekick might be inviting trouble with what was then a revolutionary proposal: 'I explained to Eric that I didn't want a standard record deal for them. My strategy was based on what I had learned from Bob Crewe. He had signed The Four Seasons direct to VeeJay Records in the USA, and they made hits but never got paid. So they went to Philips and did a tape lease deal. This meant they made the records and delivered them. Philips just marketed them.' [1]

As The Beatles were proving so lucrative an investment for EMI, Oldham and Easton decided to begin pressing on the nerve of its chief competitor, Decca. Like every other record company, it could foresee the Merseybeat ferry grounding on a mud bank before the year was out, and, therefore, might be persuaded that the Stones were the next big fish to hook.

Besides, old Dick Rowe had pulled some bold strokes lately, smiled Eric. He had an intriguing track record. After overseeing 1953's 'Broken Wings' by The Stargazers, the first British disc to top the national chart, Rowe had become recognised as a key talent spotter within the UK record industry. Later 1950s singers who also thrived under his aegis included Lita Roza, Dickie Valentine and Billy Fury.

For a while, he'd even left Decca to work for the independent Top Rank for whom he provided flagship acts in Bert Weedon and John Leyton - with whom Joe Meek had made 1961's domestic chart-topper, 'Johnny Remember Me'. When the label folded, Dick was reinstated as head recording manager at Decca, where he ministered to further hit parade entries. Why, only in February, his 'Diamonds' for ex-Shadows Jet Harris and Tony Meehan had been at Number One.

Nevertheless, for all his Top Ten penetrations stretching back a decade, Rowe was now victim of innumerable *bon mots* in rival offices across London as The Man Who Turned Down The Beatles after their test in a Decca studio on New Year's Day 1962. Just back from a business trip to New York, he'd reached the 1st January session tape while ploughing through the backlog accumulated in his absence. Jet-lagged, he considered them no better or worse than any other guitar group who conjured up back-of-beyond youth clubs with soft drinks, ping-pong and a presiding with-it curate. Anyway, he had sufficient outfits like them under contract already. All the same, best wishes for future success and blah, blah, blah, Mr. Epstein. With Roza and Valentine in non-teenage citadels of 'quality' entertainment now, Fury on the wane, and both The Beatles and Gerry and the Pacemakers poised to score another Number One each for EMI, those to whom Rowe was answerable weren't so sure about him anymore.

In fairness, executives with other labels had been just as blinkered - and hadn't even gone so far as to grant The Beatles a try-out. Presented with the opportunity too, Joe Meek had declared them 'Just another bunch of noise, copying other people's music'. [6] Yet, provoked by the failed Scouse supplicants' infuriating success with EMI, a chastised but cynical Dick Rowe had been saturating Decca with peas from the same Merseyside pod. In the last week of January alone, he'd made off with The Big Three, Beryl Marsden, singing Cavern disc-jockey Billy Butler and, because their drummer was ex-Beatle Pete Best, Lee Curtis and the All-Stars.

Soul-tortured Rowe was on the look-out for more potentially hitmaking Scousers when he and one of Best's estranged former colleagues, George Harrison were judging a 'Battle Of The Bands'-type tournament at Liverpool's Philharmonic Hall on the second Friday in May. On the panel too was Bill Harry, editor of *Mersey Beat*. Whispering to Harry and Harrison either side of him, Rowe reckoned that every one of the competing groups was much of a muchness.

Civilly, George agreed and, because Dick had been honest in not over-justifying his error in turning his nose up at the Beatles, Harrison decided to help him. There was, he enthused, this southern group he'd seen. Musically, they were 'Almost as good as The Roadrunners' [7] - which, prior to the latter tainting their act with too much 'wacker' humour, might have been absolutely true. The Rolling Stones, continued George, were far wilder visually, and having the same effect on their audience in a provincial club as The Beatles had on theirs at the Cavern. 'Dick got up immediately,' observed Bill Harry, 'And caught the next train back to London.'

During painfully slow disembarkations at stops *en route* to King's Cross, Rowe stared moodily at the dark landscape and wondered if these next Beatles had already been scarfed up by someone else. Before George Harrison had, a couple of other people - he couldn't recall who - had also spoken to him about The Rolling Stones, but it hadn't registered.

Throughout Saturday, Dick made cloak-and-dagger enquiries. Young Mike Vernon was a fan of the group, and a patron of the Crawdaddy, but others who'd heard of The Rolling Stones – and listened to the R G Jones tape - weren't so convinced that they were up Decca's alley. Cliff Richard might indulge in a little scripted playfulness when headlining on *Sunday Night At The London Palladium*, but this bunch, so it was rumoured, were downright uncouth in the manner in which they treated the crowd. It had come to the ears of certain promoters that they said things like 'fuck' and belched into the microphone. If this was the case, then it was tantamount to vocational suicide. Obviously, Mick Jagger's Mike-ish 'bloody hell' had blossomed into a music business equivalent of a fisherman's tall tale.

Dick Rowe's benchmark of pop group professionalism was Brian Poole and the Tremeloes, who he'd signed in 1962 long before this Merseybeat fad had given everyone a nasty turn. Yet, when the dust had settled, why shouldn't things carry on as normal with the tried-and-tested agenda of catchy tune, publicity build-up, pre-ordained grinning on television and Decca raking in a bit of loot at the end of the day?

Brian and his Tremeloes understood their role in this completely - that they were a link in the chain between board meeting and marketplace as purveyors of popular songs that people would hum, whistle and partly sing over a few chart weeks before the forces behind them prepared another harmless ditty for easy consumption with either the same act or a substitute with the same basic format. Moreover, in keeping with the principal stylistic dictates of the day, Poole's boys were neatly coiffeured; garbed in not-too-way-out uniform suits, most charming to everyone, and given to stage patter that didn't include bad language or overt attempts to pull front-row girls - everything a decent pop combo ought to be.

They were reliable in the studio too. Before being permitted to record under their own name, they were used, together and separately, as a backing unit in Decca's complex in Broadhurst Gardens, West Hampstead, in operation since 1938. Brian and two Tremeloes, for example, functioned as a vocal trio on such masterpieces of song as disc-jockey Jimmy Savile's 'Ahab The Arab' and, recalled Brian, 'If you listen to The Vernons Girls' cover of "The Locomotion", it sounds more like blokes apart from the lead vocal. That was us too. We also accompanied auditionees that came in. Even when we were famous, we were helping out on sessions - because it paid really well.'

This was a well-judged choice: showbusiness without the show in an era when, for a lad to go on the road with a fly-by-night beat group - nearly always all male - was almost the exact equivalent of a lass becoming a burlesque dancer. At best, it was regarded as a novitiate for a life as an 'all-round entertainer' - as The Beatles seemed to be implying with that Lenny the Lion nonsense and succumbing to joining in a comedy sketch with the hosts on *The Morecambe And Wise Show*. On amassing a stockpile of hits, a pop musician would 'mature' and be in a favourable position for personal appearances in variety, cabaret and, if of vibrant enough personality, periodic TV slots and advertising. That's why, when he and the Tremeloes began fading from the charts eighteen months later, Brian Poole was able to take it philosophically: 'We've had a good run - and even without the hits, we have managed to convince most people that we are a good enough band to book.' [8]

If these Rolling Stones could actually play, and were willing to toe a clean, winsome line - with maybe acceptably pseudo-rebellious behaviour as their gimmick - they could follow the same route. The industry would look after them when their time in the main spotlight was up, and the the circle would remain unbroken. So thought Dick Rowe as, setting aside critical prejudices, he donned Phil Spector-esque shades and took his wife to the Crawdaddy on the Sunday afternoon.

Surprising the office cleaners, he arrived at work the next day at eight o' clock. It was a matter of only a few telephone calls to breakfasting contacts to find out who handled The Rolling Stones - and then a great light dawned. Eric Easton had rung him about them at a busy time only last week - and so had some music publisher, laying them on with a trowel, having been incited to do so by this other fellow, who appeared to be a learner-manager like Epstein. While Andrew Oldham was an unknown quantity, Dick knew the type with whom he'd be dealing in Easton. He sat it out until the anticipated time that Eric's working week would start, and then picked up the receiver again.

A sufficiently strident note of urgency in Rowe's streets-of-Islington whine propelled Easton and Oldham to Decca's riverside offices just after lunch. The normally hoity-toity receptionist conducted them straightaway into the presence of managing director, Bill Townsley. He and Dick shook hands with Eric, anticipating straightforward dialogue terminating with much the same kind of agreement reached on behalf of Brian Poole, Beryl Marsden or The Big Three. They had, however, reckoned without this Andrew creature sprawled disrespectfully in a button-leather armchair, with his fast mouth and his sweeping aside of such obstacles as demo tapes and auditions. They could keep their studios in Broadhurst Gardens, he told them. The Stones would be taping their first record and those that came after somewhere else. Furthermore, they wouldn't need a Decca staff producer either. He'd take care of all that.

Just like Joe Meek or Phil Spector would too, he threatened further the very foundation of the industrial structure by saying that Decca wasn't going to own the results. They'd be leased to the company so that the Stones, through Impact Sound, could maintain artistic control and ensure that as few middlemen as possible would be entitled to a cut. No house producer, for instance, was going to earn by forcing his rotten songs or throwaway instrumentals onto the group's B-sides. Never were the Stones going to be too much in awe of a condescending voice calling them to order via the control-room intercom to splutter, 'We'd rather not, sir.'

Why was Andrew doing this? Was it self-interest or just devilment? Dick Rowe and Bill Townsley realised that it was neither, but something much worse, an anathema, a sin against tradition. It was Change.

The old unspoken intention appeared to be to buck the established strategy of making first impact with pop noise and then dropping it quickly to enter showbusiness proper. Yet Oldham saw pop not as a starting point, but the entire purpose of a career. There needn't be any higher plateau where popularity with a teenage audience had no substance. Ridiculous though it seemed to Dick Rowe, Andrew Loog Oldham viewed The Rolling Stones as a longer term prospect than commodities to be bought, sold and replaced when worn out. 'There was no precedent at that time,' agreed Keith Richards too, 'You shot up there, and you were gone. There was no possible way you could believe that it was going to last for anything more than another two years. So for us, a record deal was, like, the beginning of the end.' [9]

Nevertheless, in a half-nelson because the Stones' pressure-cooker reputation was steaming too fast from the Crawdaddy, Decca had no choice but to fix a ghastly corporate smile as this dreadful teenage loudmouth called the shots. Decca didn't want the next Beatles to go with Pye, Philips or, heaven forbid, an EMI subsidiary, did it? By the close of the week, a three year Decca recording deal guaranteed the Stones and Impact Sound a royalty of six per cent between them, a damn sight more than EMI had given their precious Beatles.

If not on the same hard bargained terms, Dave Berry and the Cruisers, Bern Elliott and the Fenmen and The Rockin' Berries were to be among further remunerative acquisitions for Decca over the next few months. Yet, for each such hitmaking unit, there was also a Beat Six, a Big Six, an Emeralds, a Tommy Bishop's Ricochets, a Dynamic Sounds, a Bobby Cristo and the Rebels, a Brumbeats, a Blue Stars, an MI5, a Sandra Barry and her Boyfriends, a Gonks, a Barry and the Tamberlanes, a Bunnies, a Gobbledegooks, a Falling Leaves...

Such disappointing investments could be absorbed by cross-collateralisation with profits amassed by the winners. In any case, the attitude at Decca was not to waste too many resources on this new strain of pop group. All of them are the same, and none of them will last long anyway. Yet, Dick Rowe, desperate to climb back on his perch, had made it a point of honour, despite finding Andrew Loog Oldham objectionable, to get The Rolling Stones into the Top Ten before this beat bubble burst and decent music reigned once more.

Notes

1. *Q*, May, 1995
2. *New York Times*, 20th December, 1964
3. Released in December, 1962 as 'Magic Star' by Kenny Hollywood

[Geoff Goddard] (Decca F11546)

4. *Stoned* by AL Oldham (St. Martin's Press, 2000)

5. *Melody Maker*, 26th September, 1964

6. *Record Collector* No. 334, March, 2007

7. *Back In The High Life* by A. Clayson (Sidgwick & Jackson, 1988)

8. *Call Up The Groups!* by A. Clayson (Blandford, 1985)

9. *Rolling Stone*, 5th November, 1987

## Chapter Nine
## Coming On

*'We were doing gigs every night, and we refused to play it. How could we go out and do our set of heavy rhythm and blues and then play this little pop song. It was too embarrassing' - Keith Richards* [1]

As it had been with the Impact Sound document, Brian's had been the only Stone signature on the Decca agreement. He was also the only member of the group present when it was decided how the assorted and incoming monies would be divided, and was thus able to winkle out of Eric Easton, holder of the purse strings, an extra few pounds a week for himself.

Andrew Oldham's only interest in Brian's little display of covert avarice was storing the information away for use against him if the situation arose. For now, however, it was mostly all smiles. If Eric anticipated little more than a detached professional relationship with his new clients, an affinity based as much on friendship as profit developed between the younger partner and the majority of the Stones, aided by episodes such as the comedy inherent in the overcoming of a difficulty that had required immediate attention. 'After everything was signed, they remembered the session Gomelsky had set up,' a middle-aged Oldham would recollect, 'The deal gave IBC a specific time period in which to do something with these tapes. So we rehearsed Brian to go to them and say he felt the band was going nowhere, and that he had this big opportunity to join some other outfit. Could IBC let him go if he paid back the £106 in studio costs - and they fell for it, thank God.' [2]

The next problem was the A-side of a maiden single. A lingering prejudice of most British record companies - Decca possibly above all - in the early 1960s was that the last thing anyone from a teenager in a dance hall to the head of the Light Programme wanted to hear was a home-made song. Nevertheless, on the bus *en route* to the studio, Cliff Richard's then-guitarist Ian Samwell had penned 'Move It', the Bachelor Boy's chart breakthrough. Yet, with Vince Taylor's 'Brand New Cadillac' and Johnny Kidd's 'Please Don't Touch' and 'Shakin' All Over', it was among few truly classic British rock 'n' roll singles in an age when the typical UK pop entertainer accepted cheerfully his second-hand and, arguably, counterfeit status to US role models.

The notion of anyone in a pop group developing composition to any marked extent had been unheard of before The Beatles, who, with an abundant internal source of self-penned items, crossed the demarcation line between composer and artiste, and were capable of fulfilling commitments to their music publisher many times over.

The Stones, however, had no intention of doing likewise, even if attempting a self-penned song was, by the latter half of 1963, no longer necessarily an unofficial intermission in which club audiences could talk to friends, get in a round of drinks, go to the toilets, anything but dance or even listen to it. 'We do not use any original material,' Mick Jagger had told *Jazz News*, adding a blithe 'After all, can you imagine a British-composed R&B number? It just wouldn't make it.' [3]

Grubbing round publishers' offices around Denmark Street was, therefore, out of the question. There was no other alternative but to rifle the vaults of the US R&B motherlode - and the more fashionable northern groups had done that already on disc. Five such items, for example, had filled needle-time on The Beatles' debut album. In March too, The Big Three had irritated the Top Fifty with a version of Richard Barrett's 'Some Other Guy', and Kingsize Taylor and the Dominoes - as The Shakers - were about to release 'Money' coupled with a reading of Chuck Berry's latest, 'Memphis Tennessee'. Though they were fronted by a sort of Norman Wisdom of pop, Keith Richards half-liked Freddie and the Dreamers' spirited revival of 'If You Gotta Make A Fool Of Somebody'. Freddie himself preferred New Yorker James Ray's original of 1961, but this R&B sing-along suited his Gerry-with-a-hernia voice and the tempo of his Dreamers' act. All Freddie needed was a spot on ITV's *Thank Your Lucky Stars* on 21st May, 1963 for his clowning to nudge it into the Top Ten.

Trying to avoid Merseybeat standards, the Stones pored over respective record collections - which had included lately an album series by Pye that was bringing many of the old delta and urban legends to a wider public. *Folk Festival Of The Blues*, for example, was an aural souvenir of a Chicago concert the previous summer, showcasing Muddy Waters, Willie Dixon, Sonny Boy Williamson, Buddy Guy and Howlin' Wolf. High street record shops were also stocking both reissued and new singles such as Bo Diddley's 'Pretty Thing' - backed with 'Road Runner' - 'Boom Boom' from John Lee Hooker and Chuck Berry's 'Go Go Go', the one before 'Memphis Tennessee'.

By process of elimination, the Stones boiled down the range of choices to the artiste whose songs still stood in boldest relief in their stage set – as well as those of countless other beat groups. To give themselves the best possible chance by not bothering with universally known favourites or anything another act might be releasing, the short-list was narrowed further, and after discarding 'Around And Around' and 'Roll Over Beethoven' - just issued by the West Midlands' Pat Wayne and his Beachcombers on EMI, and earmarked for inclusion on The Beatles' second LP, *With The Beatles* - they settled on an opus attractive for its unpopularity amongst rivals. Nobody else did 'Come On', flip-side of 'Go Go Go', but, shrugged Keith Richards, 'It was the most commercial sound we were capable of making at the time, and the song had some kind of affinity with what we were used to doing.' [1]

Into the bargain, while Berry's 'Memphis Tennessee' was to eclipse all British covers - including a Top Twenty arrangement by the confusingly-named Dave Berry - and 1964 held a greater triumph for an unopposed 'No Particular Place To Go', he, Diddley, Hooker, Waters, Wolf and all the rest of them were, overall, less appealing to UK youth than the beat groups who borrowed from them. 'One, they're old; two, they're black; three, they're ugly,' theorized Keith. [1] Therefore, for people who didn't derive deep and lasting pleasure from studying composing credits on record labels, The Rolling Stones' brisker 'Come On' would be the *only* version.

It was gingered up further with Bill Wyman's pulsating bass and Brian Jones's *waa-waa-waa* harmonica *ostinato* that, if essentially monotonal, had to negotiate a corny but tricky key change for the last verse. To the Crawdaddy crowd, 'Come On' was hardly a showstopper, and a *Record Mirror* feature-cum-review confirmed that 'it's not the fanatical R&B sound that audiences wait hours to hear'. [4] The B-side didn't set the word on fire either. Jagger sounded not unlike Elvis Presley - of whom he still wasn't particularly fond - on 'I Want To Be Loved', a Muddy Waters opus, written by Chess's house double-bass player, Willie Dixon, that also bore a passing resemblance to Jimmy Reed's 'I Ain't Got You'.

It was a re-make of a track from the IBC session. Less successful had been a second attempt at 'Come On' at Broadhurst Gardens owing to long executive faces at a master taped at Olympic Studios in Barnes that showed producer Andrew Loog Oldham's lean experience at the console in a poor light. Yet it was this first recording that was pressed - as the lesser of two evils. The Stones felt the same, but concurred with both Decca and the management that, regardless of quality, it might serve as an opportune means to an end, especially in view of a critic in *Mersey Beat* regional pop periodical, who, on hearing an advance copy of 'Come On', described them as 'a London group with the Liverpool sound.' [(5)]

For what it signified rather than what was in the grooves, Bill Wyman, especially, felt that, should the group fold, 'Come On' would be something to bequeath his grandchildren if he had any. He'd already started compiling a scrap book that kept chronological track of the Stones' hitherto short and rather erratic career. Thus far, there wasn't much to paste in its pages beyond the merest snippets of printed news and some publicity photographs - like those resulting from a joint shoot with Brian Poole and the Tremeloes to indicate, shrugged Poole, 'That the Stones were joining the Decca "family", I suppose. Our fan club secretary came in with a load of pictures for us to sign, and Mick said, "You'd never catch me doing that. I'd have a rubber stamp made".'

Jagger, however, was far from prominent in the principal portrait selected. In costumes of shiny waistcoat, white shirt, slim-jim tie, black trousers and Cuban-heeled boots that - with Andrew Oldham's consent - Eric Easton had bought and compelled them to wear, he, Bill, Keith and Charlie had arranged themselves with the Tremeloes, standing in a half-circle behind the two Brians in pride of place on stools. Poole - only twenty-two - in his jacket appeared to be imparting gesticulating advice to Jones: genial voice-of-experience to waywardly earnest young shaver.

Out of camera range, Ian Stewart looked on, his face twisted into the frown of someone biting back on his anger. He'd just swallowed what he'd decided to take as an insult dealt in the form of a management directive that under no circumstances was he to be seen either in photographs of the group or on stage with them in future. It was a cruel necessity, but he'd remain part of the team, so Brian Jones assured him - as if Brian was still in a position to do so. Ian could be chief road manager if he liked.

This relegation had been telegraphed by the rendering of the 'Come On' piano section inaudible on the instructions of Oldham, to whom fell the awkward task of telling the beefy ex-ICI pen-pusher that he lacked visual appeal. There was no denying, so Andrew tried to explain, that he was a bit, well... you know. To Ian's further disgust, while he expected nothing from Jones, no-one else in the group, not even Bill or Charlie, made more than a perfunctory attempt to insist on his reinstatement. While he'd always feel entitled to refer to the Stones as 'us' rather than them, Stewart's widow was to insist that, 'Whatever Ian or anyone else said, he did care about being relegated. The bottom line for Andrew was that his face didn't fit. Andrew loved the pretty, thin, long-haired boys. Ian felt bitter about the savage way he was kicked aside.' (2)

An understandable dark night of the ego passed, and, after he'd come to terms with this banishment - and his shaving mirror telling him why - Stewart stayed on as general factotum whose duties included humping equipment and, like an army batman without the uniform, attending to the others' food, sleep and general health requirements. Moreover, if unseen, he remained, as Brian intimated, an official Stone musically, attending when required to keyboards in the studio. 'He was the glue that held all the bits together,' was to be Keith's epitaph following Ian's death in 1985, 'Very few people realise how important he was to the Stones.' (6)

Richards had been the subject of another adjustment when the Stones were on the point of take-off. His surname was to be 'Richard' from now on, thus giving him an implied affiliation with Cliff, Britain's most successful solo pop idol. That a Birmingham combo called The Tempests also contained a guitarist named Keith Richards, however, had not been another consideration when the change was implemented by Easton and Oldham.

With an irresolute nod too, Bill Wyman, approaching his thirties, deducted seven years from his age for a personal profile put together for members of the newly-formed Rolling Stones fan club in the image of the *New Musical Express*'s 'Lifelines' tabulation - height, weight, favourite colour, hobbies *et al*. It was often a hard lie for Bill to live. If his physical appearance just about passed muster, he betrayed his maturity in what Stones accountant Stan Blackbourne perceived as 'his whole attitude.'(7) Married, a non-partaker of any stimulants more exotic than tobacco and alcohol, and having a greater affinity with Easton than Oldham, the orderly way in which he and Diane kept house was eminently satisfactory to Bill: a place for everything and everything in its place. He couldn't understand why it was beyond someone like Brian, with all his personal fastidiousness, to give the Edith Grove hovel a quick flick with a duster every now and then.

Jones's finer sensibilities extended, however, to making out he was a former 'architect' and listing Bach as a 'favourite composer' for the fans' hand-out. Eric Easton also approved of Keith *Richard*'s conventional and Beatle-esque ambition to appear at the London Palladium.

It was noted too that Keith lowered his eyes when ticked off for following Charlie's lead in loosening his matching tie - as Watts was for setting a bad example. Punctuality and back-projection were all-important too, but the group were less convinced by Eric's arguments for playing to a fixed programme in the clubs that were still the Stones' bread-and-butter.

To Easton's further dismay - and Oldham's fury - the Stones dropped 'Come On' from their repertoire, even when it was specifically requested, even after they'd submitted to miming it in the uniform attire - check coats with velvet collars on this occasion, that were abhorrent to them - on *Lucky Stars Summer Spin*, a Sunday evening supplement to *Thank Your Lucky Stars*, a month after its release on 7th June. With a predominantly female audience screaming at them as indiscriminately as they did over all male performers on the show, this crucial exposure had come about via Easton leaning on Brian Matthew. Further television slots, a full-page feature in the *Daily Mirror*, spins on the Light Programme and more muffled airings on Radio Luxembourg also allied with the stir from London to begin a yo-yo progression to the edge of the Top Twenty where 'Come On' lingered until autumn, thus fulfilling *Record Mirror*'s estimation that it 'should make the charts in a small way'. [4]

It was enough to hold on hoping, and the speed of events since Easton and Oldham's appointment at Decca in early May had already been sufficient motivation for Mick Jagger to write to Kent Education Committee, the providers of his grant, terminating his course - with a year left to go - at the LSE. He represented it as a 'sabbatical' to his parents, but as boat-burning to Dartford Grammar cronies with whom he'd stayed in touch. A consternated Peter Holland, now at the nearby University College, would recall 'him telling me he was now singing in a group. I really laughed. "What do you mean, singing?" I said, "You haven't got a voice".' [8]

As Joe and Eva were often to remind Mike, it would never be too late for him to resume his degree studies, heartened as they were by his remarks in the *New Musical Express* about the wretched group being 'an enjoyable pastime. We consider ourself professional amateurs.' [9] Making the most of an imagined finite time in the limelight, he seemed not only to take the pert *Lucky Stars Summer Spin* outfits in his stride, but was also amenable to endorsing what might be construed as a gimmick in a head-tossing at the microphone that sections of the Crawdaddy audience copied.

'It gets so crowded that all fans can do is stand and twitch,' he elucidated, 'They can't dance because there isn't room.' [10] Expediently, though more widely known as the Shake, it also resembled not so much a dance as a mass tic actually called the Twitch, and propagated fleetingly as one of many alternatives to the Twist, still going strong in 1963. There was even a Twitch Club in Birmingham which the house band, The Rockin' Berries, had just immortalised on an eponymous B-side.

Knowingly and unknowingly, Mick demonstrated the Twitch when the Stones, though bound to Sundays at Studio 51 and the Crawdaddy until late September, undertook not so much a tour as a continual and sporadic string of one-nighters, commencing in Middlesborough's Alcove Club on 13th June, and concentrated mainly on agricultural and factory towns in the north and east, and venues where the personality of the entertainers was generally secondary to brawling and the pursuit of romance. Having, deliberately, little in the way of seating, dancing was encouraged, and hall managers expected beat groups to exude a happy, inoffensive on-stage atmosphere as well as action-packed sound to defuse potential unrest amongst over-excited adolescents. Wantonly pleasing yourself - by, perhaps, not giving the mob what could be described, with a little logical blindness, as your 'smash hit' - could kindle cat-calls, outbreaks of barracking and more pragmatic reaction from riff-raff such as the many Teddy Boys that had remained at large despite the slings and arrows of fashion. Their displeasure could be most painfully expressed by a shower of pre-decimalization pennies cascading stagewards, carrying on after the lacerated visitors evacuated the boards, and throughout the master-of-ceremonies' attempts to restore order.

The Stones were most immediately conspicuous for their motley appearance, notably hair that, if only fractionally longer than Beatle moptops, was sufficient to brand them as 'cissies' or 'queers' in provincial settlements where the Second World War was about to enter its twenty-fifth year. In this Corn Exchange or that seaside ballroom, young adults, for whom even quiffed Elvis was not yet a symbol of masculinity, would be just as perturbed as their elders when confronted with the Edith Grove contingent's greaseless forelocks and ducktails-gone-to-seed - and Bill and Charlie not far behind. Screaming Lord Sutch's locks had been shoulder-length since 1959, but that was seen as part of his endless efforts to elicit career-sustaining publicity for a 'horror-rock' presentation as harmlessly amusing as a ride on a fairground ghost train. This lot didn't regard the way they looked as anything remotely funny.

Their abandonment of sartorial uniformity was causing less comment than the hair, but comment all the same at a time when skiffle icon Bob Cort's dictum about 'visual effect' - that 'you all look exactly the same' [10] - resonated still in the Midwich Cuckoo-like regularity of most beat groups' stage attire. Thus the Stones akin to the fated US movie star Frances Farmer, who flew in the face of 1940s Hollywood's rulings about glamour by arriving garbed in slacks and sweater at premieres where cameras clicked like typewriters. Just as she caused Paramount's alarmed publicity department to limit the damage by emphasising the 'eccentric habits of the star who will not "go Hollywood",' [11] so the Stones would be classified swiftly by a bemused *New Musical Express* as 'the group who prefer casual wear to stage suits and who sometimes don't bother to change before going onstage.' [12]

The *Lucky Stars* check jackets had disappeared after acquiring frayed cuffs and too many indelible stains born of sweat and spillage. Neither would there be any wonderful-to-be-here vapourings in Jones and Jagger's onstage dialogue during this first run of post-'Come On' engagements that, because of the meritocratic nature of a profession based on chart performances, included support spots to such as The Hollies, on the wings of their second hit and touted as 'Manchester's Beatles'. Certainly, they'd been the biggest fish to be hooked in the north after Liverpool had been left to rot. Nonetheless, the Stones' Top Thirty strike allowed them to lord it over a diversity of other acts - though a handful gave cause for nervous backwards glances. Preceding the Stones at Morecambe's Floral Hall - one of only two west coast engagements - The Merseybeats and Dave Berry both happened to enter the lower reaches of the Top Fifty for the first time in the same September week - the former with The Shirelles' 'It's Love That Really Counts', and Dave with 'Memphis Tennessee'.

Somewhere else, Oldham's Wayne Fontana and the Mindbenders also leaned heavily on rhythm-and-blues and earned the Stones' approbation - qualified because they preferred the US blueprints - but other couplings weren't so concordant when pop music was still seen as an off-shoot of light entertainment. 'There weren't any sub-divisions then,' said Dave Berry, 'There would have been nothing unusual for the Stones to have been on the same bill as a crooner, an instrumental group or a singing postman. No-one thought any of the new groups would last. It was the first real wave of true British pop, and no-one could guess what was in store.'

As Ian Stewart transported his grubby human cargo across six counties in his VW one afternoon, Bill Wyman, drifting into an uneasy doze with the road roaring in his ears, may have dreamt of a limousine gliding the group to a sold-out theatre where their name was in lights. He'd wake with a start as the exhausted van bumped off an early evening high street onto the gravel next to some municipal hall. From the vehicle, he and an unexpectedly large number of human shapes would emerge, numb with bearing amplifiers and drums on their laps. 'Don't go in empty handed!' a voice shouts, causing someone to haul further gear from the overloaded van before shuffling towards the building's front steps. A janitor answers their banging, but does not help lug the careworn equipment into a chilly and darkened venue that bears all the tell-tale signs of having known better days: the dust on the stage's heavy drape curtains, never unfurled these days; the padded wallpaper peeling off here and there; the front-of-house staff's depressed forbearance.

By half-past eight, the place is two-thirds full of teenagers milling around and spruced up for another small death cavorting to records and then the supporting local heroes. However, within a minute of the main attraction starting its set, a roughneck might have to be restrained physically by Ian Stewart from slamming his fist through a public address speaker, having decided to be a lion of justice, striking a blow for decent entertainment for decent folk.

Astonishingly perhaps, it was not Jagger but Jones who stoked up the most aggression with a privately rehearsed radiation of anti-everything menace laced with effeminacy. Instances were noted of Brian bucking and gyrating as if he had wasps in his pants - as if infused with an attention-grabbing desire to outdo Mick. This was easy to do then as Jagger, whose movements were often limited anyway by small stages and an undetachable skull-like chrome microphone on a heavy stand, revealed only half-hidden clues of the showman he was to become.

Jones proved capable of stealing the limelight in more subtly narcissistic fashion. While Jagger was doing his best to whip up reaction, all Jones had to do was fix his eyes on his guitar neck as if stupefied by his own note-bending dexterity, not forgetting to look up now and then to emit a rare bashful grin to trigger ecstatic squeals from girls, tits bouncing, near the lip of the stage, in repudiation of another surge of heckling further back from lads who, bold with heterosexual bluster, wouldn't dare admit finding the Stones' nancy-boy general factotum guiltily transfixing as, by slightly overdoing the subliminal obnoxiousness, he wallowed in a repellent bewitchment.

Back in the safety of the Crawdaddy, Alexis Korner had seen for himself how 'Brian went out to needle people, to really arouse them, so that they really responded. You'd see him dancing forward with a tambourine and snapping it in your face and sticking his tongue out at you in a nasty way, not in a schoolboyish way, and then he'd move back before you actually took a punch at him. Brian had more edge to him than any of the others then. He was the nasty one. He could be really evil on stage.' [13]

Jubilantly, Jones, then and later, would point out the pockets of violence he'd incited to the others, and, grimaced photographer Gered Mankowitz, 'always seemed ready for some sort of confrontation with the police when concerts got out of hand.' [14]

Local constabularies had started paying routine calls towards the end of what archaic posters billed as 'swing sessions' where fists often swung harder than groups whose music soundtracked someone being half-killed out there. Narrow-eyed bouncers - security officers - were hired to keep order, but washed their hands of incidents occurring after customers and entertainers had left the premises, even by that troublemaker who'd been raised aloft weight-lifter style and chucked out onto the pavement.

Aching to start something more, he and youths like him would watch like lynxes as the Stones loaded their equipment after the performance. Maybe that fair-haired one would reply 'Good evening' to a gruff ''Ullo', and thus warrant a beating up for being such a toffee-nosed ponce. Yet the fellows would deduce that these aliens weren't queers, very much the opposite. Limbering up for another long haul back to London, at least one of them might be against the shadowed side of the van, pawing some available girl. Coming on as the rough, untamed East Ender that he'd never been, Jagger was discovering that a fledgling pop star's life brought more than mere money, but with the qualification, 'Ugh, we used to attract such big, ugly ones. Dreadful birds with long, black hair, plastic boots and macs'. [15]

Mick would sense being observed with non-hostile interest by boys too. Some of them caught the Stones a second and even third time during this round of engagements, and, if most kept their distance, theirs would be the spatter of clapping that broke long seconds of thunderstruck hush when its final major sixth had resounded. Applause might crescendo into a whistling, cheering, stamping tumult with a sub-flavour of screams - for, under the stage lights, the group certainly looked and sounded Big Time - and though he'd never admit it, a backdated Ted couldn't really fault the musicianship or the Stones launching into unashamed classic rock from the 1950s if they felt like it - and he had to admire the nerve of that boot-faced Mick, who walked what seemed to him to be an artistic tightrope without a safety net.

The Stones' exactment of such submission from those who hadn't wanted to like them - and the gradually less scattered screams reverberating as each evening progressed - was food for thought for hipper youths. At a village institute somewhere in the eastern shires, one ogling female's nose was put out of joint when Jagger, overlooking her, introduced himself afterwards to her escort and chatted to him about the current state of pop. The bloke was Syd Barrett, waiting for his time to come as lynchpin of The Pink Floyd, who were to begin in 1965 with a familiar dipping into the Waters, Diddley and Berry songbooks.

Other entranced male converts who vanished into the night, lost in wonder, went no further than copying the Stones' looks, pooching out their lips like Jagger's - and, more particularly, fighting every literal inch of the way to grow out their short-back-and-sides over years of incomprehension, lamentation, derision, deprivation and uproar.

179

On first glance at most photographs of the early Stones, the first hairstyle - as opposed to face - to which you'd be drawn would be Brian's straight 'pageboy' cut, fringed to the eyebrows. Blond when the others were dark, he assumed that he was still the group's chief spokesman as well as their focal point. A gradually more irritating trait to the other Stones was Brian butting into conversations in order to imprint his importance to the group on outsiders. As if he alone controlled its destiny, he'd pontificate publicly and often ignorantly about matters yet to be discussed with the others, and say 'we' instead of 'I'.

'We don't want to play at the Star-Club,' he confided airily to Richard Green of the *NME*, 'This is because British groups are only booked there to fill in. The club features American names, and British outfits that have appeared there have not starred.' [16] Admittedly, The Beatles had been the main attraction on the very opening night in 1962 of the legendary Hamburg night spot, which then sought out further Britons to do the same, even hosting a week-long 'Liverpool Festival' featuring nothing but groups from north-west England's grimy pivot of industrial enterprise.

It was Jones whose borderline sarcasm was to bring the drip-drip of muttered fulminations between the Stones and Liverpool's Swinging Blue Jeans close to fisticuffs before an ebbing away that left the combatants glowering at each other from opposite ends of a BBC canteen. Generally, however, beat groups of fluctuating equality, united by artistic purpose and mutual respect, were courteous enough to each other when paths crossed in a wayside cafe or a pub over the road from the venue. Rivalry would dissolve into camaraderie as musicians boasted, spread rumours, small-talked, betrayed confidences, schemed and had a laugh - or a cry, depending on how well things were going, though all bookings, so it was frequently made out, were triumphs in retrospect.

In common confinement in frowzy dressing rooms came anecdotes about what Bill got up to with that brunette in King's Lynn; Mick telling Gary Brooker of The Paramounts how much he liked their crack at 'Poison Ivy'; Charlie deducing from a round-the-kit fill dating back to Art Blakey that, with his heart in jazz too, Bobby Elliott, The Hollies' drummer, was not just thumping out the usual four-four backbeat, but was 'a really good player'. [17] A couple of the other Hollies offered their services if the Stones needed extra backing vocals when next they convened in a recording studio, and, when flung together again days after the BBC dust-up, differences between the Stones and The Swinging Blue Jeans would be settled.

The Jeans' first single, 'It's Too Late Now' had been penetrating the Top Thirty in the selfsame month as 'Come On'. Both acts had done quite well for first-timers, but who could yet presume that they were anything other than classic local groups who'd caught the lightning once and would most likely have returned to the haphazard oblivion from which they'd emerged by this time next year?

It was a like a lottery, thought Dick Rowe, Bill Townsley and nearly everyone else at Decca's customary Tuesday morning board meeting. All these bloody bands are the same. Let's carry on snapping up as many as we can, see which racket catches on, and cash in quick. None of them will be around long anyway, so why waste resources endeavouring to prove otherwise.

Such was the spirit that pervaded discussion with Andrew Oldham about the follow-up to 'Come On'. This time, the company was adamant that the group would report to Broadhurst Gardens where a staff producer would be in clock-watching charge, and that they'd follow the time-honoured precedent of reviving an old US hit, namely The Coasters' 'Poison Ivy' which, though first issued four years earlier, was very much in the air in 1963. To give it the best possible chance it would be backed by 'Fortune Teller', a more recent *Billboard* R&B chart entry by a Benny Spellman, and now being approximated by hundreds of groups scrimmaging round all the insalubrious beat clubs that were now littering Britain's every major town.

Everywhere, it seemed guts were being ripped from old factory premises, cellars cleared and bars extended to make venues for outfits with guitars and long hair, no matter how dreadful they sounded. Dick Rowe and his team of underlings could check out up to thirty groups a night without having to leave the Home Counties where you couldn't turn around without another club opening, whether Leo's Cavern in Windsor, another Cavern in Leicester Square, Boreham Wood's Long Jon Club, the Shake-and-Shimmy in South Harrow, Eastbourne's Catacombe, the Beat Scene in Cheshunt or the Witch Doctor on the coast in Hastings.

In any one of them, hardly an evening would go by without one of the acts on the bill trying 'Poison Ivy' or 'Fortune Teller'. On disc too, simultaneous covers of the same song had prevailed since the *New Musical Express* had published the first disc chart in 1952. Thus Dick Rowe didn't even interrupt his lunch when told that, over at EMI, both The Dave Clark Five and The Paramounts were planning to release versions of 'Poison Ivy' too, and that 'Fortune Teller' had also B-sided The Merseybeats' 'It's Love That Really Counts'.

The Stones' proposed new single was allocated a catalogue number and release date, and sheet music with their picture on it put on sale. While no longer compromising on their hirsute, motley image - on stage, if not quite yet on television - they still seemed willing to be pushed in whatever direction fate, Oldham, Easton and Decca ordained. Now that beat group slants were being crowbarred into everything from ITV commercials to episodes of long-running *Mrs. Dale's Diary* on the Home Service, they wouldn't be above a jingle for Rice Krispies breakfast cereal, and raising their thumbs in photographed endorsement of Vox amplifiers in a trade magazine. Whether motivated to help the needy or not, the Stones were also to do their bit in a charity match against a Teenstar Bowling League, organised by Julie Grant, an Eric Easton client since a childhood of talent contest victories.

To uphold the notion of the Stones as outwardly Nice Lads When You Get To Know Them - the angle adopted by every pop star from Johnnie Ray to Babyshambles - it was necessary to ensure that no word of certain of their off-stage shenanigans leaked to such press as might be interested. To many within the Stones' entourage, Bill Wyman in particular was something of a lothario on the road. 'Right from the beginning,' he explained, 'my marriage was a failure so I had no guilt about fooling around. It helped me get over the boring times - and it became habitual. It was better than drugs because you couldn't overdose on it. If you'd had enough, your body didn't work anymore, and it was as simple as that - so I thought it was quite healthy.' [18]

That's isn't to say that Bill didn't care about Diane, now cooing over their infant son, Stephen, for all the muddle there had been since the breakthrough with 'Come On' between Bill the husband and Bill the 'available' pop idol. Even if mutterings about his extra-marital antics hadn't filtered through to Diane, a man so preoccupied with his job is apt to be an inattentive spouse, and it may not have occurred to Bill that there was a limit to wifely loyalty and affection, even if neither of them were infatuated newly-weds, holding hands around Beckenham.

If Wyman's marital status was not to be stressed, Andrew Oldham was desperate to suppress altogether Brian Jones's illegitimate children and his cavalier conduct towards their mothers. While his private sweetness still peeped out, many of those closest to him were nauseated by his callous treatment of girlfriends, past and present. Having closed the door on Pat Andrews, his latest flame was a builder's daughter, Linda Lawrence, who he'd met in the midst of the group's several summer Tuesdays at Windsor's Ricky Tick club.

Before the year was out, she was to announce that she was expecting a baby - her first, his third. While such a situation wasn't exactly water off a duck's back to Brian, he appeared to accept it as only slightly more of an occupational hazard than some palais scrubber capsizing the expected no-strings dalliance by getting inconveniently clingy. His desire was verging on the satyric, and he didn't need yesterday's conquest turning up unbidden at the next gig when he was emitting subliminal signals from the stage to someone else that tonight was going to be her night, either in the romantic seclusion of a backstage broom-cupboard or when they eased themselves between the sheets in a hotel that was slightly less grim than that in which the other Stones were staying.

Always on the look-out, he liked to have the evening's sex life sorted out before the last number. Then he'd disappear until the van was almost ready to leave. At the last minute, he might climb in, zipping up his flies or wiping sticky hands on his clothes. The others would eye him slyly. They knew. He'd made sure of that.

That Brian was a sexual braggart, they'd long been aware and that he was underhand and manipulative, they had strong suspicions - suspicions which were to be confirmed by Andrew Oldham when an implication in one of Jones's interminable bouts of petulance that autumn sparked Oldham's decision to expose the secret deal with Eric Easton about the division of profits.

In a bandroom somewhere in the north-east, he picked a moment when no hushing up was possible. After the game had been given away, there was a tense silence. Every face was transfixed with the amazement of someone who has suddenly discovered that a friend has been cheating and lying to him. Brian sort of smirked. That was all, but from that instance of his disgrace, he became - imperceptibly at times - the morose outsider in a group that he was to make his enemy. Though he remained chained to it, this was the only way to support his degradation. If the Stones couldn't see that he was their greatest asset, then he'd be their greatest liability. After doing so, he might then either instigate a new beginning or anticipate a more absolute fall from grace by destroying his former self. In the end, he was to do both.

Back in the present, however, Brian, deposed as *de jure* as well as *de facto* 'leader', prepared for his first night in the same bed-and-breakfast accommodation as everyone else. The next morning, he'd be snubbed as they sat at a separate table in the dining area. A spat between Jones and Richards not long afterwards culminated with fisti-cuffs. According to Wyman, 'Keith gave Brian a black eye when he ate Keith's meat pie or something.' [19]

Behind this overt act, as well as whispered off-mike spite and momentary, if penetrating, eye-contact, Jones was the unconscious victim of intensifying character assassinations over venomous pints in a pub's murkiest corner. Flare-ups in which he was central figure increased in frequency, in turns more insidious and less polite - or so it seemed to him in his worsening paranoia. Whether speaking or singing, he felt that he couldn't open his mouth without one or other of the rest criticising or contradicting him. Was it just him or was it that, as well as cold looks and cold shoulders, they'd taken to badgering him with enough minor problems to start World War III; being unnecessarily pernicketty about his volume, tone and tuning during what were becoming known as 'soundchecks'; making an issue of seeming trifles - such as Jones forgetting to sing one of the 'That's what I want' antiphonies in 'Money' - and forcing him to chat them up, almost like he would a girl, whenever he wanted the smallest favour done?

Fighting back, Brian, a minority of one, employed the same weapons, but, while he won victories, most of them were Pyrrhic, and he was always going to lose the war. Months after Andrew's revelation, Phil May would be privy to an incident when Jones, in a friend's car, travelled separately from the other Stones to an engagement in Portsmouth. An overcharging alternator brought the vehicle to a halt between Guildford and Petersfield. Anticipating the Automobile Association patrolman's shaking head, Brian hailed the group's van which happened to be passing twenty minutes later, but it nosed past, the passengers flicking vulgar signs at their open-mouthed and stranded colleague.

How could they be so nasty? How could they? The business over his - now discontinued - larger cut of concert income was rankling still, and the other Stones were quite ready to cut off their noses to spite their faces by mounting the stage at Portsmouth without one who would be missed both musically and visually.

At a time when irrecoverable schisms within groups were frowned upon - because the chemistry of the four interlocking personalities within the fortune-making Beatles had proved so potent - it was necessary for the tempest to drop, and Oldham to steer the Stones' manner towards the ostracised Jones to, if not geniality, then the grimly urbane. Though time wouldn't heal altogether, there came a reconciliation, and then long periods when Keith and Mick, if not Ian, would feel almost as close to Brian as they had during the year of struggle that had preceded 'Come On'. In-jokes side-splitting to no-one else would have the caste-within-a-caste howling with laughter, and Brian's heart would feel like it would burst through its rib-cage when Keith smiled almost gently at him when they were head-to-head over guitars again like at Edith Grove in the beginning, and the exchange of a civil word or two with Mick would give way every so often to what might be construed as a compliment.

Yet solicitude and brusque affection could swing in seconds to the re-opening of old wounds, and Brian's concentration in studio, van or tour bus would be split as his ears strained to catch murmured intrigue as the dirty tricks, the antipathy, the sleights of verbal judo and further mind games resumed.

In the more immediate aftershock of Oldham blowing Jones's cover, the dust hadn't settled when the group had zigzagged back to London for one of the final sessions of the Studio 51 residency, where The Downliners Sect were readying themselves to take over just as The Yardbirds were at the Crawdaddy. As well as an 'atmosphere' you could slice with a spade, a shift in the power structure of the Stones was perceivable to Don Craine: 'When I walked in on one of their rehearsals at Studio 51, Brian was definitely being edged out. The big huddle there was Mick, Keith and Andrew. No-one was saying a word to Brian, who was looking seriously peeved. Andrew was talking about simplifying the image. One front man worked better, he reckoned, but Brian was already starting to dislike the fact that Mick was getting the adulation - and *vice-versa*.'

Although members of The Beatles and the countless acts who copied them took turns on lead vocals, managers and producers of other groups were still singling out someone to be its implied Cliff Richard - with all the attendant resentment that was often created. There was tension, for example, when organist Alan Price - from whose Alan Price Rhythm And Blues Combo was springing The Animals - found himself skulking beyond a main spotlight occupied by singing non-instrumentalist Eric Burdon - who was to acknowledge graciously that Price '*was* The Animals to a certain degree.' [20]

Amassing as tremendous a grassroots following in Newcastle-upon-Tyne as The Beatles had in Liverpool, The Animals were to be seized by EMI in the New Year - as would be The Downliners Sect and The Yardbirds becoming almost as major an attraction of the Greater London branch of the British R&B movement as the Stones. Around the same time as Decca acquired the Stones, the rival company had already grabbed The Mann-Hugg Blues Brothers. They were to rename themselves Manfred Mann, just as the reconstituted Art Wood Combo were to become The Artwoods after Decca signed them several months later. Both were now trading likewise in worthy and open-ended arrangements of mostly R&B set-works - 'Down The Road Apiece', 'Hoochie Coochie Man', 'Mojo Working', 'Route 66', 'Smokestack Lightning' and so forth - at Studio 51, Eel Pie Island and the Marquee.

'Manfred (Mann, organist) and Mike (Vickers, multi-instrumentalist) were playing in a modern jazz quartet, and decided they weren't going to make a living out of that,' explained Paul Jones, Manfred Mann's freshly-enlisted vocalist - and the same Paul Jones who'd partnered Brian Jones at the Ealing Club - 'They had no feeling for rhythm-and-blues, but they knew they didn't want to play rock 'n' roll. So for them it was a compromise between music and money, so when you listen now to the Manfred Mann version of "Smokestack Lightning", you can hear that it's played by musicians who didn't have a terrific amount of feeling for that stuff - but we wanted hits, no two ways about it. We saw those girls screaming at the Stones, and I wanted a piece of that.' [21]

Manfred Mann's first half-year as EMI recording artistes were not encouraging. Yet, despite two flop singles, the former Mann-Hugg Blues Brothers were mutating into as much of a pop group as, say, The

Swinging Blue Jeans, complete with uniform stage outfits - albeit jettisoned as quickly as the Stones had theirs - balanced by a *soupcon* of non-irregularity in Manfred's beatnik beard as distinctive as Hank Marvin's hornrims, Johnny Kidd's eyepatch, Don Craine's perpetual deerstalker - and Mick Jagger's lips.

A Manfred Mann lookalike nowadays, Mike Cooper had formed The Blues Committee which, for all his blues purism, 'ended up doing material that the Stones did.' The Yardbirds, however, 'made a conscious decision *not* to do the same numbers the Stones did,' pronounced drummer Jim McCarty, 'though we drew our repertoire from the same albums by Jimmy Reed, Muddy Waters, Slim Harpo, Chuck Berry, Howlin' Wolf... The Stones did Harpo's "I'm A King Bee"; we did his "Scratch My Back". We did Wolf's "Smokestack Lightning"; they did "Little Red Rooster" - though we did "Down The Road Apiece", which they did eventually, but we never tried "Route 66".'

*Circa* mid-1963, The Yardbirds had risen from the ashes of The Metropolitan Blues Quartet, with McCarty, singing mouth-organist Keith Relf, Paul Samwell-Smith on bass and guitarists Chris Dreja and Anthony Topham. As it had been with Dick Taylor in the Stones, student Topham left the group in the interests of higher education. He was replaced as lead guitarist by the older Eric 'Slowhand' Clapton, once of the Engineers - as was Manfred Mann's Tom McGuinness - who'd backed a Scouse-accented singer named Casey Jones until the first indications that the Merseybeat bandwagon was slowing down.

Most consumers of today's cultured 'contemporary' pop for the over-forties have taught their children to regard The Yardbirds as a springboard for the nurtured prowess and neo-deification of Clapton, who was no more eloquent an instrumentalist than Topham, but possessed stronger stage presence at the Crawdaddy, where his overamplified Fender duelled with Relf's surging harmonica during the 'rave-ups' that would convince both onlookers and recording managers that, as the Stones were pushing R&B-derived southern pop into the hit parade, The Yardbirds were poised to do likewise.

Sniffing round them too was Brian Jones, already making contingency plans should 'Come On' really be Keith's 'beginning of the end'. [22] Jim McCarty would remember Jones furrowing a half-serious brow about nurturing The Yardbirds for greener pastures as learner-manager Andrew Loog Oldham was still trying to do with the Stones, and Bill Wyman, as far as Stones' duties would allow, was contemplating doing with a couple of promising groups local to him, in order to recoup more than memories, golden and otherwise, when the Stones' time was up. Nevertheless, such a liaison between Brian and The Yardbirds progressed no further than an informal chat round Keith and Jane Relf's parents' house in Richmond. 'It was an ego thing for Brian,' reckoned Jim, 'To show that he could cope with both playing with the Stones and managing us, but it fizzled out, probably because he realised exactly how much time and money - of which he could spare neither - needed to be invested.'

Brian - along with Ian Stewart - was also 'interested' in The Tridents, formerly Nightshift, whose lead guitarist, Jeff Beck, had borrowed from Stewart *Folk Festival Of The Blues*. However, Beck was prone to 'going off on a tangent, and everyone would laugh and say, "Play some proper blues"' [23] as he tossed in *leitmotifs* that alternated Oriental-sounding exotica with hackneyed clichés of showbiz cabaret. Beck was to join The Yardbirds in 1965 after Eric Clapton, uneasy about his colleagues' increasingly commercial outlook, transferred to John Mayall's Bluesbreakers, who'd opined that The Yardbirds were 'appalling'. [24]

Mike Cooper thought likewise about another R&B group of the same freshly-bottled vintage, The Pretty Things. 'Don't be misled by the same,' he wrote in his diary after catching them at the 100 Club, 'This group are all atrocious musicians led by a sickening effigy of Mick Jagger... Jagger and the Stones have just succeeded in making a name for themselves and already some maniac, an anaemic-looking punk, is on his tail.'

The Things' origins lay in 1962's Bricklayer's Arms rehearsals that had resulted in the assembly of the first edition of the Stones - with Dick Taylor on bass. After he quit, Dick kept in touch, and was pleased that his old mates had 'come on a lot' at the Crawdaddy, but the entry of 'Come On' into the Top Fifty on 25th July, 1963 was a disquieting moment for him. A secret relief at departing the shabbiest nook of showbusiness imaginable gave way to reflection that the rewards of being in an R&B outfit might now extend beyond beer money and a laugh.

Reverting to a more comfortable role as lead guitarist, he formed The Pretty Things - named after the Bo Diddley shuffle - in September, 1963 with fellow art student Phil May, who sang and blew mouth-organ. He'd recall that 'Dick was the first guitarist I ever played with, and, because of that, I had no yardstick by which to judge him - though it would be obvious that Keith Richards had learnt a lot from him. Only after about five years did I begin to appreciate how good Dick was. It was a bit like taking your wife for granted'.

It was necessary, however, to place a *Melody Maker* small ad for a rhythm guitarist to anchor Taylor's attractively rough-hewn solos and riffs. And, as it had been with Bill Wyman at the Wetherby Arms, trainee insurance clerk and former Dartford Grammar pupil, Brian Pendleton's splendid amplifier was a deciding factor when he was among hopefuls at the consequent auditions.

With John Stax on bass and a temporary drummer, the Things made their public debut at the Central College of Art with borrowed equipment and May's microphone fed through a juke-box. They were to pay further dues in December with 'an eight hour stint at the Royal Academy.' shuddered Phil, 'When I came off stage, I had blood coming up from my throat.' Early fans included Malcolm McLaren and punk Methuselah Charlie Harper, awaiting respective distant roles as The Sex Pistols' manager and fronting The UK Subs.

With spontaneity overruling expertise, the stage act was more open-ended than that of the Stones, becoming at one point, a continuous performance underpinned throughout by Bo Diddley's *der der-der der-der der der* beat, and May extemporizing from full-blooded screech to *sotto voce* intimacy. Phil's straining attack and natural coarseness invited inevitable comparisons to Jagger - and, as Mike Cooper had shown, not all of them were flattering.

Yet there was much fraternization between the Stones and the groups that followed in their wake as exemplified by a remarkable jam session at Eel Pie Island with a shower that included Bill Wyman, Ian Stewart, Jeff Beck and session guitarist Jimmy Page. Everybody took turns on lead vocals, but the essence of this impromptu display was Beck and Page breaking sweat on duelling six-strings. Then there was Jagger clambering on stage to duet with Keith Relf on 'Bright Lights Big City' when The Yardbirds were on at the Marquee or Phil May borrowing Mick's book containing lyrics of 'every Chuck Berry, every Bo Diddley, every Jimmy Reed song', and Mick admitting that he found Phil's onstage gyrations instructive. He noted too, Paul Jones's spasmodic crouching and jumping about with Manfred Mann, who'd just been commissioned to pen a theme for a newish ITV pop series, *Ready Steady Go*, to replace The Surfaris' 'Wipeout' instrumental. What emerged was '54321', a catchier opus than 'Come On' with *a la mode* harmonica laid on thicker.

This was yet to be cast adrift on the vinyl oceans when, with the M1 only half-completed, Ian Stewart was coping with the tactical problems of moving the Stones from A to B in order to arrive on time for a ten-minute spot twice nightly during the opening half on their first proper round-Britain tour. After purported negotiations for a support slot to Jerry Lee Lewis had fallen through, this was to consist of thirty-odd dates beginning on 29th September, low on the bill to the all-American Everly Brothers, Bo Diddley and, flown over after the first posters had been printed, a luminary who had exchanged the billowing drapes and overhanging pompadour he'd sported in *The Girl Can't Help It* for sober attire and a bristled scalp. Nothing, however, could belittle him in Keith Richards' eyes: 'The most exciting moment of my life was appearing on the same stage as Little Richard'. [25]

The trek was to finish close to home at the Hammersmith Odeon on 3rd November - two days after the Stones' next single was issued. It wasn't 'Poison Ivy' after all, but a new song that had come their way through association with The Beatles. This had become a double-edged sword, now that John, Paul, George and Ringo were about to become part of the 'Establishment' as a result of their allotted four numbers on the Royal Variety Show three days later. Short haircuts would still be forced upon sons of provincial Britain, and pop was not yet an acceptable career option, but parents laughed along with children at John Lennon's chirpy 'rattle yer jewellery' ad lib to the royal balcony, which to teenagers like David Cook - later 1970s pop star David Essex, but then an amateur drummer - 'meant that they couldn't be any good.' [26]

Closer to the heart of the matter, the Stones had an inkling that their four northern friends were now unable to step down from a carousel that was revolving too fast. They were aware too that the gift of a Lennon-McCartney composition was like a licence to print banknotes after every original track on the Beatles' debut LP had been covered by another artist, whether, say, 'There's A Place' by The Kestrels, 'Misery' by Kenny Lynch, 'I Saw Her Standing There' by both

Anthony Newley and Duffy Power or, most spectacularly of all, 'Do You Want To Know A Secret' by Billy J. Kramer.

A demo of this chart topper had been offered to Kramer prior to the album's release - and a similar favour was bestowed upon the Stones when John and Paul completed 'I Wanna Be Your Man' as the group's career-stabilising second single, virtually to order when looking in at a Stones afternoon rehearsal at Studio 51 one September Tuesday. A near-identical arrangement was to be selected for *With The Beatles*, but this wasn't to be in the shops until 22nd November, thus giving the Stones a clear run for three weeks.

'I Wanna Be Your Man' was, however, no *magnum opus*. Indeed, after visiting the Stones, Lennon taught it to Ringo Starr, suited as it was to the drummer's Johnny-one-note rant. Yet, although Starr sang and played simultaneously on this *With The Beatles* track, it lacked the hungry drive that the Stones were to invest into their improvement - with Brian's bottleneck solo loud and clear - on a slapdash composition, and, if it was a compliment, it was to be their version that would be caricatured aurally on The Barron Knights' 'Call Up The Groups' comic medley in 1964.

'We weren't going to give them anything great, were we?' was to be Lennon's rhetorical confession in one of his last interviews. [27] Had he and McCartney done so, Brian Epstein may have felt that they were giving too much of a leg up to potentially dangerous competitors. This would be justifiable on the evidence of the *NME* readers' popularity poll for 1963, which placed the Stones behind The Springfields, The Shadows, Gerry and the Pacemakers, The Searchers and The Beatles, but ahead of Freddie and the Dreamers, Brian Poole and his Tremeloes, and The Hollies.

While this was contrary to the group's standing in raw market terms then - exemplified by their one minor chart entry and a picked-to-click follow-up against Freddie's three Top Five smashes - considered ovations had unfurled rapidly into wall-to-wall screams on that all-styles-served-here package with, ostensibly, the three North American acts as the principal draws. So a pattern was set, though the Stones remained on a billing equal to that of a certain Mickie Most - back in England after four years as South Africa's riposte to Elvis Presley, and coming to prefer the retractable sphere of the recording studio to the stage - and Julie Grant, who Eric Easton had visualised as a successor to fading schoolgirl pop idol Helen Shapiro. The last of Julie's three small chart entries had stopped just short of the Top Thirty, but there'd been high hopes of her just-issued 'Hello Love' as there'd been of 'Sea Cruise', Mickie Most's follow-up to 'Mr. Porter', which had made the Top Fifty - just - in summer.

Mickie gyrated, snarled and rolled on his back like a man possessed, but still 'Sea Cruise' died a deletion-racked death, along with 'Hello Love', while Don and Phil Everly conducted themselves with observed good humour when followers of the home-grown group had, at one stop, hurled screwed-up paper cups stagewards and bawled 'We want the Stones!' in unison even as the siblings gave 'em 'Bye Bye Love', *risqué* 'Wake Up Little Susie', 1961's chart-topping 'Temptation' and further smashes as old as the hills.

By the homeward leg of the expedition, no-one could pretend that they - or Little Richard or Bo Diddley - were the main attractions any more, even if none of them would relinquish any co-headlining supremacy implied in the tour programme, despite the Brothers' last three singles fighting shyer of the Top Twenty than 'Come On'. Nonetheless, at least they had a backlog of hits - unlike Diddley whose 'Pretty Thing'/'Road Runner' single, repromoted as the tour got underway, would be his UK chart debut, touching an apogee of Number Thirty-Four. Yet this modest climb on top of a dredging-up of 'Bo Diddley' by the late Buddy Holly, which had reached Number Four in the UK charts over summer, had elevated Diddley to a little more than mere cult celebrity in Britain. Brian Jones would treasure the memory of 'actually playing harmonica with Bo. You don't forget the day a long-standing dream comes true' [28] - though Bill Wyman, keeper of the secrets, would recollect Jones's non-arrival at the *Saturday Club* session where this was supposed to have taken place.

If less revered by the Stones than Diddley, the energetic Little Richard had had considerably more commercial triumphs, though not in recent years, having gained but one minor hit since his enrolment at theological college in 1959 and a subsequent ministry. While it had been only recently that Richard's show had metamorphosed from a gospel revue to a straight rock 'n' roll presentation, albeit trading 'heys' and 'yeahs' with his audiences like a glory-bound preacher-congregation interplay. Mick Jagger would be diligent in making observations of Richard's onstage activities for incorporation into his own, even if, like a slightly batty favourite uncle, 'The Georgia Peach' was neither sinister nor sexy when 'he drove the whole house into a complete frenzy.' marvelled Mick, 'like an evangelistic meeting.' [29]

Richard was, therefore, received with an affection that was not extended to The Everly Brothers, though Bill Wyman was captivated by the duo's bass player, Joey Paige, as Charlie Watts was by their 'fabulous drummer, Jim Gordon. We'd never seen a band as slick as that.' From the wings too, both Charlie and Mick were captivated by the 'incredible' Jerome Green, who wielded the maracas that coalesced the undercurrent to Bo Diddley's eponymous signature tune. [17]

While eclipsed by the Stones, Bo, Don and Phil, and Little Richard were still paid as per contract, and stayed in pre-booked luxury suites. As well as being less certain that they'd sleep in comfortable beds each night, the Stones were short of ready cash and were driven to ingratiating themselves with others in the cast in hopes of largesse for the basic needs of palates becoming coarsened by chips-with-everything meals in roadside snack bars. 'I was impressed with how polite they were,' beamed Julie Grant, 'They were always very nice to me and my Mum, who was my chaperone with me being only seventeen. They didn't have much money, and on one occasion, my Mum gave them some money for fish-and-chips.' [30]

When the expedition had reached the Cheltenham Odeon on 8th October, because Brian stayed with his parents, the budget could be stretched so that the others could be put up at the town's Irving Hotel where the Americans were, and where Mick sat in with the resident Tony Faye and his Fayetones while Bill, Charlie, Ian and Keith held court at the bar. Yet Pat Andrews had been surprised at how close the group were to break-even point: 'I didn't have any money either, but I'd made friends with some firemen, who were in attendance at the show. They said they'd get me in. During the interval, Ian Stewart found me and said that Brian wanted me to come backstage. Once again, it was almost like Brian and I had seen each other only yesterday, and he said, "Do us a favour. Go across the road and get me some fags." All the other Stones fumbled in their pockets for just about enough change so I could buy them cigarettes too.'

There was a reunion too - for Jones anyway - with Richard Hattrell: 'After the Cheltenham show, I tracked Brian down to the Waikiki, a club patronised by the town's trendiest people. He was completely on his own in the corner. I gathered there'd been some quarrel earlier with one of the others, probably Keith, and Brian was very unhappy, very fed-up, but he invited me down to a private after-hours session in the hotel. I never saw him again after that.'

Neither did Pat, following lunch with her toddler's father in a high street cafe the next day - because it was still possible for a Stone to take the air after breakfast without public fuss. However, they'd be accosted for autographs in corner shops and be subject to acute watchfulness in lonely petrol stations with the resumption of dates in familiar haunts that were becoming less and less familiar, and in hitherto unknown venues in unknown towns like, the Urmston Baths - boarded over for dances - the Kayser Bondor Ballroom in Baldock and, on Christmas Eve, Leek Town Hall.

This jaunt was typified by a midnight matinee in Tottenham's Club Noreik four days later where Keith Neville of the supporting Moquettes - who vied with Mike Cooper's Blues Committee as Reading's boss group - was astounded when, 'On our arrival at the stage door, the girls were screaming and getting very excited, thinking that we were the Stones. So you can imagine the atmosphere inside. It was heaving, just a sea of heads.' [31]

That one-nighters were becoming ticklish operations was instanced further by individual invasions of the stage from a majority of iron-bladdered girls who'd arrived ridiculously early to queue round the block, and Charlie Watts's rage on the occasion - or, perhaps, not such an occasion nowadays - when he was almost killed with kindness by libidinous females not much younger than himself, who ripped his new pink shirt so thoroughly that he could never wear it again.

'He suddenly got thrown into the thing that was really not part of his self image,' said Keith Richards. [1] There were, however, off-stage compensations. With the Stones' second 45, 'I Wanna Be Your Man' heading towards the Top Twenty, and no steady girlfriend since drifting apart, briefly, from Shirley Ann Shepherd, Watts realised that he, as much as the others, had access to plenty of unsteady ones for whom his face on the very first edition of BBC's long-running *Top Of The Pops* - broadcast on New Year's Day - proved a powerful aphrodisiac.

Yet, with middle-aged candour, Charlie Watts would insist that 'I wasn't interested in being a pop idol. It's not the world I come from. It's not what I wanted to be, and I still think it's silly.' [32]

For those ignorant of Charlie's instant distaste for stardom, and his group's living and travelling conditions, the Stones had 'gone beyond' - maybe as far as any group of their sort could go. They'd breathed the air round Bo Diddley, been on television, and ventured into the Top Twenty interior - entering at Number Fifteen and peaking at Twelve, and this time without a borderline, yuk-for-a-buck single, and without being obliged to dress the same. As for returning there or even clambering higher, well, they'd have to cross that bridge when they came to it.

Notes

1. *Keith Richards In His Own Words* ed. M. St. Michael (Omnibus, 1994)
2. *Q*, May, 1995
3. *Jazz News*, 21st November, 1962
4. *Record Mirror*, 8th June, 1963
5. *Mersey Beat*, 14th June, 1963
6. *Q*, October, 1988
7. *Q*, October, 1988
8. *Daily Telegraph*, 10th July, 1993
9. *New Musical Express*, 23rd August, 1963
10. *New Musical Express*, 1st November, 1957
11. Press release quoted in *Will There Really Be A Morning?* by F. Farmer (Allison & Busby, 1974)
12. *New Musical Express*, 27th September, 1963
13. *Record Collector*, July, 1989
14. *Record Collector*, July, 1995
15. *Who's Really Who* by C. Miller (Sphere, 1987)
16. *New Musical Express*, 12th March, 1964
17. *Rhythm*, June, 2001
18. *Record Collector*, April, 2001
19. *Record Collector*, April, 2001
20. *Animal Tracks* by S. Egan (Helter Skelter, 2001)
21. *Rock 'N' Reel*, No. 35, winter, 2001
22. *Rolling Stone*, 5th November, 1987
23. *The Yardbirds* by A. Clayson (Backbeat, 2002)
24. *Call Up The Groups!* by A. Clayson (Blandford, 1983)
25. *The Life And Times Of Little Richard: The Quasar Of Rock* by C. White (Pan, 1985))
26. *Melody Maker*, 2nd November, 1971
27. *Revolution In The Head* by I. MacDonald, (Pimlico, 1995)

28. *New Musical Express*, 17th July, 1964
29. *New Musical Express*, 8th February, 1964)
30. *And The Beat Still Goes On*, February, 2003
31. *Reading Chronicle*, 1st May, 2002
32. *Sunday Times*, 10th August, 2002

## Chapter Ten
## Group Scene '64

*'People thought, when we started, that we were strange to look at. Now we're lumbered with the image' - Bill Wyman* [1]

Kindly, Keith Richards championed as his 'favourite band' in 'Lifelines', The Flintstones, an all-purpose horn-driven combo who, on the Everlys-Richard-Diddley package, had backed Julie Grant and Mickie Most - who also became 'very friendly with the Stones. Their music was exactly the music I liked.' [2]

As would-be record producer Mickie's new pals were spoken for, he could only be sold more profitably on the R&B and untutored stage-craft of the yet-unsigned Animals - still called The Alan Price Rhythm And Blues Combo - after he and the Stones witnessed a late-night session by the group in a local club when the tour had reached Newcastle. Exchanging contact details with them, Most was to summon The Animals to London where, in February, 1964, he oversaw the recording of 'Baby Let Me Take You Home', their debut 45, and the harbinger of 'House Of The Rising Sun', which set the group on the path to international stardom.

Most had first attempted to break cover in his new field with a demo tape by Dave Berry and the Cruisers he brought to Decca - for whom he'd been signed for one-shot 'Mr. Porter'. However, while Mike Smith, Dick Rowe's A&R lieutenant, liked Berry and the group, he found Mickie's plans for them unworkable, and decided to occupy the central chair at the console himself.

Dave was in transition from R&B to more generalised pop when he was among The Swinging Blue Jeans, The Cheynes - whose bean-pole of a drummer, Mick Fleetwood was to be the 'Fleetwood' in Fleetwood Mac - Marty Wilde and his Wildcats and the rest of a moveable feast of support acts or, as some of them preferred, 'guest stars' on 'Group Scene '64', a winter package co-headlined by the Stones and The Ronettes.

During this jaunt, whenever Keith wanted to kill time that hung heavy in the dressing rooms by picking at guitars with someone other than Brian, he sought the particular company of Alan Taylor of the Cruisers. This may have aided the sublimation of an apparent crush he'd developed on The Ronettes' Ronnie, soon to be Mrs. Phil Spector.

Still a virgin and possibly unaware of the depth of his silent worship, she found her admirer 'not so much shy as quiet. I could make him laugh, but most of the time, nothing was funny to him. He was very much himself in his own room and his own world.' [3]

Other musical youths on the tour weren't so reticent when seeking the favours of individual Ronettes, although the Stones seemed a little stand-offish at first, owing to a telegram received by Andrew Oldham from a morbidly jealous Spector insisting that there was to be no communication between the two groups that wasn't a professional imperative. After a while, however, this directive was being defied quite openly.

Deferentially, the Stones, in an inversion of 'ladies first' protocol, took the stage before The Ronettes, who were, in any case, of slightly higher rank in the gradation of pop via million-selling 'Be My Baby' the previous autumn; their latest single, similarly infantine - and Spector-penned - 'Baby I Love You', destined to be almost-but-not-quite as big, and the impending release of a debut album. Because the Stones hadn't yet harried even the domestic Top Ten, Decca hadn't been prepared to chance more than an eponymous EP, pressed up for issue a fortnight after Christmas, as a holding operation between 'I Wanna Be Your Man' and a yet-undecided third single.

Anyone awaiting seething musical outrage from this item of merchandise was to be disappointed - unless substituting harmonica for the usual guitar or piano lead instrument on 'Money' was considered so. A token Chuck Berry number, 'Bye Bye Johnny', one of his A-sides from 1960, was of more workmanlike persuasion, but 'You Better Move On', the Stones first released attempt at a slow ballad, came to be the EP's chief selling point. It was a sound rather than adventurous choice, this belated cover of the first and biggest US hit by Arthur Alexander, a black vocalist from Alabama, whose songs, if not records, had already been brought to a European audience recently via the attentions of such as Johnny Kidd and the Pirates and The Beatles, who'd already put out versions of Alexander's 'A Shot Of Rhythm And Blues' and 'Anna' respectively.

The EP was rounded off with the hated 'Poison Ivy'. Not wishing to see 'Fortune Teller' go to waste either, Decca foisted it onto *Saturday Club*, a 'various artists' compilation album in the shops on the same late January day as one containing 'Come On' and 'I Wanna

Be Your Man', and entitled *Ready Steady Go* after what had become by then, perhaps, the most innovative and atmospheric pop series of the 1960s, prospering as it did on interaction between performers and audiences.

Though the latter touched the edge of the LP Top Twenty, such collections were mere market ballast in an era when singles mattered most - though a handful of EPs, including one by The Dave Clark Five containing *their* 'Poison Ivy', were seeping into the *singles* Top Thirty throughout 1963's early spring. The Stones joined this elite, and their EP was still hovering 'twixt Twelve and Twenty when, for the next tour - titled 'All Stars '64', and beginning a week after the finish of the last one - they surrendered needlessly their headlining status to John Leyton and Mike Sarne, each of whose solitary chart-toppers, 'Johnny Remember Me' and 'Come Outside', [4] were far behind them.

While cursed too with compromising association with the wrong side of the 1963 watershed, Jet Harris, gone solo and addled with alcohol, gave himself no help whatsoever one night by introducing his backing combo, The Innocents - drawn from Bobby Angelo and the Tuxedos of 'Baby Sittin'' fame - four times before stopping during the opening chords of his latest single, 'Big Bad Bass', and stumbling into the wings. With good reason to be more justifiably apprehensive about being upstaged than Jet was, or The Everly Brothers had been, John, Mike, Billie Davis - Jet's girlfriend - Don Spencer and other solo entertainers in an age of groups, would soldier on like the troupers they were as the eclipsing howls and chants for the Stones welled up to a pitch where you drowned in noise, and girls went crazy, tearing their hair, wiping their eyes, rocking foetally and flapping scarves and programmes in the air.

Not helping either on the final night - at Morecambe's Winter Garden - was Charlie Watts and a piggy-backed Mick Jagger blundering across the stage during Billie Davis's spot, and Keith Richards stumbling upon a wind-machine in a props cupboard, and operating it with an excess of enthusiasm during John Leyton's rendition of 'Wild Wind', the then-half-forgotten 1961 follow-up to 'Johnny Remember Me'.

As if the entire audience had sat on tin-tacks, the keening volume had risen to its loudest during the Stones' performance that evening - as it had on all dates towards the end of February when the single after

'I Wanna Be Your Man' went straight in at Number Eleven. A revival of 'Not Fade Away', the Buddy Holly B-side that had so besotted a Dartford Grammar schoolboy in 1958, was to come to rest within an ace of Number One, colliding with the descent of Manfred Mann's '54321' and, of more direct interest to the Stones, overtaking 'That Girl Belongs To Yesterday' by Gene Pitney, as besuited and short-haired as Eric Easton. Nevertheless, bar the remote Elvis, he - with Roy Orbison and, though hits were thin on the ground after 1961, Jerry Lee Lewis - came to command the most devoted UK following during a lean time for North American pop artistes, respected as he was for his under-stated stage persona if not his distinctive dentist's drill-like whine that you either liked or you didn't. There were no half-measures.

Late in 1963, 'Twenty-Four Hours From Tulsa' had been Gene's first big British strike after one of that year's predecessors, 'Mecca', had arrived too late to prevent a cover by The Cheetahs, a unit from a Birmingham suburb, snatching the slight chart honours. In the hiatus between the two in November, he had met and befriended the Stones when sharing the same dressing room for an edition of *Thank Your Lucky Stars*. They were introduced by Andrew Oldham, who, after the opening platitudes, began speiling in top gear, and was to leave the building as the globetrotting American's UK publicist. When Pitney returned to Europe in the New Year, it was to him that Oldham turned to help loosen the tension at an exploratory 'Not Fade Away' session at the close of January back at IBC, where the Stones, after months on the road, seemed to be getting on each other's nerves too much to achieve any satisfactory result. For the next studio date - 4 February - Andrew was going to humbug them into a more constructive frame of mind by bringing in Pitney, an outside party of such eminence that, like a vicar in a BBC situation comedy, his mere presence would compel them to rein their nonsense.

Breaking the strike-happy mood too was Oldham, escorting into the studio the more self-important Phil Spector, for whom Pitney, a songwriter of some merit, had composed 'He's A Rebel', a hit for The Crystals in 1962. Spector had crossed the Atlantic to keep an eye on Ronnie, and to assess whether The Everly Brothers, Little Richard, Roy Orbison, Del Shannon and other US icons' round-eyed accounts of recent first-hand experiences of what was gripping Britain's beat-crazy teenagers had enough substance to be worthy of the attention of the Svengali of Sound.

After Gene poured everyone a shot of brandy from a duty-free bottle, the shirtiness and provocative indifference dissipated as the group, aided by their distinguished visitors, buckled down to 'Not Fade Away', now reworked by Richards on acoustic guitar to sound more like Holly's vibrant revival of 'Bo Diddley', and with Jones adding piquant harmonica icing just as the cake was baked. With this task completed, there was sufficient adrenaline left to tape further tracks including 'Now I've Got A Witness' (Like Uncle Phil And Uncle Gene)' - a twelve-bar instrumental with Brian extemporising on harmonica over a riff borrowed from Tommy Tucker's just-released 'Hi-Heel Sneakers', and 'Little By Little', essentially a jammed rehash of Jimmy Reed's 'Shame Shame Shame' with different lyrics, which were put together in a studio alcove by Jagger and Spector in the time it took for the other Stones to put down the backing.

During the evening's idler moments, 'Uncle Gene' and 'Uncle Phil' lent critical ears to some unaided compositions by Jagger and Richards. Belying Mick's earlier assertion about the Stones' disinclination to attempt self-penned material, their breaking cover, however reluctantly, as a songwriting duo at last had been down to Oldham's steady incitement, bringing up the subject seemingly every time they spoke - which was frequent as the three had been sharing, since autumn 1963, a second-floor flat that, if in a rather shabby 1930s terrace in West Hampstead's bedsit land, was palatial compared to 102, Edith Grove.

If Keith is to be believed, it was at 33, Mapesbury Gardens that Andrew 'just locked us in a kitchen for a day, and said, "When you come out, make sure you come out with a song". To me - and to Mick - writing a song was as different as someone who makes a saddle for a horse, and someone who puts the shoes on [but] it gives you the confidence to think, well, if we can write one, we can write two.' [5]

As neither had learned to write musical script, they were relatively untroubled by the formal do's and don'ts that traditionally afflict creative flow. There were only the stylistic clichés and habits ingrained since they'd first strummed guitars as teenagers. They hadn't much of a clue how to go about what they'd taken on, but, muddling on, they applied themselves to getting a clearer picture from the confusion, learning what they could *in situ* and unwittingly dismissing many ingrained preconceptions and introducing new ones as they grappled with their - initially shallow - muse, drawing from virtually every musical idiom they had ever encountered and endeavouring to disguise sources of inspiration in hopes that nothing would remain too embarrassingly familiar. In a spirit of evaporating bad grace - and handsomely endowed with a capacity to try-try again - they were soon as bereft of ante-start agonies as Ernie Wise when penning one of his awful plays, and had the misplaced confidence to send a tape of a ditty entitled 'Give Me Your Hand' - which was 'nothing great' either - to The Beatles.

Among other churned-out efforts, 'Tell Me (You're Coming Back)', if a slightly drippy ballad, was the only one considered even marginally usable by the Stones, while the most risible was 'When A Girl Loves A Boy'. From its very title, you may be able to guess what it was like. Without exception, the rest of these early attempts at matching John and Paul's difficult yardstick had, like 'Tell Me', more to do with Bobbies Vee, Vinton and Rydell than Muddy Waters, Bo Diddley and Chuck Berry.

Possibly for this very reason - and with wrong-headed expectations of striking Lennon-McCartney gold - demonstration tapes were submitted and accepted by aspiring stars grubbing round Denmark Street offices for format songs, impressive principally, for instant melodic familiarity and lyrics just within the bounds of acceptable boy-meets-girl ickiness. The otherwise unsung George Bean and his Runners' second 45, for instance, was Mick and Keith's repetitive 'It Should Be You', while Bobby Jameson, a Paul McCartney lookalike but fair-headed, tried their 'Each And Every Day Of The Year'. Then there'd be 'So Much In Love', 'Blue Turns To Grey' and '(Walkin' Thru' The) Sleepy City', successive A-sides by Rugby's Mighty Avengers, and, as late as spring 1965, 'I'd Much Rather Be With The Boys' - attributed to Richards and Oldham - by The Toggery Five, runners-up to The Bo Street Runners in *Ready Steady Win!*, a televised national talent contest. Among finalists, incidentally, were The Birds in which Ronnie Wood played guitar.

Though 'So Much In Love' was to snatch slight chart honours, monetary rewards for Richards and Jagger as composers were meagre until another number given the George Bean treatment, 'My Only Girl', was revamped as 'That Girl Belongs To Yesterday' by Gene Pitney, who'd been as Bobbyish as they come in his time. He'd discerned that there might be a hit there if he altered the melody, but left the words as they stood - though their investigation of vaguely the same emotional area as 'Tell Me' compounded the stereotyping of Pitney as a merchant of melancholy. Yet, while lost in the enduring shadow of the famous 'Twenty-Four Hours From Tulsa', 'That Girl Belongs To Yesterday' was neck-and-neck with 'Not Fade Away' in the UK chart race, and even sneaked into the US *Hot 100*, affording the songwriting Stones some quiet pride.

At Andrew Oldham's request, Uncle Gene spent a long evening trying to tease workable compositions from Brian Jones, who got not further than talking about what his head hadn't yet formulated in simple terms. 'There was nothing there', reported Pitney the next day, thus providing Keith and Mick with an excuse supported by authority, to cease taking Jones seriously as a composer - as they had already his singing abilities, not so much for the quality of his light baritone as it falling silent at inopportune moments. 'Brian was meant to be doing backing vocals,' Dave Berry had gathered on the 'Group Scene '64' trek, 'but he kept shying away from the microphone - which annoyed the others.'

Nonetheless, Jones had sung lead on 'Sure I Do', a late 1963 demo penned completely by himself. Other straggling remains of Brian's endeavours to muscle in on the songwriting action have also surfaced in recent years. Collaborations included 'No One Knows' - with Mick and Keith - and, with a lyricist from the advertising agency, 'Wake Up In The Morning', the thirty-second Rice Krispies doggerel. In 1964, an equally negligible, if unique, Jones-Richards piece, 'Dust My Pyramids', half-a-minute of Elmore James-esque noodling, was to kick off *Rhythm And Blues*, a series hosted by Alexis Korner for the BBC World Service. [6]

Of Brian's lost pop songs, the only one that was ever accorded release was 'Thank You For Being There', one of his last, as title track of a self-financed 2005 album by Dutch singing guitarist Diderik Groen - and even that was a combination of Groen's music and a libretto by Brian that owed much to Dylans Thomas and Bob, touching as it did on 'the lashing tail of paranoiac fears' and 'the maniacal choirs that screamed out a warning' - thus bearing out Pat Andrews's contention that 'Brian preferred to think of them not as lyrics but as poetry.'

As for the melodies, 'Brian always made his songs too complicated,' thought Jagger, 'One hundred chords a minute like a jazz progression'. [7] This, however, bolstered Pat's defence that 'no-one he knew had the ability to play his songs - including the Stones.'

Furthermore, for all his noted criticisms of Brian's 'too complicated' offerings, Jagger would make the later confession - a doubtful one perhaps - that he'd never heard a Jones opus from start to finish. He and Richards weren't very receptive to the work of other members of the group anyway, 'so it was quite hard to know if Brian really wanted to do songs with us that he'd written,' sighed Mick, 'I think he did, but he was very shy, and found it rather hard to lay it down to us - and we didn't try to bring it out of him.' [8] Keith Richards' corroboration was blunter: 'As far as I know, Brian Jones never wrote a single finished song in his life. He wrote bits and pieces. No doubt he spent hours, weeks, working on things, but his paranoia was so great he could never bring himself to present them to us.' [3]

Andrew Oldham, however, was a little more patient with Brian in case Gene Pitney's evaluation hadn't been totally accurate. Maybe Brian's *forte* was instrumentals. After all, 'Now I've Got A Witness' had been mostly his brainchild. What's more, he'd fallen in with Jet Harris - as Keith had with Alan Taylor - during the All Stars '64 expedition. It was an amity founded not so much on artistic concord as kindred spirits finding each other. It was easy to draw parallels. In The Shadows, Jet - or Terry, as Brian knew him - had been blond - albeit dyed - when the others were dark. They'd also found him 'difficult'.

Like Jones too, he was promiscuous, later revealing to a Shadows biographer that 'I made five appearances there [a London VD clinic], and in the end they gave me a membership card. I'm probably immune to penicillin now.' [9] However, Cliff Richard's affair with Jet's first wife was 'another excuse for me to have a drink. It was bloody hard standing up on stage every night behind Cliff, thinking that he was having it off with Carol. I couldn't really stand the pressure, so I started drinking fairly heavily until it became a state of mind.' [9]

1963 had been a bitter-sweet year for the gifted if self-destructive Jet. Shortly before accepting a music press award as 'Britain's top instrumentalist' at a Savoy hotel luncheon, he and Billie Davis were badly injured when his chauffeur-driven Humber collided with a bus. As a consequence, his boozing - and intake of amphetamines - increased, and were central to his disastrous stage comeback as part of the All Stars '64 package when he was fresh from his first court appearance for being drunk and disorderly.

A booker's risk, Harris would have been the proverbial 'bad influence' if Jones himself hadn't been accelerating down the slippery slope already via a gradually more immoderate consumption of his favoured tipple and worse. 'Brian had a tendency to hang around with people who were out on the edge,' surmised Dick Taylor, 'He was already plumbing the depths then, out of his head a lot of the time.'

To entertain Jet as much as the other unseen millions, Brian was to don black horn-rims for a take-off of Hank B. Marvin just after the commercials on a Stones special in 1965 on *Ready Steady Go!* - and, on 3rd May, 1964, the *NME* had stated plain as day that Harris was going to record a tune penned by Jones and Andrew Oldham. Three weeks later, readers weren't sure whether to believe the same newspaper with its 'Brian Jones is likely to record a single on his own next month.' [10]

Learning about these extra-mural projects only when information about them appeared in print, his fellow Stones shrugged them off as nothing more than Brian shooting his mouth off, as usual. After the non-events of the Jet Harris instrumental and Brian's solo single - if they ever existed - on top of that depressing evening with Gene Pitney as well as Mick and Keith's amused indifference, Jones's explorations as a solo composer were no longer to come into the Rolling Stones equation, no matter how dogged his persistence.

He was, however, to receive publishing royalties for numbers attributed to 'Phelge' or, more commonly, 'Nanker-Phelge', a corporate name for items to which all Stones personnel contributed. 'Phelge' was after the Edith Grove flatmate, while 'Nanker' was Brian's word for a particularly horrible face he liked to pull. Much of this amalgam's output consisted of instrumentals such as 'Now I've Got A Witness' and 'Stoned', B-side of 'I Wanna Be Your Man', which was, in essence, Jones blowing harmonica over a riff borrowed from the reptilian crawl of Booker T and the MGs' 'Green Onions'. It also adhered to the contemporary cliche of a spoken utterance breaking a silence at the end of each verse. [11]

Yet, if these tended to go in one ear and out the other - with 'Little By Little' a borderline case - other Nanker-Phelge numbers were by no means as disposable. Dating from 1964's unsettled June, 'Off The Hook', for example, was to be an inspired and solidly *bona-fide* song, born of Phelge and Nanker slinging in rhymes, rhythmic ideas, fragments of tune and further twists to the plot when standing over, say, Brian or Bill at the piano or watching Keith and Mick pacing up and down, bedevilled with an impulse that might have manifested itself at some inconvenient moment on a punishing itinerary during which they saw nothing of Brighton, Glasgow, Plymouth, you name it, apart from what was glimpsed as they walked across the pavement from vehicle to stage-door. When asked about what such-and-such a town had been like, even Ian Stewart was damned if he could even find it on a map.

As it had been with 'Not Fade Away', only breaks in this unforgiving round of driving, driving, driving to strange towns, strange venues and strange beds allowed them time to record the long-awaited maiden LP. Most of the sessions took place at IBC where the Stones transgressed union stipulations by running over into open-ended graveyard hours during which there was room for such tentative experiments as Charlie swathing his drums with an overcoat.

Yet, while the five visible Stones cut appositely baleful figures on the front cover, the album's prosaic title - *The Rolling Stones* - was reflective of its content being as weighty with routine if frequently exciting versions of R&B standards with side-servings of soul as each of the first LPs yet to come by The Animals, The Yardbirds, The Kinks, The Downliners Sect, Them, The Pretty Things and The Spencer Davis Group. In this respect, the methodology and selection of material was on similar lines to that of Elvis Presley on his album debut, 1956's *Rock 'N' Roll*.

As the King had done, the Stones had picked and chosen from current releases by black artists, whittling these down to Bo Diddley's latest, 'Mona', [12] which they shrouded in reverberation; 'Walking The Dog' by comedian-*cum*-blues man turned soul singer Rufus Thomas, an avenue for Brian's aptly piercing whistles and his harmonising with Jagger, and 'Can I Get A Witness' from Marvin Gaye, the most recent signing to Tamla Motown. Though it was lingering still in the US *Hot 100*, this worthier companion piece to 'Now I've Got A Witness' - like

'Mona' and 'Walking The Dog' - meant nothing in the British charts or to the Light Programme - which pushed it towards the top of the Stones' short-list.

Jagger's slightly strained 'Can I Get A Witness' vocal may have resulted from him having to dash to a high street shop to purchase the sheet music. He needed no music-stand prompt, however, for the LP's opening track. As inevitable as Valentino's recording of 'Kashmiri Song' or Vera Lynn's of 'Land Of Hope And Glory', the Stones 'Route 66' led a friend of mine to deface a school atlas, trying in vain to figure in biro exactly how it 'winds from Chicago to LA' - because, as we discovered years later, the only version on which you could make out all the words was by Bing Crosby and the Andrews Sisters from the 1940s. Chuck Berry's arrangement, however, was the prototype for the Stones, who paid further homage on side two with a lively near-xerox of 1958's 'Carol', which was to be a fixture in the stage repertoire until *circa* 1965, and was exhumed in the next decade.

Muddy Waters was represented by a speeded-up 'I Just Wanna Make Love To You' – considered near the knuckle in 1964, not simply for its lyrics but for only faintly estimable widenings of vibrato during sustained notes on Jones's harmonica that were as loaded as the lewdest of vocal innuendos by Jagger.

It was Mick's imported *I'm Jimmy Reed* LP that was the source of the Stones' 'Honest I Do' - but to the moon-faced girl at a Nottingham bus stop on an overcast April Saturday with a newly-purchased *The Rolling Stones* under her arm, the origin of 'You Can Make It If You Try' was more completely unknown. Gene Allison's template had leaked into Britain in 1958 and thence to obscurity - as did Gene himself - though it crossed over from the US sepia chart to spend a solitary week in the mainstream Top Forty.

Likewise, 'I'm A King Bee' was recognised only by the R&B specialist, who realised too that, while Jagger wasn't trying consciously to copy, his absorption of the Louisiana blues giant's laconic style - and, though not heard here, his expressive harmonica wailing - had been too thorough for him to escape being an imitator. Yet he coped well with the insidiously feverish lechery over an appropriate backing epitomised by a suggestive lowdown riff from Richards.

If some of its selections pre-empted those on the LPs of others, *The Rolling Stones* didn't include any of their three 45 rpm chart strikes. This was commendable because, though attitudes were changing in 1964, the pop album was regarded generally not as a rounded entity in its own right, but as a cynically padded-out collection, hinged on a hit single that had maybe just left the Top Forty. A testament to commercial pragmatism rather than quality, it was targeted at consumers so beglamoured by an act's looks and personality to be rendered uncritical of frankly sub-standard product, haphazardly programmed, short on needle-time and of inappreciable cultural value.

While the Stones' LP embraced a time-consuming instrumental - as, perhaps, an exhibition of 'versatility' - they dared to let 'Tell Me (You're Coming Back)' stick out like a sore thumb in the middle of side two, where it provoked responses ranging from the *NME*'s 'a sad song which will compel people to really listen to the words' [13] to Bob Dawburn, *Melody Maker*'s in-house grumpy old man, cold-shouldering it as 'second-hand Liverpool'. [14]

While 'Tell Me' was being considered for release as a single in the yet unchartered USA, other tracks were the equal of A-sides too. Issued as an Australasia-only single, 'Walking The Dog', for instance, reached the continent's Top Ten that summer. At home, the entire album clawed its way to an astounding Number 19 in the singles chart, demonstrating that huge sales of fiddly little 45s bought by schoolchildren were but surface manifestations of the respect accorded to the group by sixth form and undergraduate siblings, while prototype Mods heard the Stones as fair interpreters of the Americans. This remarkable feat oiled the wheels for the appearance in high street newsagents of a glossy monthly periodical devoted solely to the group; only The Beatles and - for four editions only - Gerry and the Pacemakers had also been accorded that honour by the same publishers.

It was instructive literature for an increasing number of fans seeking insight and information about what made the Stones tick. As it had been for schoolboys Brian, Keith and Mick with their blues passion, and Charlie with his jazz, hundreds of hours of intense listening to the three singles, the EP and the new album had less to do with pleasure than with being as surely dependant as others can be on drugs.

Part of the attraction was that the Stones had become as despised and as condemned by adults for their noise and looks as Elvis had been when *The Ed Sullivan Show* - the USA's *Sunday Night At The London Palladium* - had only dared screen him from the waist up, and Methodist preacher, trad jazz buff and *Six-Five Special* pundit, Dr. Donald Soper, had wondered, belatedly, of 'Heartbreak Hotel' 'how intelligent people can derive satisfaction from something which is emotionally embarrassing and intellectually ridiculous.' [15]

What would the good doctor have made of the Stones? Not so much famous as notorious now, 'the caveman-like quintet' [16] had been threatened with an ITV ban for 'unprofessional conduct' after rolling up two hours late for the final run-through for *The Arthur Haynes Show*, a comedy series with musical interludes, transmitted on Fridays an hour after *Ready Steady Go*. Then there were snooty restauranteurs at pains to point out that any male not wearing a tie was not to be served lunch; auditorium janitors promising to pull the main electricity switch the second that horrible racket over-ran, and night porters unwilling to leave their desks unattended to prepare sandwiches when the young twerps flopped in after the show. That sign says you're to hand them room keys in when you go out. Can't you read? No, I don't suppose you can.

In readiness for that evening's screaming at the Stones, girls getting used to mini-skirts may have trimmed newly-styled fringes with nail-clippers to make them as enviably straight as Brian Jones's, and - so a psychiatrist wrote - 'to identify with these characters as either other girls or as sexual neuters'. [17] This may have been why all-boys schools like Dartford Grammar had become especially strict about imposing short haircuts as a mark of sobriety and masculinity. It also labelled those who didn't mind as supportive of a kind of official, malevolent neutrality towards intellectually-stultifying pop groups - who compounding their disrepute, were now inclined to gesture with cigarettes and let loose the odd mild, but un-Cliff Richard-like expletive like 'cr*p' and 'bl***y' during television interviews and press conferences.

The Beatles were as guilty of such behaviour as the Stones, but, if they put themselves in the way of potentially damaging publicity - like a Liverpool woman's imputation of her baby's irregular kinship to Paul McCartney - their investors would ensure that no nicotine-stained fingers would bang out lurid coverage of it for the following Sunday's *News Of The World*. Besides, even if it was true, nothing too sordid was likely to be yet brought to public notice about John-Paul-George-and-Ringo, Gerry, Brian Poole, Dusty Springfield, Billy J. Kramer and other manifestly wholesome pop stars by a scum press who considered any besmirching of cheeky but innocent personas as untimely: save the scandal for The Rolling Stones, to be cited by one tabloid - which set all the others off - as 'the ugliest group in Britain', [18] following their languid and off-hand judgement on the latest singles - voting every one of them a 'miss' - on BBC television's *Juke Box Jury* on 27th June, 1964.

No edition of the show had ever been as controversial, and, watching it, Eric Easton drew on a cigarette and exhaled with a sigh. He'd failed miserably to turn the Stones into 'personalities' as outwardly likeable as The Beatles or Brian Poole and the Tremeloes. Take Keith Richard: a nice enough lad, he'd given his former profession as 'post office worker' in an *NME* article not quite a year earlier. [19] But now he was telling interviewers that he'd been a 'layabout' and was listing 'policemen' among his pet hates. [20] If a stranger came up to him and said, 'Hello Keith. How is your brother Cliff?', Eric would rather a polite lie along the lines of 'Fine, thanks. He's keeping well' than Keith asking the enquirer why he didn't bugger off.

Finally, Easton gave up, deciding instead to place that side of things on the more with-it shoulders of Andrew Loog Oldham, whose judgement was that the more brutish the Stones were seen to be, the more they were pilloried by Authority and the more avidly the fans would swoop to their defence. On 27th November, 1964, Jagger was to be be convicted of a second driving offence in six months. This time, his counsel's plea prompted a not altogether relevant discussion, which would be reiterated in a schoolgirls' comic: 'The Emperor Augustus Caesar was another with long hair [*sic*], and he won a great many victories. Put out of your mind the nonsense talked about these young men. These boys are highly intelligent, not long-haired idiots as some people care to refer to them. Mick's shaggy mane is a grade A asset to Britain.' [21]

Outside school, the group - and beat music in general - was gaining ground in the most unlikely settings. With an ear to the ground, Adam Faith had switched from lightweight neo-Bobby ditties to ersatz Merseybeat, as heard on 1963's Top Ten restorative, 'The First Time'. It now read 'Adam Faith with The Roulettes' on the record label, and, over the next three years, Adam and this two guitars-bass-drums unit were to prove a competent team, both on disc and on the boards with some idiosyncratic cracks at black R&B as well as an assertive 'I Wanna Be Your Man'.

Enough of the old Adam remained to satisfy the faithful, but, compelled to appear straight after the Stones on 1964's *New Musical Express* Pollwinners spectacular at Wembley Empire Pool, Adam, ready to murder his own grandmother, built on his predecessors' foreplay and all but out-Jaggered Jagger. Was this the same young man who, in pantomime as 'Dick Whittington', had led a children's chorus through 'Lonely Pup In A Christmas Shop' as 1960 rolled into 1961?

Top Twenty selections were thundering now from the PA system at Tottenham Hotspurs soccer pitch. The Dave Clark Five's early hits were particularly popular there - since, not only had local lad Dave called his publishing company 'Spurs Music', but he was also leader of a group with a sporty outlook as shown in the keep-fit scene that would open their 1965 celluloid vehicle, *Catch Us If You Can.* [22]

This was much at odds with the fey aura emanating from the likes of The Rolling Stones - 'The Five Shaggy Dogs with a brand of "shake" all their own,' as one local rag had it [23] - the cause nowadays of blazing rows between parents and once tractable sons about hair. If he could get away with it, a boy might approximate a Brian Jones feather-duster or try to look like someone who looked like Mick - whose appearance was chief among reasons why Bob Geldof, then a Dublin teenager, identified with 'The Rolling Stones, the first band I considered my own. Mick Jagger's hair was a mess, and my hair was a mess, even when it was short.' [24]

Yet Jagger had protested in interview that he and the other Stones had their hair cut 'not short, but regularly'. [25] A statement that some took as vague approbation came from Mr. Scowcroft, president of the National Hairdressers Federation: 'Men's hairdressers do not object to youth wanting to wear its hair long, provided it is shaped.' [26]

'It seems so ridiculous now,' chuckled Phil May, then the wearer of the longest male hair in mid-1960s Britain, 'There was trouble in the streets all the time. If I walked down the high street, people would jeer and try to pick a fight.'

Like Winston Smith yelling abuse at Goldstein in *1984*, a provincial youth, whose short-back-and-sides broke his heart, would, when the family was transfixed by the miming of 'You Better Move On' on *The Arthur Haynes Show*, suppose that his father was right in remarking that the Stones were morons. He'd also join in the sniggers two days later when, during one 1964 edition of *Sunday Night At The London Palladium*, English showbiz treasure Max Bygraves poked fun at the Stones with the aid of an overhead projector and a blow-up of Jagger with a superimposed Yul Brynner pate. Yet the boy would scorn inwardly funnymen such as Bygraves and Ted Rogers who, knowing the prejudices of their audience, would only have to hold their noses and twang 'Ah wanna be your lover baby, ah wanna be your man...' to get a laugh.

Passively expressed loathing in the living room for the sake of domestic harmony became private admiration in the bedroom, though no amount of backcombing, pulling or applications of a thickening gel called Dippety-Do could disguise your shearing at a time when - similar to how it had been with Jack Good and Vince Taylor - a BBC producer refused to allow a vocalist to appear on television unless he had his shoulder-length locks abbreviated, and eleven boys were suspended from a Coventry secondary school for having 'Mick Jagger' haircuts. An editorial in a tabloid newspaper advocated a law that made short-back-and-sides compulsory for men, and a nasty rumour filtered round about Jagger's impending sex-change, thus enabling him to marry Brian Jones. 'They are not looked on very kindly by most parents or by adults in general,' added the *Daily Mirror*, 'They are even used to the type of article that asks big brother if he would let his sister go out with one of them'. [27]

Just as their spiritual descendants would over 1970s outragers The Sex Pistols, 'manly' types, relaxing over a game of darts in the pub, would plan a hypothetical raid, armed with scissors, on one of these Rolling Stones' houses, wherever it was. Such silly, harmless stuff was at root deadly serious; symptomatic of a feeling that it was a bounden obligation to put action over the simple debate of certain Sunday newspapers. In August, an ITV regional news magazine was to report a scuffle between the Stones and one such posse of these Alf Garnetts-in-embryo on an early evening beach when it was becoming clear now that darkness was the group's sole shield against the havoc that would accumulate round them now if blithe fatalism tempted them to walk abroad between soundcheck and show.

Yet many of the older Alfs, ineffectual and otherwise, were eating their hearts out, either because their dreary wives were the only women they'd ever 'known' in a Biblical sense or because their lives had been blighted by the war - and today you heard some little twit answering back when his poor old mother told him to get off to the barber's for a four-penny all-off! What sort of world was it when you switched on the telly and that Mick Jagger flashed into the front parlour, hair all over his surly, lippy mug, poncing about in his tat, and caterwauling that he was a king bee buzzing around some tart's hive or something? That was if you could make out the words - which you couldn't.

Notes

1. *Melody Maker*, 8th February, 1964
2. *The Record Producers* by J. Tobler and S. Grundy (BBC, 1982)
3. *Keith Richards In His Own Words* ed. M. St. Michael (Omnibus, 1994)
4. A duet with Wendy Richard, future mainstay of television soap-opera *East Enders*
5. *Q*, October, 1988
6. Then known as the General Overseas Programme
7. *Melody Maker*, 23rd November, 1969
8. *Rock & Folk*, French journal, May, 1984
9. *The Story Of The Shadows* by M. Read (Elm Tree, 1983)
10. *New Musical Express*, 24th May, 1964
11. The Dave Clark Five were to rework the basic idea of 'Stoned' for 'Move On', flip-side of 1965's 'Catch Us If You Can'.
12. Entitled 'I Need You Baby' on some pressings
13. *New Musical Express*, 10 April, 1964
14. *Melody Maker*, 23rd May, 1964
15. *Melody Maker*, 29th March, 1958
16. *New Musical Express*, 8th February, 1964
17. Quoted in *Beat Merchants* by A. Clayson (Blandford, 1996)
18. Quoted in *Who's Who In Popular Music* ed. S Tracy (World's Work, 1984)
19. *New Musical Express*, 2nd August, 1963
20. *New Musical Express*, 27th November, 1964
21. *Boyfriend Book 1966*, (City Magazines, 1965)
22. US title: *Having A Wild Weekend*
23. *Watlington Gazette*, 11th March, 1964
24. *The Guardian*, 11th June, 2004
25. *Disc*, 19th May, 1964
26. *The Guardian*, 31st March, 1964
27. *Daily Mirror*, 3rd May, 1964

## Chapter Eleven
## Junior Birdmen

*'Friday night, we played Cleethorpes. Saturday, we played with The Who on the West Pier at Blackpool. Sunday night was Salisbury, right down the other end of the country. Then two nights at Leo's clubs around Windsor. Then straight back up north for the weekend'* - Tony Munroe of The Birds [1]

If the Stones were above one-nighters by the middle of 1964, they had already started to punctuate round-Britain tours with roots-affirming dates in venues of comparable size to the Crawdaddy of blessed memory - though never the Crawdaddy itself. However, as early as the Everly Brothers jaunt, the group had returned for one night only to Studio 51 where The Downliners Sect now held sway, and wall-height photographic blow-ups of both themselves and the departed Stones had been hung.

Very much rising stars then, the Sect were more fully mobilised than The Pretty Things to follow the Stones into the hit parade. Like The Animals, they had financed the pressing of an EP of selections from their club set. EMI, the company that signed them, were impressed too by a diverting and frequently hilarious stage act, and took the word of informed fans that the Sect were, arguably, Britain's foremost Bo Diddley executants, and that their Ray Sone ranked with Brian Jones as a recognised master of blues harmonica.

One March evening in 1964, the Sect had been on the boards when Van Morrison, Herbie Armstrong and other members of an Irish showband with a night off during a string of engagements in England, decided to sample a session at Studio 51. The story goes that, enchanted by the Sect, Morrison was lured to another of the group's engagements, and so coveted Ray Sone's job that he asked point-blank to take over as mouth-organist, quite content to attend to overall effect rather than dominate proceedings. Whatever the truth of this, he sailed back to his native Belfast with a half-formed but distinct ambition. 'When he saw The Downliners Sect, he said "That's the sort of group I want to have!"', remembered Armstrong. Morrison himself corroborated this statement with, 'They were really doing it then. I heard The Pretty Things, but The Downliners Sect were *it*!' [2]

It was, therefore, quite in order for the Stones to be supplicatory towards the Sect just after a Sunday afternoon spot when, detailed bass guitarist Keith Grant, 'Mick and Keith - who were a bit of a double act - walked into Studio 51. They asked if they could appear with us as they missed the atmosphere of the small clubs, so we picked a date when they were free to do so. However, on the night, after they'd done a couple of songs, someone pulled the plug on them - possibly because they were upset that the Stones had "deserted" the place by becoming famous. The plug was put back in, but was pulled out again after a few more numbers, so I stationed myself by the plug to stop it happening again.'

When the Sect ventured forth into a wider world too, they were to be lost amongst those also-rans that they had influenced as the Stones had influenced them, and lent credence to Marquee manager Bill Carey's gripe in *Record Mirror* that 'every beat group with money enough to buy a harmonica and hire a four chord guitarist is calling iself R&B. It's a cast-iron certainty that, in 1964, the great heaving mound of Tin Pan Alley-controlled beat groups will attach itself to the R&B label.' [3]

The usual summit of short careers would be a trivial round of recurring engagements and a smattering of airplay that might precipitate a fleeting foray into the lower reaches of the Top Fifty for one, maybe two singles that often demonstrated musical ability at odds with overweening expressive ambition. Yet, without vanity, mere awareness of worth in the teeth of ill luck was enough to feed hope, though with every passing day, you were less likely to become The Rolling Stones. Then the bass player leaves, and a group that used to support you turns up on *Top Of The Pops*. If only there hadn't been a power cut when Andrew Loog Oldham was there; if only the singer hadn't had a sore throat at the Marquee; if only we hadn't lost our way...

Pop is an unfair, erratic business. Arbitrary isolations - a producer's stomach ache, a manager's procrastination, a drummer's hangover, an agent's extended lunch break, an amplifier packing up, a flat tyre - all these unrelated trivialities can inflict so much damage until, with even an encore no longer sufficient to feed hope, the group throws in the towel, having decided to make a proper go of their day jobs and college courses, instead of yearning for any more glittering future that might result, however indirectly, from the next feedback-ridden, drum-thudding evening.

Bitter was the poverty that was to compel one such outfit from Worcestershire to organize a jumble sale to cover accumulated parking fines. A few weeks later, the final blow was the liquidation of its fan club. The entire line-up of one northern R&B group who'd landed a recording contract and enjoyed transient fame too, wound up working together, stacking and loading newspapers in a W.H. Smith's warehouse.

The Primitives from Oxford managed three UK singles for Pye, beginning with a respectable go at Sonny Boy Williamson's 'Help Me' at a time when most would-be UK bluesmen copying the black, US masters were discovering still that the results weren't anything like. The group also worked up a following in Italy before all was lost by 1967. That was good going.

*In extremis*, vocalist Jay Roberts had had his girlish tresses cut before millions on a TV chat show, a publicity stunt that was a giant step from the circulated photographs of Manfred Mann dragging their most hirsute *mann* into a barber's. Other R&B outfits weren't as eager to demean themselves so crassly - though, craving for the hit that might lift them off the northern ballroom treadmill, The Hullaballoos - from Hull - peroxided the hair that was soon to splay halfway down their backs, and Worthing's T-Bones had a lesser gimmick in their front man, champion boxer Tommy Farr's son Gary, introducing the tambour to British pop. As a popular club act, they were on a par with The Artwoods, whose stylistic approach was almost two decades ahead of 1983's brief jazz craze, spearheaded by Carmel and Animal Nightlife. This may explain why, as Art Wood recalled, 'We'd been the first R&B group to be taken on by the London City Agency, who'd concentrated until then on trad jazz bands. It was through them that Decca signed us, Mike Vernon became our producer, and we got on *Ready Steady Go!* - the first group ever to play live on the programme. We were everywhere... Leicester, Manchester, Redruth, Newcastle, back at the 100 Club...and we ended up playing every night on the same circuit as people like Zoot Money, Graham Bond, Cliff Bennett, The Downliners Sect, The Birds...'

Cracks began to appear when studio time booked for The Artwoods to record 'The House Of The Rising Sun' had to be reallocated after Decca, not quite so nonchalant about such matters any more, got wind of versions on Pye and EMI respectively, by The Sundowners, pride of Great Malvern, and The Animals, who Art Wood had known as just another group on the circuit: 'When we were at the Club-A-Go-Go in Newcastle, we became friends with The Animals, who showed us around and we did the same for them when they came to London.'

Other chances came and went. 'When we at the Marquee one night,' remembered Art, 'Cat Stevens came into the dressing room and gave us some demos of some songs he'd written - which included "Matthew And Son". At the next rehearsal, we tried it, but it wasn't our sort of music. A year later, Cat had a hit with it. In 1964, we were also offered and, for the same reason, turned down 'Funny How Love Can Be' before The Ivy League did it themselves and got into the Top Ten.'

Becoming too clever for the charts, Art and his musicians were to be commended for overlooking outright commercial concerns, but such an uncompromising stance was to provoke an eventual tailing off of engagements and any serious attention by the business.

Groups formed by Art's younger brothers weren't especially fortunate either. While these and The Artwoods could all be filed under 'pop' and repertory outlines dissolved on occasions, there was no pronounced conflict of interests or inter-related avenues for noisome home truths. 'It wasn't a case of sibling rivalry, very much the opposite,' grinned Art, 'I was so pleased for Ted when his trad band toured the continent and he recorded with Chris Barber, and we were both pleased when Ronnie started with The Birds - though we couldn't have functioned in the same band because Ted was trad, I was primarily rhythm-and-blues and Ronnie was more rock 'n' roll.'

A decade Art's junior, guitarist Ronnie had been studying graphics at Ealing Technical College in 1963 when personnel from two local outfits, The Renegades and his own Rhythm And Blues Bohemians amalgamated as The Thunderbirds - after 'The Jaguar And The Thunderbird' on a Chuck Berry LP, but a standardised name anyway. The line-up was two guitarists - with Wood doubling on harmonica - bass player, drummer and lead vocalist. Just like The Rolling Stones too, they jettisoned stage uniformity with indecent haste.

A youth club in their native Yiewsley, a crowded satellite of the London borough of Hillingdon, accommodated their first recitals, until triumph in a regional battle of the bands gained them regular Saturday nights in a community centre close enough to the two streets where all Thunderbirds bar one lived, for the equipment to be carried there - which was just as well as nobody was old enough to drive.

One of the first quests outside their neck of Middlesex was an egg-on-the-face second-billing to Chris Farlowe and the *Thunderbirds*, fully professional since 1962, at Eel Pie Island, which necessitated the Yiewsley group becoming just plain Birds. Their accustomed routine came to be typified by a Monday night residency at the Aquarium in Brighton after they'd been taken under the wing of Leo de Clerck, proprietor of Leo's Cavern in Windsor and other small venues in the south-eastern shires. The outside of the van he provided for The Birds was emblazoned by signwriter Ronnie with the group's name, but was soon defaced with affectionate messages scrawled in lipstick and nail-file during a constant run of engagements over the next three years as far away as Scotland. 'We were huge in Cheshire,' boasted guitarist Tony Munroe. [1]

Their youthful metabolism made it easier to endure trunk road odysseys that were truly hellish: washing in streams, shaving in public conveniences and trying to enjoy as comfortable a night's repose as possible maybe on the front passenger seat after nothing better had come of the usual, 'Do you know anywhere we can rest tonight?' enquiry. This was showbusiness. It was also staring fascinated across a transport cafe's formica table as the drummer makes short work of a greasy but obviously satisfying fry-up while you pick at your dish with less enthusiasm. 'We lived on sausage, egg and chips,' laughed Tony Munroe, 'We were professional musicians on ten pounds a week, when the average wage was fifteen. Out of that, we had to pay our own accommodation, which was why we used to sleep in the van. There again, we loved it.'[1]

Wherever they played, it always seemed to be one week after The Primitives and one week before The T-Bones - and sometimes, as Ronnie's big brother recalled, on the very same night as The Art-woods: 'Once, we were on at one of three boat clubs on the river Trent in Nottingham. That same evening, Cliff Bennett was playing in the second and The Birds were in the other - all of us from the same part of Middlesex. Unbelievable! During the interval, The Birds and The Art-woods swapped our musicians around, and each group did the second set as half Birds, half Artwoods. On the way home, all the groups used to run into each other at the Blue Boar greasy spoon on the M1 - which petered out around Birmingham in those days.'

An attempt by The Birds to move up to the next level was a qualified success. While failing to seize the ultimate prize of a one-shot recording deal on *Ready Steady Win!*, the group landed an out-of-character slot on the BBC television variety show *ABC Of Britain* performing what would be their debut A-side, 'You're On My Mind', penned by Ronnie, when Dick Rowe got round to contracting The Birds to Decca in autumn 1964 - for longer, incidentally, that he had *Ready Steady Win!*'s victors, The Bo Street Runners. It was, however, *BC Of Britain* today and back on the endless one-nighters tomorrow - but at least they could bill themselves 'Decca Recording Artists' now that 'London's Newest R&B Sensation!' was starting to wear thin.

Somewhere within the Hertford – Welwyn Garden City – St. Alban's triangle, they rubbed shoulders with The Juniors, who, less a commercial merger than a bunch of town boys playing together for the hell of it, had become parochial celebrities since lip-synching what turned out to be their only single, 'There's A Pretty Girl', on a recent edition of the ITV children's programme, *Five O' Clock Club*.

On the boards at, say, Welwyn's Free Church Youth Club or the Co-op Hall in St. Alban's, it was noticed that the wildest ovations were saved for numbers in which the lead guitarist featured heavily. He was none other than the now teenage Mick Taylor, remarkable to Ronnie Wood for the chronic stage fright he tried to assuage by chain-smoking. It didn't seem to affect a fretboard style that was more than the mere equal of Wood's, having gone far beyond the countrified picking of Bill Haley - in whose presence his heart had opened in 1957 - to the terse soloing and passagework that echoed T-Bone Walker, B.B. King and other principal black post-war guitarists. Taylor's love of the blues was reflected too in his frequent commutes to Dobell's, and, specifically, in the time and money he had just expended to acquire King's *Live At The Regal* album on import, months before its release in Britain.

With 'There's A Pretty Girl' and *Five O' Clock Club* the zenith of The Juniors' corporate ambition, Mick wasn't to be entirely surprised by the sundering of the group before 1964 was over - though most of its members were to regroup within weeks as The Gods. Taylor, nonethe-less, passed through the ranks only fleetingly as he looked out for more attractive prospects as not a week seemed to go by without another R&B outfit breaking loose of local orbits and ringing some changes. Some of those he heard acquitted themselves well, made nice music. Even so, a lot of them were just like The Birds, just like The Rolling Stones.

Yet, glancing in his armchair at *Melody Maker*, Taylor was drawn to a review of 'Dimples', a John Lee Hooker xerox on 45 by The Spencer Davis Group, whose leader was a proficient, even distinctive singer and guitarist. It was, nonetheless, Spencer Davis's misfortune that his sidekick, Steve Winwood, no older than Mick, and pop-eyed at the microphone, was in another league via an instinctive Brian Jones-like command of any fretboard or keyboard instrument put in front of him - plus a voice of strangled, lived-in passion.

Gravelly ranting was the ace up the sleeve of Joe Cocker, who, under his adolescent *nom de theatre* 'Vance Arnold', was lauded in the *Sheffield Telegraph* as 'surely a star of the future' [4] after he and his backing Avengers held their own whilst warming up for the Stones at the Town Hall.

Among those who supported The Downliners Sect before the going got erratic, was a Muswell Hill ensemble, The Kinks, who were about to be grabbed by Pye. 'Decca turned them down,' snarled co-manager Larry Page, 'Because they had the Stones already'. To Pye's annoyance, The Kinks' first two singles, tinged with Merseybeat, had bitten the dust, but the quartet 'arrived' with a vengeance in August, 1964 when 'You Really Got Me' kicked off a run of smashes that adhered mainly to similar jerky riffing.

Advantaged too by being in the right place, i.e., London, at the right time, The Pretty Things' time was about to come too. Their abandoned drive, extra-long long hair and androgynous image, offset only by Dick Taylor's beard, held instant appeal for record company moguls looking for an act to combat the Stones as well as the groups like them that EMI had just grabbed. With Dick Taylor's affinity to those very Stones as useful in negotiation as a demo of 'Route 66', newly-acquired managers Bryan Morrison and Jimmy Duncan got the group on the Fontana label in spring 1964 after only a fourth paid booking.

Projected as wilder, fouler and more peculiar than the Stones - kind of Terry-Thomas to their David Niven - the Things were to warrant both a centre spread in *Fabulous* pop magazine and an in-depth article in the new *Sunday Times* colour supplement. Furthermore, it was the Things rather than the Stones who were central to TV God-slot discussions concerning the depth to which pop had sunk with its championship of such degenerates - who were themselves hauled in by ITV to answer clerical criticisms. However, their verbal retaliations were hastily restricted when Phil May and Dick Taylor began capsizing the programme's intentions by using long words and speaking nicely.

If they weren't animal-like retards, then it must be made out that they revelled in higgledy-piggledy filth and slept in their vests. Thus the *News Of The World* galloped into the fray, sending a couple of its hacks to brave the Belgravia *demi-monde* of 13, Chester Street, the Things' communal flat - and a freeholding of the Duke of Westminster. Yet if doorstepping press on a moral crusade imagined aristocratic portraits gazing down reproachfully on a tip occupied by depraved reprobates, they were to be disillusioned. 'They came round when we were having afternoon tea,' chuckled Dick, 'You could eat off the floor there.'

However, because of the bad name they were giving the place, the noble landlord served notice on his Chester Street tenants; an eviction held at arm's length only briefly by a *Checkpoint*-type television probe. The Things hadn't spent much time there anyway. 'It was only a crash-pad,' admitted May, 'As we were working nine days a week. We'd get back at five in the morning, and leave at noon.'

By August, an uproarious evening with The Pretty Things at St. Andrew's Hall in Norwich would prompt the *Midland Beat* headline 'R And B Ousts Rock In East Anglia!' [5] Illustrating further that not only was the swing away from Merseybeat complete, but that the Things were likely to supersede the Stones as anti-Beatles-in-chief, a single, 'Rosalyn', a Duncan composition that owed much to Bo Diddley, had peaked already on the edge of the Top Thirty, and, in autumn, the next one, stop-start 'Don't Bring Me Down', riven with *dig-it-man* beatnik slang, was in the Top Ten. Destined to climb almost as high as 1965 got out of neutral, a third 45, self-composed 'Honey I Need', lived in a careering chordal lurch, thrashed at speed behind May's ranted vocal: punk or what?

Perhaps sniffing a perishable commodity in this slight falling-off, Fontana rush-released a big-selling Pretty Things LP that some critics, both then and in retrospect, considered more raw and exciting than the Stones' album debut almost a year previously. Furtheremore, if in the frame too early for the deification of high-velocity guitar heroes like Jeff Beck, Peter Green, Eric Clapton and Alvin Lee, Dick Taylor was placed on a par with George Harrison, who, for as long as Clapton, Lee and other fast-fingered virtuosi fermented hitless in the clubs, would continue to win polls as top guitarist. Though in a different stylistic league than Harrison, Taylor's solos and ostinati were similarly constructed to integrate with the melodic - and lyrical - intent of each track rather than the technical challenges of underlying chord patterns.

'On the early Pretty Things records, Dick should never be mistaken for a mere blues copyist,' opined Wreckless Eric, then a Newhaven schoolboy, 'Even playing Jimmy Reed, he had a style that was entirely his own. Later, when he was free from the constraints of the blues structure, his playing was positively symphonic.'

Yet, for all Taylor's fretboard dexterity and the well-argued accounts the group gave of themselves in the media, grown-up Britain reasoned still that, if teenagers had to like beat groups, let it be the more palatable ones such as The Beatles, The Dave Clark Five or Herman's Hermits. These combos, however, seemed to hold less allure for the more privileged adolescents than the Things and the Stones, partly because socialites, *nouvelle vague*, A-list celebrities and even aristocracy had, like the Crawdaddy's intellectual contingent, discovered that there was an inverted social cachet, a certain outlaw chic, about hanging around with the more degenerate beat groups.

In London especially, it was cool for everyone who was anybody to not only dig but also to socialise with The Rolling Stone and The Pretty Things. Chauffeur-driven vehicles disgorged names of the calibre of Lionel Bart, Diana Dors and Judy Garland outside 13, Chester Street, where Garland, near the end of a badly frayed tether, air-kissed Brian Jones. She put him, plus one on the guest list for one evening of her month in cabaret at the Talk Of The Town, where he snapped mickey-taking fingers to the big band keeping studio-smooth pace to egocentric Judy, pleased that a Stone - one of her entourage had to remind her which one it was - had shown interest.

Then there was Phil May and drummer Viv Prince's double date with Garland and 'someone for me,' reminisced Phil, 'who turned out to be Rudolf Nureyev. He danced like a woodentop at the Ad-Lib. All I remember of Judy is her gripping my wrist in her claw-like hand.

As she spoke, I could see blood coming from under her nails as they dug into my skin, but it seemed impolite to pull my hand away.'

Always the Things expected their celebrity to end as much as Fontana did, but they resisted temptations to adjust themselves along more mainstream lines, thus precluding the public accepting them - as it would the Stones in time - as a tolerable if unsavoury part of the national pop scene. 'The Pretty Things had everything it took to overtake the Stones,' pontificated veteran outrager Screaming Lord Sutch, 'but in those days "all publicity is good publicity" didn't always apply because, though they were years ahead of their time image-wise - the Sex Pistols of their day - it was too much for the general public in the mid-sixties. The Stones just about walked the line; the Pretty Things went way over it. This was a time, remember, when simply getting married could still ruin a pop star's career. The man-in-the-street couldn't imagine any of the Pretty Things ever being married - except to each other.'

The Things and the Stones were actually neck-and-neck for only a few months, but, purportedly, Andrew Oldham took the challenge seriously enough to issue a directive that the rival act was not to be rebooked on *Ready Steady Go!* upon pain of his Stones boycotting the series. Such bullying by the bigger apes in the UK pop jungle was not unique, but the *esprit de corps* of old would reassert itself still - as it did when, following a set truncated by a riot at the Palace Theatre in Manchester, Keith and Mick taxied across the city to 'sit in' with the Things, who happened to be appearing at the Manchester Cavern that same evening. The Stones also sold the Vox amplifiers - to which they'd given the thumbs-up in 1963 - as a job lot to the Things, who gladly lent the equipment back to the Stones, whose own was being held in transit in the Netherlands, for an engagement up north.

Outside the context of work too, personnel from both groups would be seen drinking at the same tables in fashionable clubs in central London from which the pop elite and their trailing 'liggers' could select a night out: 'night' defined as round midnight to dawn; 'fashionable' meaning that the supercool Ad-Lib near Leicester Square would be 'in' for a while before the inscrutable pack tranferred allegiance to the Speakeasy or, just down the road from Studio 51, the Pickwick before finishing up at the Cromwellian in SW7, the Bag O' Nails off Carnaby Street, the Scotch of St. James and maybe four other hangouts, attractive for their strict membership controls, tariffs too high for Joe Average, spy-holes on the doors, and no photographers admitted.

Amused by the memory, Phil May would reconjure how 'us and the Stones also used to go to the Freddie Mills Nite Spot, the Starlite Rooms and these rather strange watering holes that were patronised by a mixture of leftish stars and gangsters - and CID flying squad funnily enough. People like the Krays were drawn to us because, if they were Public Enemy Number One, we were Number Two.'

Brian Jones didn't find his status of social pariah who kept company with criminals as entirely distasteful as, say, Charlie Watts or Dick Taylor might have done. He had been keeping what might have been a benevolent rather than wary eye on The Pretty Things as he had on the more insidiously threatening Yardbirds, who, if lacking 'image', were to gain a toehold on the Top Fifty in October with a revival of Sonny Boy Williamson's 'Good Morning Little Schoolgirl'.

In turn, the Things were providing Brian with a safe house when required now that the pregnant Linda Lawrence's parents, as charmed by him as Mr. and Mrs. Andrews had been, were trusting that Brian would not decline the honour of their daughter's hand in marriage. They had made their gentlemanly prospective son-in-law most welcome in their home in Windsor and treated him as if he belonged there, going so far as to rename the place 'Rolling Stone' and permit him use of their motor car. If 'Rolling Stone' was not as handy for West End nightclubbing as 13, Chester Street, the rest of the household, Linda and younger sister Carole, could not have been more hospitable either - or more understanding when, for example, the Dracula hours of Brian's job meant pre-dawn disturbances and groggy, dressing-gowned breakfasts in the late afternoon.

The Lawrences, however, were to discover that Brian Jones was no longer a gentleman - but perhaps he'd never been one in the first place. To Linda's sorrow, he had been furtively negotiating a move back to London via go-between Jimmy Phelge, who had moved from Edith Grove to a Knightsbridge mews house shared with P.J. Proby, an expatriate Texan with a magnificent if mannered vocal style and an outrageous public demeanour, who was on the wings of his first - and greatest - British hit, 'Hold Me'. 'We had a non-stop river of naked women and rock 'n' roll crooks and geniuses,' laughed Kim Fowley, one of the other co-tenants, 'and it was great times. We had lots of visitors including Brian.' [6] Yet, while this seemed just his sort of place, Jones decided in the end to ensconce himself permanently in the basement beneath The Pretty Things in Belgravia - 'sleeping with the enemy', to use Phil May's roguish expression - around the time that his and Linda's baby was born on 23rd July 1964. While she was in labour, he was posing with his guitar at a Stones photo session - though, apparently, he dashed to the maternity ward as soon as the last shutter clacked.

Whatever inner debate had motivated Brian and Linda to name their son Julian, rather than maybe Elmore - or Chester or McKinley, the respective baptismal names of Howlin' Wolf and Muddy Waters - who could begrudge Pat Andrews horrifying Jones - and Andrew Loog Oldham - by telling her sad tale to trashy Sunday newspapers, and taking part in an edition concerning illegitimacy of *Man Alive*, a current affairs series on the BBC's brand-new second TV channel? Two telling sentences in her 'talking head' interview were, 'He's got no feelings for anybody. He just uses people and throws them aside.' [7]

With the candour of middle-age, Pat was to admit, 'I would have kept quiet because it felt it was nobody else's business, but then Linda had this child - which was fair enough - but what hurt me was that they'd called him "Julian" like his half-brother. Instantly I thought Brian was getting back at me - but why? The last time we'd parted, there was no animosity. Without stopping to think about it, I went straight to the newspapers. Then Georgio Gomelsky suggested I should find a solicitor to help get some money for Julian Mark. After a lot of messing about, the Stones organisation made me an offer of x pounds per week on condition that I sign a contract promising never again to speak about Mark in connection with Brian. I refused and set a paternity order in motion.'

Charlie Watts of all people had been troubled too by a similarly aggrieved lady during the little period of giving in to nature's baser urges that had ended after Shirley Ann Shepherd, quite unchanged, re-entered his life on being allowed past backstage security when the Stones were at the Hammersmith Odeon at the finish of their first tour. With old affections flooding their hearts, the two resolved to marry as soon as the sweep of events permitted, and were to enjoy a week's holiday together in Gibraltar the following spring regardless of Charlie's professional obligations. The Stones, therefore, weren't quite the full shilling at the Invicta Ballroom in Chatham on 15th March, 1964 when Mickey Waller, then with Marty Wilde's Wildcats, had to be wheeled in to deputise.

As Charlie and Shirley's romance rekindled, Bill and Diane's marriage muddled on simply because neither had sufficient motivation to finish it, and nothing of any substance yet suggested that the couple's life together was less than endurable.

Since March, they'd been Mr. and Mrs. *Wyman* as Bill had changed his surname by deed poll to that of his now well-known stage alias. Out of the cradle, Stephen couldn't help but become at least faintly aware of a celebrity exemplified by the image of Daddy holding his bass in the near-vertical manner peculiar to himself, being used as the emblem for the Top Twenty listing in *Merseybeat*, now subtitled 'Britain's leading beat paper', but dying like a sun going nova. While his workload meant that their famous friend wasn't able to give his child as much paternal attention as he'd have liked, Tony Chapman, Brian Cade and others of the fellows from his old life with whom he'd stayed in touch agreed that fatherhood suited Bill when he was able to let it.

Stephen may have stirred in Bill onsets of tickling, pillow-fighting high spirits, but a mist of resigned despair would begin to thicken gradually over the Wymans' new detached house, still in Beckenham, but, in accordance with an established pattern of graduating to an abode that was an improvement on the one before. It stood on an exclusive estate and encompassed the bathroom the indoor toilet and the immersion heater of which every one of Bill's childhood homes had been bereft. Little inside a relatively capacious dwelling indicated its owner's profession, apart from the electric musical instruments and amplifiers. With its modern furnishings and home help, it might have been the property of a marketing executive so admired by his superiors that he could get away with eccentricities like the near-shoulder-length hair that would render less able men ineligible for promotion.

He'd provided Diane and the boy with everything they could possibly want, hadn't he? To a detached observer with no stake in whatever busied the affluent rooms *chez* Wyman, it could have been an epitome of marital bliss - indeed appreciating what an ordeal of conviviality Bill's job could be, Diane was understanding when he didn't want to go out much. Nonetheless, she hoped that he might unwind a little, talk to her and enjoy their brief leisure with Stephen. Yet too soon would come his hand-squeezing departure for another distant stage and, whenever the opportunity presented itself, routine unfaithfulness.

'It was usually me and Brian that would go to the clubs to see the local groups and try to pick up the ladies,' he outlined, 'Mick and Keith would stay in the hotel, working on songs, while Charlie would usually go off to an art gallery or something.' [8]

Though there were episodes of the kind of laugh-a-minute ambience that prevailed, purportedly, when The Beatles were hurtling through the British countryside in their customised Austin Princess, there was little in the way of more profound dialogue when the late-night radio stations went off the air in Ian Stewart's Volkswagen and, next, the Dormobile with fitted record-player, and the ever more splendid vehicles that bore the Stones. 'We never talked on a deep level to each other,' shrugged Wyman, breaking into Damon Runyonese present tense with 'Me and Charlie do, but not the others. It's all peripheral stuff unless it's Stones business.' [9]

Often, the high command of Jagger, Richards and Oldham would choose to travel separately, thus allowing themselves close discussions about strategies that would be presented as *faits accomplis* to the others, and money-spinning creative activities involving other artists from Gene Pitney downwards. 'I didn't have Andrew Oldham behind me, like Mick and Keith did,' sighed Bill, 'I was always left on my own to write and produce, so I had to learn the hard way. That meant I failed a lot, producing these unknown bands who remained unknown, most of them.' [10]

He'd promised to oversee a single for Joey Paige if ever they were on the same land mass at the same time again, and had been equally taken with The Innocents, who'd gone beyond the call of duty backing Jet Harris in the Group Scene '64 tour, and, *sans* the ex-Shadow, would be on the bill of another Stones expedition in the late summer. By autumn, however, they weren't much of a group anymore, but multi-instrumentalist Colin Giffin and bass player Dave Brown were putting together a new ensemble, The End, [11] having taped 'I Want You Around', a Beatle-esque original.

Further demos of Brown-Giffin compositions were to impress Bill Wyman, who, with Glyn Johns, 'had been talking for some time about putting a production company together. Everybody else was doing it so he brought me in on that, and I just popped in at the end of a session. We formed Freeway Music, but Glyn soon dropped out so I was lumbered with looking after them.' [12]

No record The End made with Wyman was to make anyone rich, though 'Please Do Something' was to enter the Spanish Top Ten. Neither would Wyman and Johns' one-shot single with The Cheynes. Its A-side, 'Down And Out', had dripped from the pens of Wyman and Brian Cade, the ex-member of The Cliftons, who, as the Stones were to The Pretty Things, were connected genealogically to The Preachers, going strong since formation by Tony Chapman and Steve Carroll in September, 1963 for much the same reasons as Dick Taylor had started the Things that same month

The Preachers were becoming too hot for Penge and Beckenham to hold by the following March when they made a tape of a show at Beckenham Public Hall - where they headlined over The Cossacks and two other local combos - and put it before Bill Wyman, along with two IPC studio recordings. Bill didn't get round to doing anything about it for the best part of forty years when, contacted by bass guitarist Keith Temple, he organised and wrote sleeve notes for the release of the material on vinyl. [13]

In the meantime, Bill had lent an intrigued ear to The Preachers' fourteen-year-old Peter Frampton, as prodigious a guitarist as Mick Taylor for 'these wonderfully innovative jazz solos. He used to come knocking on my door and say, "Please can I come in and play guitar?", or he'd say, "Got any old stage clothes you don't want?" Then he'd say, "Great! Got some spare Beatle boots?" We've stayed in touch ever since. He seems to treat me like his mentor or uncle.' [13]

Peter, later of The Herd, Humble Pie and then a solo star, was a member of a Preachers that had taken stock after Tony Chapman had sustained head injuries and Steve Carroll, only nineteen, been killed when the group's van had crashed into a telegraph pole on the way to an engagement in Stourbridge on Wednesday 3rd June, 1964. There but for fortune went Bill Wyman, who'd been three days into the Stones' first tour of North America when it happened.

Notes

1. *Record Collector*, No. 239, July, 1999
2. Booklet notes to *The Definitive Downliners Sect: Singles A's & B's*
(See For Miles SEECD 398, 1994)
3. *Record Mirror*, 7th January, 1964
4. Quoted in *Swinging Sheffield* by A. Clayson
(Sheffield Museum, 1993)
5. *Midland Beat*, No. 11, August, 1964
6. *Ugly Things*, No. 19, summer 2001
7. *The Rolling Stones As It Happened*
(Chrome Dreams CIS2002/1, 2001)
8. *Mature Times*, December, 2004
9. *The Guardian*, 10th March, 2006
10. Whose guitarist Terry Taylor would be in Bill Wyman's
Rhythm Kings with Peter Frampton and Gary Brooker from
The Paramounts and Procol Harum.
11. *Record Collector*, No. 212, April, 1997
12. *Nod, Shake & Stomp* by The Preachers
(Tenth Planet TP053, 2002)
13. *Record Collector*, No. 231, November, 1998 (see note 10).

*Chapter Twelve*
**Gathering Moss**

*'As a male, I personally don't like feminine hair on men - and I imagine women don't like it either. If the fellows are wearing their hair, not just to be different, but because they like it, then I say that's great. The important thing is to be yourself' - Roy Orbison* [1]

In the Deep South 'Bible Belt', hellfire sermons were preached of the divine wrath to fall on communicants who did not subscribe to the casting out of the Limey pop pestilence and its flaunting of Corinthians xi.14: 'Doth not nature itself teach you that if a man have long hair, it is a shame unto him?' Out of earshot of the church bell too, not everyone below the Mason-Dixon line was as benign as Roy Orbison. As a registered protest against boys that looked like girls, Jerry Lee Lewis sheared back the long, crinkly wavy mane which had kept falling over his eyes since first he Hit the Big Time, while, back on the streets, contempt for men trying to ape the coiffeur of this new breed of 'musical' longhairs was expressed by actions that went further than merely bawling 'get yer 'air cut!' from a passing car. There was much suffering at the hands of white, 'redneck', good-'ol-boys, who laced right-wing militancy with pious fear of, not so much 'God', as of 'The Lord', a homespun prairie Plato with a crewcut, a Charles Atlas-like build and a hatred of commies, niggers - and queers like The Rolling Stones, whose natal tour of North America took place in June, 1964.

Visits by The Beatles and The Dave Clark Five earlier in the year had announced what has passed into myth as the 'British Invasion' of the sub-continent, an eventuality predicted by Gene Pitney when he'd landed in New York with the screams from that edition of *Thank Your Lucky Stars* with The Rolling Stones, still ringing in his ears.

On 22nd November, 1963, the day before the programme was transmitted, President Kennedy had been assassinated in Dallas, Texas. Some were to argue that the consequent hysteria centred on British beat groups was an antidote to the depressing Christmas that had followed the shooting - and also a reaction to the formulaic Bobby ballads and interchangeable surf instrumentals forever running up and down an unexciting *Hot 100*. John Lennon's more forthright theory was 'Kids everywhere go for the same stuff and, seeing as we'd done it in England, there's no reason why we couldn't do it over there too.' [2]

The rest of the world would be a walkover after Uncle Sam capitulated. His wonderment at all things from our sceptred isle was to peak in the 1964 week when two-thirds of the *Hot 100* was British in origin. Yet, as a phenomenon, this had less to do with the stars themselves than the behaviour of a public, who, once convinced of something incredible, exhibited a fanaticism for it that left the British themselves swallowing dust.

Many weeks before the Stones threaded through customs at New York's Kennedy Airport on 1st June, 1964, the US media had emphasised their notoriety to such a pitch that adolescent North America and its exploiters had anticipated a resounding outcry from the old and square that here were not four but *five* Horsemen of the Apocalypse, spreading plague and destruction wherever they passed. Certainly, the Stones tour is comparable in retrospect to the chaotic fortnight in the USA that was to finish The Sex Pistols in the next decade, if not The Beatles' quasi-regal progress in February, when they'd been greeted by the unison banshee scream they'd mistaken for engine noise on touchdown.

The Stones' welcome was muted by comparison, mainly because, unlike John, Paul, George and Ringo, the way hadn't been paved by a Number One in *Billboard*. 1964 was half over, and the Stones' progress in that same chart had been negligible. 'Come On' had not been deemed worthy of a US release, and 'I Wanna Be Your Man' had B-sided 'Not Fade Away', which, beginning a creep around the *Hot 100*'s lower reaches at Number 98, became chief selling point of *Britain's Newest Hitmakers*, a pot-shot at the LP list.

A few hundred fans converged, nevertheless, on the airport's upper terraces as the newcomers faced long corridors of light and shadow, cameras clicking like typewriters, and stick-mikes thrust towards their mouths in hopes that they'd crack back at the banal, ill-informed and damned impertinent questions - mostly about whether they were wearing wigs - with a Beatle-esque combination of zaniness, unsentimentality, unblinking self-assurance and the poker-faced what-are-you-laughing-at way they told 'em.

Coming across as more rivals to The Dave Clark Five than The Beatles, nothing particularly funny or even significant emerged from the Stones' lips, either then or during the first jet-lagged radio inter-view - at cock-crow on New York's WINS station - an episode of wryly deadpan shallowness conducted by a yapping presenter with the *nom de turntable* Murray the K. The brashest of them all, he'd had the unmitigated audacity to proclaim himself 'the Fifth Beatle' and now 'the Sixth Rolling Stone'.

From Manhattan's Astor Hotel, Brian dared a stroll around Times Square on the afternoon prior to an internal flight to Los Ange-les for a mismatching on a television variety show hosted by Dean Martin, one of Frank Sinatra's back-slapping 'Rat Pack', who dished out derogatory quips at the Stones' expense. Next up was a US con-cert debut before a crowd of not quite five thousand at San Bernandi-no's Swing Auditorium on a bill with Bobby Vee, Bobby Goldsboro and Bobby Comstock, all blow-waved human digests of stolid Pat Boone maxims.

Generally, the remaining shows were either like that or poorly-attended headlining affairs like Minneapolis's half-empty Excelsior State Ballroom. Yet, as it had been when punishing seasons in Ham-burg's red-light district clubland had toughened up The Beatles in readiness for what lay ahead, weeks of exploratory hard graft in the States were the Stones' 'Hamburg' in that they were often arduous but contained hidden blessings. Hitless, the group was obliged to melt the *sang froid* of non-screaming curiosity-seekers - and, though they were judged and found wanting on a couple of occasions, other audiences felt a compulsion to dance only a few bars into the first number, and Jagger was twisting 'em round his little finger by the finish on the evi-dence of the bedlam that you could hear back in the dressing rooms.

During two performances, compered by the Sixth Rolling Stone, at Carnegie Hall, New York's premier auditorium, on 23rd June, capac-ity crowds went crazy enough to provoke a ban on pop extravaganzas there for the foreseeable future. On this final day of their most harrow-ing public journey thus far, the group had been determined not to quit the stage until the entire place was jumping. They made a run of the most frantic ravers all the more piquant by hanging fire midway and inserting doe-eyed 'Tell Me', which, as a US-only single, was inching into the national Top Thirty, which meant that a rapid follow-up, 'It's All Over Now', would be guaranteed a fair hearing - and *England's*

*Newest Hitmakers* began its pedantic climb to Number 11, warranting a second US album - *12x5* - soon afterwards.

Nonetheless, while the likes of The Dave Clark Five, The Kinks, The Animals and, of course, The Beatles were ensconced in the singles Top Ten, the Stones would still be struggling as US chart propositions when they undertook another jaunt before the year was out. Into the bargain, there was a worrying psychological undertow: the danger of being superseded in the interim by a group that would make them look tame. On the strength of sound alone, let alone its makers' more deranged appearance, 'Don't Bring Me Down' wiped the floor with twee 'Tell Me', didn't it? Yes, the ubiquitous Pretty Things were being primed to so delightfully horrify the Land of the Free that the Stones might be lost in their shadow.

Appetites were being whetted by filmed snippets, including an interview direct from Dick Taylor's parents' front room, allied with US radio censoring the line 'I laid her on the ground' from 'Don't Bring Me Down', and the issue of a 'decent' version by something called 'On Her Majesty's Service'. The group's management office rang with proposed tour schedules from US entrepreneurs yelling 'Klondike!' at the notion of a freak carnival of even greater magnitude than those dreadful Rolling Stones. An advert extolling the Things' virtues - 'Proof positive that long hair *can* be popular' - filled half-a-page in *Billboard*. Dollars danced before gleaming eyes. Fortunately for the Stones, however, the moment was lost forever through executive dithering: big place, America, isn't it?

With most of the Union's fifty states comparable in size to the the whole of Britain, it did no harm for London, Decca's US outlet, to hurl at such a wide sales domain singles of any Stones tracks from forthcoming or already big-selling LPs that took their fancy. Thus 'Time Is On My Side' from *12 X 5* - a mixture mostly of the contents of a second British EP, *Five By Five*, and tracks from the yet-unissued second UK album, chart-topping *Rolling Stones No. 2* - intruded on the national Top Twenty in autumn 1964.

Four of *12 X 5*'s twelve selections - and further items for purposes that were then mainly non-specific - had resulted from the non-public highlight of the Stones' first US trip, when they spent two days in the studio where Chicago blues lived as pungently and as pragmatically as it did in the down-and-out State Street busker lilting an unaccompanied and never-ending 'Hoochie Coochie Man' as if optimistic of sexual congress, possibly on the very pavement.

The hirsute young Englishmen could scarcely believe that they were inside Chess under the aegis of the same house team that had forged the definitive works of Waters, Wolf, Diddley and Berry. Jagger especially could not come to immediate terms with the reality of standing within the postal address - 2120 South Michigan Avenue - to which his schoolboy self had sent saved-up money for the otherwise unobtainable discs that had made life halfway bearable then. Although these days, if the group had soundchecked inside a ballroom on Pluto, it mightn't have seemed all that odd. Neither would mixing socially with Chuck Berry, who dropped by, all sweetness-and-light, and with cause to be thankful for further hard evidence of the Stones' devotion in their revivals of royalty-earning 'Around And Around' and 'Reelin' And Rockin'' plus non-negotiable 'Down The Road Apiece' and 'Confessin' The Blues' from the catalogue of Jay McShann's Kansas City Orchestra, which, like 'Down The Road Apiece', Berry had covered as the Stones had covered his 'Come On'.

The group attempted another fusion of urban blues and nascent rock 'n' roll in 'Don't Lie To Me', a Fats Domino single from the early 1950s, and framed crackerbarrel philosophy in the context of a broken romance within a straightforward blues structure for the Nanker-Phelge combine's 'Empty Heart' and Richards and Jagger's 'Good Times Bad Times'. This was the B-side in almost all sales territories to the jewel in the crown of the Chess sessions: a stirring improvement on 'It's All Over Now', a minor US hit by soul combo The Valentinos - so minor that it didn't warrant a release in Europe. It had been recommended, as he'd tell you himself, by Murray the K, a Sixth Rolling Stone indeed on that occasion.

Almost as small a US hit in 1961 had been Wilson Pickett's soul ballad 'If You Need Me'. With Ian Stewart on organ and piano, the Stones' version was to compete with 'Around And Around' as the most played *Five By Five* track on UK pirate radio. It was similar in style to Irma Thomas's much more recent 'Time Is On My Side'. Though the group copied its arrangement, their overall delivery was impregnated with an individuality inherent in Jagger's emotion-charged spoken passage.

This was to be included on *The Rolling Stones No. 2*, and was noticeably different from another version of the same number that, with piano instead of organ, and greater emphasis on guitar and backing vocals, had been recorded earlier in London, and was, therefore, able to be included on *12 X 5*.

At the last minute, so was salutatory '2120 South Michigan Avenue' - an instrumental of like persuasion to 'Now I've Got A Witness'. Remaindered, however, was another vocal item, 'Look What You've Done', from the venerated Muddy Waters, who chanced to be present too when the Stones were also working on his downbeat 'I Can't Be Satisfied'.

It featured what Brian Jones was to cite as 'one of the best guitar solos I've ever managed.' [3] Yet, while it was selected for *The Rolling Stones No. 2*, it wasn't to appear on its US counterpart, February 1965's *The Rolling Stones Now!*. This was because North American LPs tended to include fewer tracks, but why was 'I Can't Be Satisfied' one of the omissions? Jagger and Richards' lacklustre 'What A Shame' could have gone without any hardship.

Such an affront, however unintentioned, fuelled Brian's growing worries about how dispensable a Stone he was becoming - so much so that there was an apparent 'I'll show 'em'-type suicide attempt not long after the return from the States. Yet, in particular territories there and elsewhere, Jones rather than Jagger was The Man. Somewhere among audiences as amorphous as frogspawn lurked many a musician who Jones was to outfit with musical - and visual - personality. While Lowell George - one of The Standells, a Los Angeles outfit before postpsychedelic recognition as mainstay of Little Feat - first attempted bottleneck through Brian's inspiration , it was Jones's hairstyle as much as his instrumental skills that captured the imaginations of myriad other US males who, after gazing with yearning at the sleeves of *England's Newest Hitmakers* and then *12 X 5*, grew out their crew-cuts as far as they dared and, with lacquer and cellotape, tortured it into a straight, all-round fringe just like Brian's.

Some formed groups that seized upon whatever aspects of the 'Invasion' idioms they felt most comfortable. The Seeds, The 13th Floor Elevators, ? and the Mysterions, [4] The Shadows Of Knight and myriad less renowned Anglophile 'garage bands' were to crawl from the US sub-cultural woodwork, owing much to the Stones, who, if relatively slow to gain ground in North America in hard financial terms, would amass widespread fundamental support between their first and second visits.

More and more frequently, in out-of-the-way dance halls in Wisconsin or Arizona, you'd be coming across a quintet that had reinvented itself as a Stones-style combo. The Jagger-esque singer would be standing sideways-on to the microphone, and, when he wasn't either blowing mouth-organ or wielding maracas, would be clapping hands above his head and kicking one leg backwards as if dancing a half-hearted Charleston. To his right, the blond - possibly peroxided - fellow transfixing the girls with his Brooding Intensity would be playing, in imagination at least, a Vox Teardrop Mk. VI which, with its sensuous if lozenge-shaped table, was to be as synonymous with Brian Jones as the Fender Stratocaster with Hank B. Marvin.

Though being like Brian was becoming so ultimate an objective for such exquisites, it was less fun for the lad himself for reasons connected with the gnawing away of his self-worth as a musician. Theoretically, his formal training put him a cut above Mick and Keith, who had had to *dah-dah* 'head' arrangements to each other rather than score them out in musical script. Nevertheless, as much as it was with The Beatles, Stones albums were being scoured for potential hits by other artists, who were also courting Richards and Jagger for any of the compositions that were still pouring forth from them, that were unsuitable for the group.

Yet while it may have been feasible for Keith and Mick to order a guitar-shaped swimming pool each for supplying Gene Pitney with 'That Girl Belongs To Yesterday', whither the likes of further cracks at 'Blue Turns to Grey' by both The Epics and, from California, Dick and Dee Dee - not to mention Vashti's 'Some Things Just Stick In Your Mind', 'Wastin' Time' by comedian Jimmy Tarbuck or 'You Must Be The One' from The Greenbeats? Either they made deflated journeys into the bargain bin or were buried on B-sides. If released by the Stones as a catchpenny A-side in Germany, 'Congratulations' - nothing to do with Cliff Richard's renowned Eurovision Song Contest entry - was also part of life's loose change in almost every sense of the phrase.

Never designed for public consumption, demonstration recordings - 'demos' - of these syndications were knocked together, assembly-line-like, during the summer of 1964, mainly in the Decca complex, conveniently close to Mapesbury Road, by Jagger and various makeshift backing groups. Usually, these consisted of whatever Stones were available plus session players with close knowledge of each other's work via countless daily recording dates, punctuated by Musicians Union-regulated tea-breaks. Among reputed helpers on 'Some Things Just Stick In Your Mind', for example, were guitarists John McLaughlin - to be a jazz-rock colossus in the 1970s - and the sometime leader of The Big Jim Sullivan Combo, who'd covered Ral Donner's Presley-esque 'You Don't Know What You've Got' in 1961. Big Jim had since emerged as one of the brightest stars in the metropolitan studio firmament.

Led Zeppelin's guitarist-in-waiting, Jimmy Page, fretted subordinate rhythm chords to Sullivan's lead picking on 'Each And Every Day Of The Year'. As a fish beneath the waves of the burgeoning beat boom too, Led Zeppelin's future bass guitarist, John Paul Jones - who, alongside McLaughlin, was fulfilling existing engagements with the fading Tony Meehan Combo - engineered 'We're Wastin' Time', a vague waltz-time fusion of Merseybeat and C&W, notable for someone - probably Sullivan - finger-picking a twelve-string acoustic.

In more familiar guise, John Paul was plucking bass on 'Try A Little Harder', a Jagger-Richards attempt at ersatz soul, with other personnel from The Andrew Oldham Orchestra, assembled by the Stones' co-manager earlier in the year for easy-listening *melanges* of mostly current hits and acclamatory originals such as 'There Are But Five Rolling Stones' [*sic*] and '365 Rolling Stones (One For Every Day Of The Year)' - which, incidentally, featured Steve Marriott, yet to front The Small Faces, on harmonica. These were shoehorned onto a 1964 LP, *16 Hip Hits*.

Jones had shouldered responsibility for most of its creative donkey-work gladly because 'I wanted to arrange, Andrew wanted to produce, and neither of us was very choosy. I was grateful because he trusted me with these sessions and all these musicians. I was allowed to write them nice, interesting little things, especially for woodwinds. We'd always have a couple of oboes or French horns. He gave me a chance to do all these weird things. He kind of let me get on with it, but he had a very clear idea of what he wanted. The records we made were more the underground really. The very fact that they didn't sell actually gives you a certain freedom; you can do what you like, having a good time, getting paid for it. His sessions were always fun. So many others were banal, mundane, very boring. You couldn't wait to get out of them.' [5]

John Paul had replaced the arranger first appointed by Oldham, Mike Leander, who'd accepted a post as a Decca staff producer. According to Leander's close friend, Paul Gadd, *Ready Steady Go*'s floor manager [6], his relationship with one of his clients was 'something more than professional. At times, it got a bit complicated, and there was always a lot of whispering when she was there.' [7]

'She' was Marianne Faithfull, a filly that Andrew Oldham had just added to his managerial stable. Marianne was what George Bernard Shaw might have called a 'downstart' in that she came from a family that had once been better off. With her mother, a lady of Austrian aristocratic stock, she dwelt in one of the more forlorn suburbs of Reading, the Berkshire county town reckoned by makers of television documentaries to be the most 'average' in Britain. By the time she reached the sixth form at St. Joseph's Convent School, Faithfull was omnipresent - as was Mike Cooper - singing in floor spots at local folk clubs.

While she acquitted herself admirably on these occasions, Marianne as an A-level student was, as she herself would ruefully admit, 'No egghead. What I really want to do eventually is settle down and get married' [8] - presumably to University of Cambridge undergraduate John Dunbar, her 'steady', who was consistent with her liking for 'tall men with glasses'.[9] A Londoner, he was an acquaintance of Peter Asher, brother of Paul McCartney's then-girlfriend, and half of Peter and Gordon, who, in spring 1964, were heading for Number One with 'World Without Love', penned for them by Paul with John Lennon.

'In' with the innermost in-crowd of all, Dunbar had showed off Marianne, blonde, pulchritudinous and just seventeen, at a launch party in March for 'Shang A Doo Lang', the second Decca single by a young actress, Adrienne Posta. Its composers, Mick Jagger and Keith Richards, were there too, but Marianne was introduced first to the disc's producer, Andrew Loog Oldham - who saw pop star potential in her convent-educated loveliness.

He set Keith and Mick to work on a made-to-measure song, and they came up with what Richards considered 'the sort of song we'd never play. We were trying to write "Hoochie Coochie Man", and came out with a song that's almost like "Greensleeves".' [10] Wan

'As Tears Go By' was then demoed with just a session guitarist picking arpeggios behind Jagger - who was extraordinary to Marianne then only as a spotty and rather coarse youth whose tearful girlfriend had been shouting at him at the Adrienne Posta do. [11]

Proving Oldham's judgement to be correct, Marianne's 'As Tears Go By' prowled the British and, eventually, the US charts during the latter half of 1964, aided by an image - not completely assumed - of an instinctively upper class and slightly scatty provincial maid, amused, if bewildered by her sudden fame. Yet this breakthrough was dampened by the failure of her ill-chosen second 45, 'Blowin' In The Wind', an anti-war opus from *The Freewheelin' Bob Dylan*, and a hit previously for Peter, Paul and Mary.

As he'd developed quite a fondness for Dylan - who was about to upset folk pedants by 'going electric' and exposing rock 'n' roll influences - Keith Richards was delighted to provide backing acoustic guitar on Faithfull's 'Blowin' In The Wind'. Moreover, his moptop-gone-to-seed was often covered with a peaked cap like Bob's when he was seen squiring Linda Keith, a photographic model and 'wild child' daughter of a Light Programme presenter, around late-night London watering holes. Linda was twenty-year-old Keith's first 'serious' girlfriend, and the peaks and troughs of their two-year entanglement would embrace his disapproval of her frolicking with heroin, a summer holiday in the south of France, and him looking through the eyes of love when facial scars of a car crash in which she was involved were still raw.

Lack of complete privacy had been very much the way of things at Edith Grove, and even at Mapesbury Road there'd nearly always be someone else hovering should a tenant and his paramour choose to canoodle on the living room settee. However, after Andrew married in September, 1964, only Mick would be party to any of Linda and Keith's sweet nothings when he and Richards moved to a chalet-style apartment with an extended lounge and fitted wardrobes in a more verdant part of North London. It was also sufficiently up-market to attract burglars - who turned the place over when the Stones were on their fourth national tour in almost as many months.

Between record dates and television plugs, Marianne Faithfull was also busy with country-wide expeditions with the likes of The Hollies, Freddie and the Dreamers, Gene Pitney, Cliff Bennett and the Rebel Rousers, The Rockin' Berries, Gerry and his Pacemakers, Roy Orbison, The Kinks and the low-billed Manish Boys, fronted by the young man destined to be David Bowie. Knowing looks were exchanged about Marianne and a married member of The Hollies, and Gene Pitney, mixing work with pleasure, was to be romantically linked with her too.

Other rumours also abounded. As well as the one about her and Mike Leander, there was even one about her and Mick Jagger, though to many of both their pop star equals and the readers of the music press, it was inconceivable that a posh bird like Marianne would go out with a Rolling Stone, unless it was an attraction of opposites, akin to the desire pregnant woman have sometimes for an otherwise sick-making morsel of food.

While all this was or wasn't going on, John Dunbar was enjoying a long holiday in Greece which might have involved more than just sight-seeing and sunbathing. Frank exchanges on his return culminated in a marriage proposal that was accepted. Within a year, Marianne was a married mother, living in Knightsbridge where their social circle was wide enough for an uneasy embrace of both showbusiness sorts and her husband's old university pals.

Although he was giving hearsay substance by openly cherishing a caprice to entice Marianne into bed, Mick Jagger was on the periphery of her life then, even as his *amour* with the volcanic Chrissie Shrimpton deteriorated, mortified as she was by 'friends' and press gossip informing her of his group's supposed satyric exploits when away from wives and loved ones.

If anything, the Stone of strongest allure for Marianne seemed to be the more devil-may-care Keith - and she was to conclude, on the strength of a purported later one-night stand, that he might be the sex stud of the century. Some noticed also a certain friskiness between Faithfull and Brian Jones, although she was aware of the uglier aspects of his inner nature, and that he was the loser in the group's power struggle on the evidence of the - often justifiable - conduct of the others towards him.

There were, nonetheless, episodes akin to a schoolyard situation in which a child teased mercilessly through the spring term, is suddenly popular when his playmates return to class after Easter, a sense of 'Brian has been tormented quite enough. Let's start being nice to him.' Mick spared an unknowing Brian the anxiety of another paternity suit by helping Andrew Oldham draft a letter to the woman in question's solicitor, settling the matter - while Keith could be less conspiratorially protective towards Brian, once lashing out with a chisel-toed boot at a youth close enough to have spat at Jones when the Stones appeared before a mob of nine thousand in Blackpool's Empress Ballroom a month after flying back from the States.

Rather than acknowledge protection and defence, Brian would pounce with a kind of despairing triumph on a perceived slight like the 'I Can't Be Satisfied' matter - and there were plenty more to come - and seek tawdry compensation after a fashion, by pulling birds on a grander scale than ever before, and stressing his 'fear' of marriage in interviews. This was motivated too by resentment that Jagger, if simply a team player - albeit a vital one - in the studio, had been singled out, however unwillingly, as not only the Stones' central figure, but a separate entity.

At a televised 'Rave Mad Mod Ball' at Wembley's vast Empire Pool in April, the five were introduced by Jimmy Savile as 'Jagger M. and the Rolling Stones', while, in September, a Mick Jagger impersonation contest was held at Greenwich Town Hall in which the day was gained by a 'Laurie Yarman' - who turned out to be Chris Jagger. However, unlike Paul McCartney's younger brother, Mike McGear, he had no qualms about sticking with a talismanic surname when he launched his pop career in earnest a decade later.

While Chris's eyes may have shone with pride, Brian Jones watched the elder Jagger's onstage cavortings sourly. He should have been the Stones' principal sex symbol, not Mick, and he took pleasure at the quicksilver front man's continued irritation whenever he, Brian, stoked up a fresh tidal wave of screams by just standing there. Off-stage, competition raged too when trying it on with female artists on any given tour, and the suaver Brian seemed to have the edge over Mick who, with Chrissie not looking, charged in, unafraid of being repulsed by such as Margo Lewis of Goldie and the Gingerbreads, one of the USA's few hit girl vocal *and* instrumental outfits. 'She almost punched his head off his neck,' gasped the group's guitarist, Carol MacDonald, '"Who do you think you are? How dare you!" - because he thought he's the star so he could do that.' [12]

He didn't get very far either with sixteen-year-old British singer-songwriter Twinkle, even though he tried very hard, going so far as to dedicate 'If You Need Me' to her from the stage. Thinking him 'very vulgar', she was more taken with Brian, who offered scintillating conversation rather than Mick's pseudo-rough diamond toilet-talk.

More conventionally handsome than Jagger, Jones was channelling much of his creative energy into being the best-looking member of the group - of *any* group. As such, he adhered to 'Mod' orthodoxy from late 1964, ordering suits made-to-measure with a discreet correctness so uttermost that Brian would have earned praise for a smart turn-out at Matins from the vicar of his Gloucestershire boyhood, almost like a previous existence now. As narcissistic as any Regency dandy, he was treating his appearance more than ever as a work of theatrical art, made afresh before he faced each day.

Everything had to be just so: back vents precisely seven inches one week, five the next. How wide are lapels now? The jacket covered either a roll-necked nylon pullover or a shirt with a tie inclined to be plain or patterned rather than op-art. Such attire could be impractical under the particularly sweaty arc-lights on *Ready Steady Go*, so he added insult to Andrew Oldham's injury to The Pretty Things by purloining Brian Pendleton's striped matalot's jersey to wear on a Stones appearance on the programme on 26th June, 1965, causing it to became a wanted fashion accessory.

The poet Henry Thoreau reminds us, however, that 'when a soldier is hit by a cannonball, rags are as becoming as purple'. No matter how fine a figure he cut, Brian could find no constructive remedy for his atrophied position in the Stones, though, now and then, he'd recover scrapings of his stolen inheritance in the sweet torment of screams. During two performances at the Odeon in Cheltenham on 10th September, the very day that the Stones had been voted the most popular British group in a *Melody Maker* readers poll, the pitch of those screeches soared to its most stinging after Brian delayed sauntering onto the boards a calculated second or two after everyone else. It was he too who was the target of nearly all the votive offerings, some inscribed with messages of undying love that rained onto the stage.

Outside, where an enterprising chap with a pile of monochrome A3 photos of individual Stones was doing brisk business, pictures of Brian outsold those of any of the others, and, before the lights had dimmed for the Local Boy Made Good's latest 'home game', he posed backstage for the *Gloucestershire Echo* between sports-jacketed 'old band mates'[13] who he hardly knew, namely Mick Bratby and Buck Jones of a still-functional Ramrods, who'd risen from the youth clubs to recent supports to The Merseybeats, The Hollies and Brian Poole. 'We were always on the threshold of greater things,' a middle-aged Buck would surmise, 'But as semi-professionals, we had to consider our jobs. In the end, I had to make a decision between being an estate agent and carrying on with the group.' [13]

Other than the fuss over Brian, the Stones' performance and all that surrounded it were not atypical of any on that specific tour. Three girls had started a queue nearly a week before the box-office opened. On the night, even many without tickets were milling round the Odeon's art-deco entrance, and the streets surrounding it were closed to traffic as police with walkie-talkies co-ordinated the group's admittance into the building. The overflowing show itself was pop hysteria at its most intense with fainting and heightened blood pressure bringing on nose-bleeds. On the sodden carpeting afterwards, cleaners would come across soiled knickers among smashed rows of tip-up chairs.

At all the other stops, hundreds ringed themselves days in advance round theatres, cinemas and city halls to guarantee admission. Those lacking such clubbable stamina recoursed to buying tickets from touts at up to eight times the marked price. At Plymouth, it was necessary to smuggle the Stones along underground tunnels leading from Westward Television's studios, two blocks away, to a lane beside the ABC. At a given signal, a fire exit was flung open and the group was striding purposefully and unobserved along the passageway towards it when a female let out a shriek and brought an adoring crowd down on them.

Not everyone was so besotted with the Stones. Putting action over pub debate, short-maned males, maddened more than ever by the Stones' now shoulder-length tresses, were now actually arming themselves with scissors and trying to inflict depilatory barbarity on the five poufs who'd taken the mick by placing an ad in a December edition of the *NME* wishing starving hairdressers and their families a Happy Christmas. No such aggressor got past the stage door, but had he succeeded, he may have been repulsed by what Keith had learned from a dabbling in karate with Andrew - or, more insidiously, his ability to outface unwanted company in the dressing rooms where he and the others would be incarcerated until, with the cadence of the last number still reverberating, they bolted pell-mell to a getaway car ticking over in a back-alley. A police cordon with helmets rolling in the gutter would hold back clamorous fans who chased the vehicle up the high street.

'Basically, we'd turn up, and all we'd think about is, "What's the exit strategy?"' explained Keith, 'And then we'd take bets on how many songs we'd get through before it all collapsed. Usually, it was ten minutes - three songs and it was all over. We'd walk into some of those places, and it was like they had the Battle of the Crimea [*sic*] going on. "Scream power" was the thing everyone was judged by. We couldn't hear ourselves for years.' (14)

During one autumn month, The Beatles were traversing the country at the same time, but no bother was expected by police patrols from the occupants of the sleeping bags that lined the pavements with their thermos flasks, transistor radios and comics. Once they might have wrung their hands, but now Mums and Dads would bring provisions to their waiting children. Well, it was only The Beatles, ritualised and cosy. In the auditorium, their daughters let rip their healthy, good-humoured screams - though, during one of those abrupt lulls that occur sometimes, some buffoon yelled 'Down with The Beatles!' His portly girlfriend swiped him with her handbag. Everybody laughed. After 'Twist And Shout', the squealing would cease for the National Anthem, and everyone would file out fairly quietly.

Contrast that to those sinister Rolling Stones at that ballroom in Blackpool in summer, which had ended in a shambles of broken chairs, an up-ended grand piano and smithereens of footlights, drum-kit and guitar amplifiers. This damage was but a fraction of the final assessment after the crowd was driven outside where they let off steam in a two-hour orgy of brawling and vandalism. There were four arrests and twelve times as many injuries - and, as if in judgement, one of those was Brian Jones with a gash millimetres under an eye.

At that precise moment on the other side of the world, The Beatles were the darlings of a grinning Australian media after 'it seemed that the whole population had turned out to meet us.' (15) Thus spake Jimmy Nicol, the drummer who deputised on this tour for a hospitalised Ringo, before vanishing from the pages of history.

Another drummer, Viv Prince of The Pretty Things was to leave a deep and lasting cultural wound Down Under a few months later, setting a standard then for rock 'n' roll excess during a tour of New Zealand by his group with Eden Kane and a laryngitic Sandie Shaw. Tales are told still about Prince, say, pissing on Shaw's feet [16], bringing the same very dead crayfish to every press conference or crawling beneath a proscenium, slurping whiskey from a shoe and attempting to set fire to the stage. Following the last date, a *woomph* of flashbulbs immortalized Prince being escorted from a - grounded - aircraft after an altercation with its staff.

Perhaps it might have been a similar story in macrocosm had the Things traced the Stones' scent to the States. Maybe the furore would have been an ignition point for global success. Then paths might have diverged differently; the Things putting up with international acclaim and supertax while the Stones began over thirty years of struggle and heartache that might have destroyed a lesser group.

If the Things bothered the Stones, the Stones bothered The Beatles more. At grassroots, while there'd been plenty of Merseybeat acts at the *NME* Pollwinners Concert, The Beatles - and The Hollies - apart, none were able to take the Top Twenty for granted anymore. Interest was waning even on Merseyside itself as epitomised by Liverpool lass Eileen Lawton's letter to *Mersey Beat*, complaining that all local groups sounded the same, so much so that 'I am now a fan of The Rolling Stones. Mick, Brian, Bill, Charlie and Keith are all individualists in their own right, and they make their contemporaries look insipid.' [17]

Both Mick-Brian-Bill-Charlie-and-Keith and John-Paul-George-And-Ringo were now famous enough to be the subjects of the first of more biographies - albeit neither of them a triumph of linguistic ability nor penetrating insights into the human condition - than anyone could have imagined then. At the Liverpool premiere in July of *A Hard Day's Night*, the northern outfit's first movie, master-of-ceremonies David Jacobs had popped in a couple of *bon mots* at the expense of the Stones. For weeks, the film's title theme by The Beatles and 'It's All Over Now' had monopolised the first two positions in Britain's hit parade, necessitating the avoidance of such revenue-draining clashes in future.

If economically foolish, Brian Jones's honesty seemed, therefore, to be commendable when, on running into the *NME*'s Richard Green - not really by chance - he'd seized the opportunity to stick a pin in 'It's All Over Now': 'I'm not that keen on the record. It's all right, but, I don't know...it's just something.' [18]

If it had flopped, perhaps the Stones would have needed him again, rather than continuing to push him slowly but surely further into the background while strengthening the dominance of the Mick-Keith-Andrew axis to a point where first Jagger-Richards A-side for the Stones, 'The Last Time', was less than a season away. Yet, just as 'Not Fade Away' had been mostly at Keith's instigation, so 'Little Red Rooster' - the single that plugged the gap between 'It's All Over Now' and 'The Last Time' - was Brian's, his most palpable and lasting affirmation of his love for the blues.

So it was that, in November, 1964, Willie Dixon - given to aphorisms like 'The blues is the roots. Everything else is the fruits' [19] - topped the British charts by proxy as composer of a piece whose pedigree could be traced through a rendition by Sam Cooke in 1963 to The Griffin Brothers' US 'sepia' smash in 1951 to the first recording by Howlin' Wolf. The risk that the Stones took in putting out a slow blues as an A-side was confirmed when it was the cause of one of the most major discrepancies between the two principal national music journal charts, entering at Number Fifteen in *Melody Maker* and going directly to Number One in the *New Musical Express*.

It nestled uneasily in a Top Twenty peopled by the likes of Gene Pitney, Val Doonican, Jim Reeves and The Helmut Zacharias Orchestra as well as 'hairy monsters' like The Kinks, Wayne Fontana and the Mindbenders and The Pretty Things, who, owing to exposure on Radio Luxembourg, not to mention the newer pestilence of off-shore pirate stations, were all making it ever harder for the BBC to give the public the 'decent' music it ought to be enjoying.

Brian experienced a sense of a mission accomplished in that, as well as this upset and something like 'Little Red Rooster' reaching a far, far larger audience than it would have done in the normal course of events, the Top Fifty was also accommodating a single each by Howlin' Wolf and John Lee Hooker, justifying the latter's comment, 'the best time ever for the blues was in England in the sixties,' [20] and Keith Richards' original simple aim, when the Stones were still smouldering into form, 'to turn people onto the blues. If we could turn them onto Muddy, Jimmy Reed, Howlin' Wolf and John Lee Hooker, then our job was done.' [21]

Well, the job *was* done, and somehow, the group was all over now - or at least what it could have been had Brian remained in charge. That phase had peaked and started its painful and lingering decline before they'd even left the Crawdaddy. In a way he would never have wished, the wildest dream of all those that had driven the early Rolling Stones became a reality, and was thereby taken away from them.

Notes

1. *Melody Maker*, 13th August, 1966
2. *Playboy*, 19th October, 1964
3. *Record Collector*, April, 2001
4. In the 1990s, a middle-aged ? and the Mysterions - with a keyboard player who looked just like 'Captain Mainwaring' in *Dad's Army* - released a revival of 'Empty Heart', and made a British concert debut at London's Royal Festival Hall.
5. *Stoned* by A.L. Oldham (Vintage, 2000)
6. Who was to trouble the world in the 1970s as glam-rock overlord Gary Glitter
7. *Leader* by G. Glitter and L. Bradley (Warner, 1992)
8. *New Musical Express*, 2nd October, 1964
9. *Ready Steady Go* annual, (Beat Publications, 1965)
10. *Q*, October, 1988
11. Despite Keith Richards' remarks, a Stones version of 'As Tears Go By' was to B-side to 1966's '19th Nervous Breakdown' in Britain, and reach the US Top Ten as an A-side.
12. *She's A Rebel* by G.G. Gaar (Blandford, 1993)
13. *Gloucestershire Echo: The Sixties* souvenir guide, August, 1998
14. *The Rolling Stones In Their Own Words* ed. D. Dalton and M. Farren (Omnibus, 1995)
15. *Melody Maker*, 20th June, 1964
16. Though the culprit was actually Kane
17. *Mersey Beat*, 9th April, 1964
18. *New Musical Express*, 17th July, 1964
19. *Sunday Times*, 11th February, 2007)
20. *The Guardian*, 8th December, 2006
21. *Blues Guitar* ed. J. Obrecht (Miller Freeman, 1993)

*Epilogue*
## Yesterday Men?

*'We're a terrible band really, but we are the oldest. That's some sort of distinction, isn't it?' - Charlie Watts*

As the turn of the century edged nearer, long hair on men was common in English country towns and the American Mid-West - as was a received conviction that the 1960s groups that pioneered it have never been as great as they were 'in the beginning'. Yet there were fiscal advantages in this. As commodity began to assume more absolute sway over creativity, the history of pop was seized upon more tightly than ever as an avenue for shifting records - and books - as demonstrated by the chart performance of 1975's *Metamorphosis*, an LP collection by The Rolling Stones of demos, out-takes and alternative versions, which, while fizzling out at a lowly Number 45 at home, reached Number Eight in *Billboard*.

That wasn't a bad result for tracks that were up to twelve years old and not meant for public consumption in the first place. Neither was a chart-topping album of new material, *A Bigger Bang*, in 2005. After all, no beat group was built to last, was it, let alone still be having hits and dominating concert platforms nearly half a century after it was formed? What's more, if augmented by horn sections *et al* and susceptible to boarding convenient bandwagons, the Stones continued to draw from the eternal verities of Jagger's half-caste singing, Richards' forceful rhythm, Watts's economic cohesion and, prior to his amicable departure in 1993, Wyman's fluid and workmanlike throb.

A lingering hip sensibility and a pulling of unexpected strokes has also kept the Stones' heads above the waters of mere nostalgia, and enabled them to live down all manner of artistic follies and *faux pas*, although they made certain mistakes that other groups would be proud to call their own. Your opinion about what these are is likely to be more valid than mine because I'm one of these heretics who thinks that 1967's psychedelic *Their Satanic Majesties Request* might be one of the Stones' finest albums. Most consumers of today's cultured 'dad rock', however, have taught their children to regard it as the work of musicians who had swum out of their depth, and I have to admit that the following year's 'Jumping Jack Flash' - a raw three-chord bedrock turfed with *Satanic Majesties* lyricism - was more commensurate with an impending return to touring after a lay-off of almost three years.

The same was true of the unvarnished directness of 1968's *Beggar's Banquet*, Brian Jones's last album before he was asked to leave by Mick Jagger and, the Napoleon to Brian's Snowball, Keith Richards. Soon to die by drowning, Jones was superceded by Mick Taylor, now an established young guitarist, having proved the equal of Eric Clapton and Peter Green, his immediate predecessors in John Mayall's Bluesbreakers, whose leader had heard The Gods playing at a venue local to Welwyn Garden City, and exchanged contact details with X-factor Mick.

Taylor was a Stone until 1973 when he became the second member with the same surname to leave. Debating the group's future, the press put forward many potential replacements, but all fingers pointed ultimately at Ronnie Wood.

A long-disbanded Birds were far behind him now. The rot may have set in when the powers at Decca decided to confine Wood originals to B-sides, and chose 'Leaving Here', a Tamla Motown cover, as the follow-up to 'You're On My Mind'. A correlated *Thank Your Lucky Stars* slot involved a poorly-judged descent onto the stage set, suspended on wires. There was also such a mix-up by record retailers with The Byrds that those ordering 'Leaving Here' were presented too frequently with the other lot's contemporaneous - and more appealing - 'Mr. Tambourine Man'. Making the best of a bad job, Ronnie's group - billing themselves as 'The English Birds' - served an infringement of copyright subpoena the hour a bemused Byrds alighted in England from their native California, but this publicity stunt did not lift 'Leaving Here' above Number 45 while 'Mr. Tambourine Man' flew to pole position.

When a third and then a fourth 45 missed altogether, The Birds - now calling themselves Birds Birds (!) - held an inevitable disbandment at arm's length via a cameo in a 1966 horror flick, *The Deadly Bees* - pop singer holidays on lonely farm where she is menaced by titular insects - before Kim Gardner and then Wood joined another group on its last legs, The Creation, whose two minor UK chart entries, 'Making Time' and 'Painter Man', were lacquered with the sound of a violin bow scraped across an electric guitar. A hasty LP, *We Are Paintermen*, had been issued only in continental Europe where, as a 1967 press release insisted, The Creation were 'Germany's third top touring group'. Yet, somewhere along the autobahns, they ran out of ideas, and elected to quit while they were ahead commercially after farewell treks round Holland and Denmark in April, 1968.

Following a subsequent spell as bass player with The Jeff Beck Group, Wood had, with Rod Stewart, joined forces with what was left of The Small Faces after Steve Marriott's resignation in 1969 to form a 'supergroup', Humble Pie, with Peter Frampton. With no attributive adjective, The Faces had, after a sluggish start, emerged as the Wood-stock Nation's very own Brian Poole and the Tremeloes, but were going off the boil as chart contenders by 1974 when Ronnie Wood became a temporary and, next, a full-time Rolling Stone.

By then, the Stones were no longer represented by Andrew Loog Oldham and Eric Easton, thanks chiefly to a divide-and-conquer ploy by Allen Klein, a showbusiness accountant from New Jersey appointed initially to undertake the administrative donkey-work of Oldham's business affairs. More inclined to fire than hire, Allen soon convinced Andrew that Eric's face no longer fitted. However, Easton had been a loyal and essentially honest servant, trustful too, so it wasn't surprising that an attempt to buy out the man who had shared the Stones' fortunes since 1963 was thwarted, and a mess of writs ensued. If tiring of ideas that were intriguing conceptually but ill-conceived in practice, Oldham would cling on longer - until the day in 1968 when he rang Mick Jagger from a telephone booth to wish him a good rest-of-his-life.

Drifting rather than breaking away from the Stones' orbit were The Pretty Things, though there would always be occasional encounters, such as one in the 1990s when, during one of his group's tours of Europe, Dick Taylor spent a night off in the VIP enclosure at a Stones recital near Brussels, chatting to his two old mates from Dartford as if the aeons that had passed since grammar school and art college had been but nothing.

For a while, the Things had been in uncertain musical transition since the fragmentation in the mid-1960s of the 'Honey I Need' line-up, most dramatically with the sudden disappearance of Brian Pendleton, who jumped onto a nameless platform during the group's train journey to some dates up north. 'We got through them as a four-piece,' sighed Phil May, 'Then Dick went round to Brian's flat, and the door was swinging open like the Marie-Celeste. He and his wife and baby had just vanished. We next saw him at a business meeting about four years later.'

With the enlistment of personnel from Bern Elliott's Fenmen, the Things' raw, blueswailing ferocity was soon deferring to subtlety of structure and studied artistic progression. This was manifest further in self-consciously 'weird' singles paving the way for *SF Sorrow*, the brainchild of Taylor and May, and unquestionably the first 'rock opera' - though, technically, a song-cycle. However, with the group no longer an overnight sensation, a tired Taylor quit the treadmill of the road, following a flash of celluloid glory in 1969's *What's Good For The Goose*, starring Norman Wisdom, at a cinema near you.

Years passed. Contradictory and far-fetched rumours abounded about what had happened to Dick Taylor. One powerful rumour was that he was down to rejoin the Stones now that *Mick* Taylor had gone. Other stories had firmer foundation in fact, but, as the next decade beckoned, Dick had anchored himself to the notion that he was going to be a Pretty Thing again, even if the old fire was down to embers. By the late 1980s, however, the group was knocking an astonishingly young clientele dead every Tuesday in a room above a London pub, even if a middle-aged joviality had replaced 1964's angry scowls. Into the bargain, there were guest performers of such diversity as Ian Stewart, Pink Floyd's Dave Gilmour and Glen Matlock, whose Sex Pistols had owed much to the early Pretty Things' thrillingly slap-dash verve.

A return to contemporary prominence was to climax in October, 2002 with a sensational exhumation of *SF Sorrow* at London's Royal Festival Hall. Engulfed by applause for a particularly *bravura* solo, Dick seemed in his quiet way as ecstatic as the capacity crowd that he and the group were so rabidly remembered. 'He looks like an ancient mad professor on stage,' smiled Arthur Brown, the opera's narrator on that night-of-nights, 'But he comes out with some of the most vital guitar playing you'll ever hear: very eclectic, totally authentic, true to the old blues, but taken into a different dimension. Without doubt, one of the great guitarists of our time.'

Like Phil May, the Stones had taken Taylor's abilities for granted. It was the same with his successor as bass player, the only Stone to reach the British Top Twenty with a solo single - 1983's '(Si Si) Je Suis Un Rock Star'. Now in his seventies, Bill Wyman has settled into the peaceful life he feels he deserves with third wife Suzanne and their children. His thwarted ambition as a songwriter - for the Stones anyway - provokes a measure of sympathy, even if his monetary wealth, like Charlie's, owes much to the Jagger-Richards A-sides that consolidated the group's market advances in the all-important United States.

Though 'The Last Time', three positions lower at Number Nine, had been a bit of a comedown compared to the Number Six tide-mark set by 'Time Is On My Side' in 1964 - and it was decided not to chance 'Little Red Rooster' as a US single - '(I Can't Get No) 'Satisfaction', the Beethoven's Fifth of 1960s pop and featuring the rasp of the fuzz-box guitar accessory that Keith had bought on the first US tour, would be the Stones' first US Number One and would be voted 1965's Best Single Of The Year in the *NME*'s readers poll. This was a momentous feat in an age when the ordained strategy for keeping up a pop group's momentum was to rush-release as many 45s - usually four per fiscal year - as the traffic would allow.

Under pressure to capitalise on 'Satisfaction', Jagger and Richards came up with what, to Jim McCarty of The Yardbirds, were symptomatic of 'a bit of a lull artistically then, what with all those hits that were similar, 'Satisfaction', 'Get Off Of My Cloud', '19th Nervous Breakdown'...'

That was OK by the fans, who sent all three of them to Number One - or as near as dammit - on both sides if the Atlantic. The rest of the public, over the initial shock, began slowly to stop fighting the situation, even grudgingly accepting the incorrigible Rolling Stones not as a pop group as transient and gimmicky as any other, but - marginally - a tolerable part of Britain's national furniture, like Promenade Concerts, *Coronation Street*, The Beatles, the first cuckoo of spring and *Sunday Night At The London Palladium* where, a few weeks before the Stones' predictably infamous headlining spot, Margo Henderson, a cabaret singer of the old school, belted out the traditional gospel song, 'Down By The Riverside', updated to include a reference to 'the good old Rolling Stones'.

They'd Made It, almost despite themselves. Nothing thrown at them afterwards - drug busts, deaths, divorces, knighthoods, you name it - could bring them down. And the wounds they inflicted, not only on pop, during the murky pageant of the early campaigns were gouged so close to the bone that, in the greater scheme of things, most of what The Rolling Stones have done since has been barely relevant.

# Discography

*Key: Decca * London #*
*Unless otherwise stated, all discs are in vinyl format.*

## BRITISH RELEASES 1963-1964

## Singles

F 11675* Come On/I Want To Be Loved (7th June, 1963)

F 11764* I Wanna Be Your Man/Stoned (1st November, 1963)

F 11845* Not Fade Away/Little By Little (21st February, 1964)

F 11934* It's All Over Now/Good Times Bad Times (26th June, 1964)

F 12014* Little Red Rooster/Off The Hook (13th November, 1964)

## Extended Play

DFE 8560* *The Rolling Stones*
Bye Bye Johnny; Money; You Better Move On; Poison Ivy.
(10th January, 1964)

DFE 8590 *Five By Five*
If You Need Me; Empty Heart; 2120 South Michigan Avenue; Confessin'
The Blues; Around And Around. (15th August, 1964)

255

## Long Play

LK 4554 *Thank Your Lucky Stars*
Come On; tracks by other artists (27th September, 1963)

LK 4583* *Saturday Club*
Poison Ivy; Fortune Teller; tracks by other artists (24th January, 1964)

LK 4577* *Ready Steady Go*
Come On; I Wanna Be Your Man; tracks by other artists (24th January, 1964)

LK 4605* *The Rolling Stones*
*Side One*
Route 66; I Just Wanna Make Love To You; Honest I Do; Mona; Now
I've Got A Witness; Little By Little.
*Side Two*
I'm A King Bee; Carol; Tell Me (You're Coming Back); Can I Get A Witness;
You Can Make It If You Try; Walking The Dog. (17th April, 1964)

Decca LK 4695 *Fourteen*
'Surprise Surprise'; tracks by other artists (21st May, 1964)

## US RELEASES 1964

## Singles

9657# Not Fade Away/I Wanna Be Your Man (6th March, 1964)

9682# Tell Me (You're Coming Back)/I Just Want To Make Love To
You (19th June, 1964)

9687# It's All Over Now/Good Times Bad Times (2nd July, 1964)

9708# Time Is On My Side/Congratulations (25th September, 1964)

9725# Heart Of Stone/What A Shame (19th December, 1964)

## Long Play

PS 375# *Britain's Newest Hitmakers*
*Side One*
Not Fade Away; Route 66; I Just Wanna Make Love To You; Honest
I Do; Mona; Now I've Got A Witness; Little By Little.
*Side Two*
I'm A King Bee; Carol; Tell Me (You're Coming Back); Can I Get A Witness;
You Can Make It If You Try; Walking The Dog. (3rd May, 1964)

PS 402# *12 x 5*
*Side One*
Around And Around; Confessin' The Blues; Empty Heart; Time Is On
My Side; Good Times Bad Times; It's All Over Now.
*Side Two*
2120 South Michigan Avenue; Under The Boardwalk; Congratulations;
Grown Up Wrong; If You Need Me; Susie Q. (23rd October, 1964)

## POST-1964 RELEASES CONTAINING TRACKS RECORDED 1963-1964

## British Singles

F 13195* Everybody Needs Somebody To Love/Surprise
Surprise/another track (25th June, 1971)

F 13203* Surprise Surprise/another track (20th July, 1971)

## British Long Play

LK 4661* *The Rolling Stones No. 2*
*Side One*
Everybody Needs Somebody To Love; Down Home Girl; You Can't
Catch Me; Time Is On My Side; What A Shame; Grown Up Wrong.

*Side Two*
Down The Road Apiece; Under The Boardwalk; I Can't Be Satisfied; Pain In My Heart; Off The Hook; Susie Q. (30th January, 1965)

LK 4733* *Out Of Our Heads*
*Side One*
Mercy Mercy; Hitch Hike; other tracks
*Side Two*
Oh Baby (We Got A Good Thing Goin'); Heart Of Stone; other tracks (24th September, 1965)

## US Long Play

PS 420# *The Rolling Stones Now!*
*Side One*
Everybody Needs Somebody To Love; Down Home Girl; You Can't Catch Me; Heart Of Stone; What A Shame; Mona (I Need You Baby).
*Side Two*
Down The Road Apiece; Off The Hook; Pain In My Heart; Oh Baby (We Got A Good Thing Goin'); Little Red Rooster; Surprise Surprise (12th February, 1965)

PS 451# *December's Children*
*Side One*
You Better Move On; Look What You've Done; Route 66; Blue Turns To Grey; other tracks
*Side Two*
Other tracks (4th December, 1965)

## British and US Long Play

UK: SKL 5212*/US: ABKCO ANA 1 *Metamorphosis*
*Side One*
Some Things Just Stick In Your Mind; Each And Every Day Of The Year; Heart Of Stone; (Walkin' Thru') The Sleepy City; We're Wastin' Time; other tracks
*Side Two*
Other tracks (6th June, 1975)

## British Compilation Long Play

TXS 101* *Big Hits (High Tide And Green Grass)*
*Side One*
It's All Over Now; Heart Of Stone; other tracks.
*Side Two*
Time Is On My Side; Little Red Rooster; other tracks.
(4th November, 1966)

SKL 5084* *Stone Age*
*Side One*
Look What You've Done; It's All Over Now; Confessin' The Blues;
other tracks
*Side Two*
If You Need Me; Blue Turns To Grey; Around And Around; other tracks.
(6th March, 1971)

SKL 5149* *Rock 'N' Rolling Stones*
*Side One*
Route 66; The Under Assistant West Coast Promotion Man; Come On;
Bye Bye Johnny; Down The Road Apiece; another track.
*Side Two*
I Just Wanna Make Love To You; Everybody Needs Somebody To Love;
Oh Baby (We Got A Good Thing Goin'); Carol; other tracks.
(13th October, 1972)

SKL 5173* *No Stone Unturned*
*Side One*
Poison Ivy; Stoned; Money; Congratulations; 2120 South Michigan
Avenue; other tracks
*Side Two*
Other tracks (5th October, 1973)

ROST 1/2* *Rolled Gold*
*Side One*
Come On; I Wanna Be Your Man; Not Fade Away; Carol; It's All
Over Now; Little Red Rooster.

*Side Two*
Time Is On My Side; other tracks.
*Sides Three and Four*
Other tracks (14th November, 1975)
Arcade ADEP 32 *Get Stoned: 30 Greatest Hits 30 Original Tracks*
*Side One*
Not Fade Away; It's All Over Now; Tell Me (You're Coming Back);
Good Times Bad Times; Time Is On My Side; Little Red Rooster;
other tracks
*Side Two*
I Wanna Be Your Man; other tracks.
*Sides Three and Four*
Other tracks (21st October, 1977)


## US Compilation Long Play

NPS 1# *Big Hits (High Tide And Green Grass)*
*Side One*
Time Is On My Side; It's All Over Now; Tell Me (You're Coming
Back); other tracks.
*Side Two*
Heart Of Stone; Not Fade Away; Good Times Bad Times; other tracks.
(11th March, 1966)

2PS 606/607# *Hot Rocks 1964-1971*
*Side One*
Time Is On My Side; Heart Of Stone; other tracks
*Sides Two, Three and Four*
Other tracks (11th January, 1972)

2PS 626/627# *More Hot Rocks (Big Hits And Fazed Cookies)*
*Side One*
Tell Me (You're Coming Back); Not Fade Away; The Last Time; It's
All Over Now; Good Times Bad Times; another track
*Side Two*
Other tracks
*Side Three*
Money; other tracks.

*Side Four*

Come On; Fortune Teller; Poison Ivy; Bye Bye Johnny; I Can't Be Satisfied; another track. (1st December, 1972)


## British and US Compilation Long Play

UK: TAB 30*/US: 820 455-1# *Slow Rollers*
*Side One*
You Better Move On; Time Is On My Side; other tracks.
*Side Two*
Under The Boardwalk; Heart Of Stone; other tracks. (UK: 19th August, 1981/US: 21st August, 1981)

UK: ABKCO 92312/US: ABKCO 1218-1 *The Rolling Stones Singles Collection: The London Years*
*Side One*
Come On; I Want To Be Loved; I Wanna Be Your Man; Stoned; Not Fade Away; Little By Little.
*Side Two*
It's All Over Now; Good Times Bad Times; Tell Me (You're Coming Back); I Just Want To Make Love To You; Time Is On My Side; Congratulations.
*Side Three*
Little Red Rooster; Heart Of Stone; What A Shame; other tracks
*Sides Four, Five, Six, Seven and Eight*
Other tracks (15th August, 1989)


## British And US Compact Disc Compilation Long Play

Virgin 13325.1.1/13378.2.0 *Forty Licks*
*Disc One*
Other tracks
*Disc Two*
It's All Over Now; other tracks
(UK: 30th September, 2002/US: 1st October, 2002)

261

**German Album**

Polygram 6.30125 Best Of The Rolling Stones (The Rolling Stones Story Part 2)
*Side One*
Stoned; Come On; I Want To Be Loved; Poison Ivy; Fortune Teller; Money; Surprise Surprise; another track
*Side Two*
Little Red Rooster; Tell Me Baby; Time Is On My Side; Congratulations; *two Andrew Oldham Orchestra tracks*; another track
*Side Three*
Route 66; Everybody Needs Somebody To Love; other tracks
*Side Four*
Other tracks
*Side Five*
Look What You've Done; Blue Turns To Grey; other tracks
*Sides Five, Six, Seven and Eight*
Other tracks (11th September, 1983)

# Index